British Women Film Directors in the New Millennium

Stella Hockenhull

British Women Film Directors in the New Millennium

palgrave
macmillan

Stella Hockenhull
Department of Film Studies
University of Wolverhampton
Wolverhampton, United Kingdom

ISBN 978-1-137-48991-3 ISBN 978-1-137-48992-0 (eBook)
DOI 10.1057/978-1-137-48992-0

Library of Congress Control Number: 2016962789

Printed on acid-free paper

This Palgrave Macmillan imprint is published by Springer Nature
The registered company is Macmillan Publishers Ltd.
The registered company address is: The Campus, 4 Crinan Street, London, N1 9XW, United Kingdom

To Sam and Thea

Acknowledgements

My thanks go to friend and colleague Fran Pheasant-Kelly for her unceasing support of my work and careful proof reading of this book. Similarly, I would like to thank friend and mentor, Ulrike Sieglohr, for her insightful comments and advice on this project. I would also like to express gratitude to the following for supplying the images: Franny Armstrong for the book cover; Agatha Nitecka for *Wuthering Heights*; Clio Barnard for *The Selfish Giant*; Megan Davis from Rise Films for *Dreamcatcher* and *Rough Aunties*; Will Wood for *Belle*. In addition, I acknowledge the University of Wolverhampton for its generous support of my research and, finally, the staff at Palgrave, including Lina Aboujieb, Kannayiram Ganesh and Karina Jakupsdottir, for facilitating this publication.

Contents

List of Figures

UKFC & Andrea Arnold

New Labour positive strategy

Notion of being an auteur

Sophie Mayer – Fish Tank

CHAPTER 1

Introduction

The British Academy of Film and Television Arts (BAFTA), formerly the British Film Academy, was formed in 1947 and includes an annual awards ceremony with a Best Director category.[1] Since its inception there have been few female nominees for this honour and even fewer winners, the exception being in 2009 when American director Kathryn Bigelow was successful with *The Hurt Locker*.[2] The only female British nominee for the award is Lynne Ramsay in 2011 for *We Need to Talk About Kevin*. This not only reflects the fact that there are not many female film directors currently working in Britain, or indeed the world, but also that their productions escape recognition even though their output is innovative and diverse. There is no easily stated thesis in this book, but my overall aim is to present a survey of British women film directors making films post-2000 (or women working in Britain making British films), and to broadly review their output at a time of significant change within the UK film industry. Amid a period of increased awareness of the paucity of women in above-the-line[3] positions, I identify key female film directors and analyse the rich potential of their productions through various dimensions, taking into account funding strategies, production, distribution and exhibition methods, as well as aesthetics and genre.

Prior to 2000 the proportion of women directors compared to men was minimal, and statistically their numbers remain meagre, although they peaked in 2009 when women comprised 17.2% of all British film directors.[4] I suggest that this is partly attributable to UK Film Council (UKFC)

S. Hockenhull, *British Women Film Directors in the New Millennium*, DOI 10.1057/978-1-137-48992-0_1

funding, which not only addressed serious concerns over diversity from as early as 2003 but also increased spending in general on low-budget films. Whether coincidentally or not, this rise in women filmmakers also corresponds to New Labour's positive strategies regarding women in the workplace, thus making the post-millennial period a fruitful one to discuss.

Some of the films featured in this book offer a feminist stance or present a female perspective, although I do not propose that all the directors included here are feminists or that all the films analysed are feminist texts. Rather, the filmmakers discussed are judged auteurs in the broadest sense of the word, the notion of authorship itself engendering a position that is critical for feminist Film Studies because, historically, women have not enjoyed easy or full admission to the industry. This is not to argue that the women directors that I consider here correspond to the auteur notion of an individual patriarchal controller, a transcendental figure revered in Hollywood discourse. In reality, many work collaboratively and I acknowledge unequivocally that the production team is equally important to the completed work. Those discussed demonstrate authorial control in various ways, not least because they often write, produce and are camerawomen on their own films. As the title *British Women Film Directors in the New Millennium* suggests, this study focuses on women film directors or women making British films.[5] However, those that I include do not necessarily seek a female audience, although the subject matter is often directed at women, particularly in the work of many of the documentary filmmakers. Furthermore, I argue that these films are empowering in some way for the female spectator, either implicitly or explicitly incorporating a significant message. This occurs either by means of their subject matter, through the representation of characters or the use of real people, or via the visual strategies deployed. Thus, arguably, a distinctive aesthetic is created, interpreted here as a female imprint and, as Cecilia Sayad notes:

> They [women filmmakers] reclaim a voice in the theoretical articulations of cinematic authorship by inviting us to think of it [the film] not as critical construction, but as self-construction – not as an artificial attempt to humanise the source of the film's discourse through a reading practice, but as the filmmaker's performance of the processes that lead to the fabrication of meaning. (2013: xxii)

Although some theoretical input is deployed in this examination of British women's films, the focus is not on feminist theory. Indeed, much has already been written about women and film over the past 40 years, particularly with the introduction of theories on representation, some of which have been used here as a framework for analysis. Early feminist criticism was aimed at Hollywood stereotypes (Haskell 1974; Johnston 1973 [2008]) which were perceived as negative misrepresentations. Claire Johnston, for example, draws on the work of Roland Barthes to argue that woman as sign is ideological and represented as 'not man' and is therefore absent from the text. However, perhaps the most groundbreaking work in feminist film theory emanates from Laura Mulvey (1975) and her psychoanalytical approach to Film Studies in relation to Hollywood cinema. According to Mulvey, the text denies a female point of view, and implicates the spectator as colluder in the patriarchal act of voyeurism, thus producing a male authoritarian sexual power relationship. As a result, she proposes an oppositional women's cinema to offer a counterpoint to the dominant mode of filmmaking. Mulvey's arguments are seminal to Film Studies, and they provide a theoretical paradigm which is furthered by Mary Ann Doane (1987) who regards the representation of women as a response to male fear and anxiety. Alternatively, Teresa de Lauretis's work, written as a series of essays in the 1980s, purports that narrative cinema goes hand in hand with feminist awareness, advancing the notion of a text which addresses the female spectator (de Lauretis 1987), and, in turn, actual communities (de Lauretis 1990). Other feminist theory on representation, particularly the work of Tania Modleski (1999) and Christine Gledhill, examines the ways in which women engage with particular genres. Gledhill's (1987) edited collection focuses on melodrama, expressly in relation to a female audience. Her later, 'Image and Voice' (1994), notes that female discourse may be articulated in a film through a mixture of its aesthetics, semantics, and/or an ideological and social stance.

Apart from the wealth of published material on feminist theory, a large number of books focused on women directors also use theoretical paradigms as their overarching narrative. Geetha Ramanathan, in *Feminist Auteurs: Reading Women's Films* (2006), for example, considers feminist filmmakers from a diverse variety of countries in Africa, Latin America, Europe and Asia, as well as Hollywood. Her thorough analysis of a large number of films directed by women demonstrates how female authority surmounts established academic concepts in the field. Indeed, she challenges rather than documents the historic and what she perceives as the recurring problematic analysis of women in cinema, which, she argues, is an inveterate characteristic of film theory. She reintroduces the notion of authorship in her discussion of the relationship between female auteurs and feminist texts, and her treatment of feminist cinema as a genre incorporates the production, reception and cultural significance of the films.

Whereas Ramanathan's work covers cinema on an international scale, Yvonne Tasker and Diane Negra (2007) explore what they perceive as, a 'distinctive … contemporary post-feminist culture' (2007: 1), specifically in Western popular culture. In this, Angela McRobbie, a key figure in debates around post-feminism, considers Sharon Maguire's *Bridget Jones's Diary* (2001) as an example of post-feminism's exploitation of feminism as a concept. Later analysis in Chap. 5 of this book draws on her ideas in connection with this film and two other mainstream examples directed by British women, *Mamma Mia!* (Lloyd 2008) and *Bridget Jones: The Edge of Reason* (Kidron 2004). In addition, and in another reassessment of feminism and popular culture entitled *Feminism at the Movies* (2011), editors Hilary Radner and Rebecca Stringer produce a collection focused on the ways in which contemporary cinema reflects changing gender roles, and in Radner's monograph entitled *Neo-feminist Cinema* (2011), the author reconsiders feminism in a number of mainstream and popular Hollywood examples from *Pretty Woman* (Marshall 1990)—the 'girly film' (Radner 2011: 3)—to films that rely on international success such as *Sex and the City* (King 2008). Sophie Mayer's more recent work foregrounds women film directors as feminist filmmakers, documenting their style and practices. Her book, *Political Animals: The New Feminist Cinema* (2016), contains a chapter on British cinema which considers the trajectory of women's film production in the new millennium as a journey, and she also introduces the notion of 'lost girls', an aspect that includes analysis of work such as Samantha Morton's *The Unloved* (2009), Mania Akbari's *Dah* (2000), Andrea Arnold's *Fish Tank* (2009) and Amma Asante's *A Way of Life* (2004).

Thus, historically and more generally, analysis of the text has taken precedence over analysis of the industry in Film Studies, although these latter processes have more recently been brought to the fore. For example, *British Cinema Past and Present*, Justine Ashby and Andrew Higson's (2000) edited essay collection, considers various aspects of nation and film. In that volume Sue Harper reflects on actresses in 1930s' Britain, whereas Justine Ashby focuses on Betty Box's career as a producer in post-war society. While such studies are highly significant in providing a backdrop to women's contribution to British cinema, the collection's focus concentrates on the period pre 2000. Melanie Bell and Melanie Williams's seminal edited collection, published in 2009 and entitled *British Women's Cinema*, includes a selection of essays ranging from 1910 to the present, concentrating on female stars and audiences. In a related vein, but adopting a broader perspective, in *Women in British Cinema: Mad, Bad and Dangerous to Know* (2000), Sue Harper analyses the ways in which the British film industry has operated in terms of female creativity from 1930 to the present. She deals systematically with different historical periods in British cinema, and the first part of her book has proven invaluable as a study and touchstone for the research here.[6] Similarly, *Women on the Edge* (Tay 2009) explicitly explores the work of twelve international women filmmakers including Sally Potter and Jill Craigie, and is a springboard for ideas in this book.[7]

Recently, there has been a wealth of academic activity on the work and role of women in the British film industry workplace, particularly through the Women's Film & Television History Network-UK/Ireland (WFTHN). This organisation consists of a group of researchers, teachers, archivists, collections managers, students, professionals, and enthusiasts who are examining the contributions that British and Irish women working in the UK/Ireland or abroad, and overseas women working in the UK, have made within the film and television industries. This includes above- and below-the-line jobs, with the organisation attempting to gain recognition for and awareness of women's work, and to provide access to women's films and television programmes. It is affiliated to Women & Film History International and encourages British and Irish contributions to international initiatives such as the Women Film Pioneers Database, the biennial international Women and Silent Screen conferences and the women's television conference, Consoling Passions.[8]

Although this book concentrates specifically on the period from 2000 to the present, when the number of women directors working within the film industry rose substantially for a short period of time, there were notable female filmmakers working in Britain prior to this era. Indeed, a trajectory is traceable dating back to cinema's early beginnings, when women were not only involved in the UK film industry as actors or below-the-line workers but also, albeit on a small scale, as directors. The early 1900s, for example, are marked by films produced mainly by the rich and ruling classes, such as aristocrat, Elizabeth Alice F. Le Blond (Mrs Aubrey Le Blond) (1860–1934).[9] Le Blond was a mountaineer, photographer and travel writer who made a number of short documentaries (between 50 and

100 foot long), driven by her hobby: the winter sports in Switzerland. As Roland Cosandey suggests, 'Although Le Blond's interest in moving pictures was more ephemeral than her practice of photography … it does evidence the close ties between cinema, tourism and sports during these early years' (2004: 378). While Le Blond's work drew on sport as the topic for her films, her contemporary, Jessica Elvira Borthwick (1888–1946), concentrated mainly on the war between the Ottoman Empire and the Balkan states. She was a traveller and an adventurous character. In order to make her films she accompanied the Bulgarian army to record battle scenes, producing considerable quantities of amateur footage as a result. On her return home, Borthwick embarked on a lecture tour, eventually showing her films at the Scala Theatre in London, though her career in filmmaking was short-lived. As mentioned, both Le Blond and Borthwick were wealthy society women and had the ability to fund their own projects. In fact, both were pioneer figures of their time but their films did not gain widespread theatrical release and, in the case of Borthwick, she did not pursue film directing as a profession any further.

Filmmaking seemed to be the preserve of the affluent in cinema's infancy, and other women working in this field at that time were Rosita Forbes (1890–1967) and Stella Court-Treatt (1895–1954). Each directed during the 1920s, and again their work was largely devoted to documenting their own travels. Court-Treatt was a travel and wildlife filmmaker, co-directing at least two films in the Sudan with her husband, Major Chaplin Court-Treatt,[10] including *Cape to Cairo* (1926). The couple made two more films with Stella's brother, Errol Hinds, including *Stampede* (1929) for which she also wrote the screenplay, and *Stark Nature* (1930). In relation to the latter, what had originally commenced as a safari trip, culminated in a film shoot. *Stampede* and *Stark Nature* were sold to British Instructional[11] for general release and, as Emma Sandon points out, via filmmaking such as this, women were able to make a direct contribution to British national identity and colonialism through their work (2010).[12]

While some women filmmakers used travel to set their careers in motion, others, such as Ethyle Batley (1879–1917), commenced work in the theatre. Batley was formerly an actor with a touring company, travelling between theatres in the provinces. Described as 'a unique figure in the expanding British film industry of the 1910s, a pioneering woman filmmaker' (Turvey 2009: 359), she married Ernest Batley who, in a similar vein to Ethyle, had been employed in theatre; together the couple moved into film directing, although she was often overshadowed by her spouse.[13]

The above might appear to herald the success of women as filmmakers, yet many experienced prejudice as well as difficulties breaking into the industry, and it was not until the 1920s that a number of female directors aimed at a more widespread theatrical release for their work. Producer, writer and director Dinah Shurey (1888–1963), founded Britannia Films in 1924, first producing the film *Second to None* (Raymond) in 1926. She continued her career as a director, and went on to work on a number of films including *Carry On!* (Shurey and Peers 1927) and *The Last Post* (1930). In 1930, Shurey set up a distribution company, Showman Films, which also handled the sound version of *The Last Post*. In the same year, she brought a lawsuit against *Film Weekly* concerning a defamatory article, the author of which asserted that it was 'obvious' that women could not direct films although they could be invaluable for their ideas (Gledhill 2007: 13), citing *The Last Post* as an example. Such discrimination against women was common at the time, a point observed by Sue Harper who also maintains that: 'In the 1930s, women experienced extreme difficulties breaking into the technical side of production, and also into the union, the ACT' (2000: 191).[14] Showman Films subsequently folded, leaving Shurey bankrupt.

British-born Elinor Glyn (1864–1943) had a relatively short directing career as well. She was primarily a novelist and screenplay writer, and wrote a filmscript based on her 1907 novel for the film *Three Weeks (The Romance of a Queen)* in 1923. Glyn coined the term 'It' in her novel *The Man and the Moment* (1914), a 1920s euphemism for sex appeal, and which was embodied by the actress Clara Bow, who became known as the 'It girl'. Glyn herself was a vivacious woman who wrote high-spirited romances that dealt with the aristocracy and issues of morality in society, and critics responded favourably towards this aspect of her work. Her screenplays had a middlebrow appeal, and consisted of 'popular romantic fiction aimed squarely at the entertainment market' (Barnett 2007: 321). Glyn also worked in Hollywood, forming her own organisation entitled Elinor Glyn Productions, Inc., specifying that she would 'supervise and direct the sequences, settings, titles, costumes and the making of the films in general from an artistic and dramatic standpoint' (Barnett 2007: 322).[15] Returning to Britain in 1929, she formed her own production company entitled Elinor Glyn Ltd, subsequently producing and directing two romantic comedies at Elstree. *The Price of Things* (1929) was an unsuccessful project that was never released, and *Knowing Men* (1930) concerns an heiress (Elissa

Landi) who evaded fortune hunters by masquerading as a companion. Written from a feminist standpoint, this film met with unfavourable critical reception (Barnett 2007), but decades on, the idea of the 'It girl' continues to have great pertinence in the post-feminist discourses of the twenty-first century.

Many films in the early years of cinema sought to be educational, and women were often employed to make instructional films: for example, this is true of the filmmaker Mary Field (1896–1968). Field worked initially as an adviser, and then as a director on educational and documentary films for British Instructional which, in 1925, created an Education Department making Field its head. From then on, the company was instrumental in ensuring that film was at the forefront of its agenda. Field's work included a nature series entitled 'Secrets of Nature' (1922–33) which 'took the less scientific subjects including zoo films, to which she added a touch of humour' (Low 1971: 131).[16] When British Instructional was taken over in 1933, Field moved to the newly created educational unit at Gaumont-British Instructional, and commenced a new nature series entitled 'Secrets of Life' (1934–50). These films, along with the 'Secrets of India' series (1934) (renamed 'Indian Town Studies' in 1935) were accompanied by a voice-over and, innovatively for that time, treated the animals they featured anthropomorphically. Her later historical journey series, 'Empire Story in Cartoon' (1939), echoed the travelogues of some of the earlier filmmakers, although in this case the films were made expressly for children.

During the Second World War, Field was active as part of a team making government films, and unsurprisingly the subject matter for these was derived from the 'Secrets of Nature' films. *Marshland Birds* (1939) was one such example, and, while this film is not obviously propagandist, it shows a variety of British breeding grounds for birds with the emphasis on the protection of the young against predators, clearly implying the safeguarding of children against invasion. Her later *Carrier Pigeons* (1941) shows pigeons being ringed for racing, their significance in the war more palpable this time, and *Wisdom Wild* (1940) draws analogies between the ways in which animals store food and the necessity for self-discipline in wartime. Shot on 16 mm film, images of flora and fauna abound and, as Sarah Easen suggests, 'These homefront propaganda films demonstrate the clarity of thought and assured direction that became Field's hallmark in over fifteen years of educational filmmaking' (Easen n.d. c). Between 1944 and 1950, Field's career veered towards children's entertainment when she became head of the Rank Organisation's Children's Entertainment Division, before her role as executive officer at the newly created Children's Film Foundation (CFF).[17]

While British women film directors clearly played a role in the early years of cinema, it was the period following the outbreak of the Second World War which witnessed a more substantial growth in their numbers. Although there were already females employed in the industry at the time, they were predominantly working in fields other than directing. The requirement to make information films, however, meant that with the outbreak of war in 1939 there were more opportunities available because, as Jo Fox, in her illuminating account on women in documentary film production from 1929 to 1950,[18] points out:

> While the war extended opportunities for women, accelerated their progress and diversified the nature of their assignments, this was, in part, due to increased demand for information films. The idea that women simply filled positions vacated by men responding to the call-up is unhelpful and reductive, not least because, for skilled professionals over 30, film was a reserved occupation. (Fox 2013: 586)

It was the British documentary movement that had provided a training ground for many of the women who directed films during the Second World War and, from its establishment in the early 1930s, the 'movement operated as a creative collective with a social purpose, namely to bring the everyday experience and heroism of ordinary man and woman to the screen' (Fox 2013: 589).

A number of women, including the sisters Marion (1907–98) and Ruby Grierson[19] (1904–40), worked as documentary filmmakers during this time. Marion had introduced her contemporary, Evelyn Spice (1904–90),[20] to the GPO film unit, and commenced her own career as a writer and then a reporter, moving to Canada to work in newspapers. Eventually she returned to Britain to work with her brother, John Grierson (1898–1972), editing Canadian films for the Empire Marketing Board Film Unit.[21]

Whereas Marion created a lengthy career out of filmmaking, her sister Ruby's life was tragically cut short. Ruby trained as a teacher before assisting on Edgar Anstey's 1935 film *Housing Problems*. Her directorial debut, *London Wakes Up* (1936), was one of a series for the Strand Film Company about life in London. Her later films consisted of *Today and Tomorrow* (1936) and *Today We Live* (1937), both collaborations with Paul Rotha about the work of the National Council of Social Service. The latter film, described as 'warm, personal and involved, with a richness of observation and feeling and a persuasive expression of social ideals' (Low 1979: 100), was part funded by the Carnegie Fund United Kingdom Trust, and shows idyllic rural scenes interspersed with images of urban sprawl and grime. Ruby directed the second part of the film, which concerns the raising of finance for a village hall, 'with a final happy scene of the village ladies in their hall doing PT in tweeds and stockinged feet' (Low 1979: 101). She too joined the Realist Film Unit, but not before she made two zoological films entitled *Animal Kingdom—The Zoo and You* (1938) and *Animals on Guard* (1938). In 1939 Ruby made *Cargo for Ardrossan*, a commentary film for the Petroleum Films Bureau and, from 1940 onwards, she began making Home Front propaganda films as part of the war effort, including *Choose Cheese* (1940), *Green Food for Health* (1940), *Six Foods for Fitness* (1940) and *What's for Dinner?* (1940). Humorous in tone, these films demonstrate the ways in which good home cooking could be achieved even with rationing. Her final film,[22] *They Also Serve* (1940), is a 10-minute documentary dedicated to the 'Housewives of Britain' and follows the daily life of a wartime mother, tending to her family and growing vegetables.

Jill Craigie (1911–99) and her contemporary, Muriel Box (1905–1991), who made her directorial debut with Ministry of Information short documentaries, were also prominent filmmakers during wartime. Craigie was a staunch feminist and socialist, directing a number of films during and immediately after the war, including her documentary debut *Out of Chaos* (1944), the later *The Way We Live* (1946), *Children of the Ruins* (1947) and *To Be a Woman* (1951). Many of these films, and in particular *The Way We Live*, demonstrate Craigie's ability as a director of high-quality productions, although she was not provided with any opportunity to realise her talent in the world of fiction film. The only feature Craigie directed was *Blue Scar* (1948), a Welsh coal-mining drama, for which she also wrote the screenplay. Described as 'a sincere effort deserving wide recognition' (L.H.C. 1949: 8), the film demonstrates in documentary style the conditions before and after nationalisation, making criticism of management and the post-war situation in the coal-mining industry. Following *To Be a Woman*, Craigie moved back into screenplay writing, only returning to directing over 40 years later, in her final film, a political analysis of the outbreak of war in former Yugoslavia entitled *Two Hours from London* (1995). The film, which focuses on the war in Bosnia and the suffering of people undergoing ethnic cleansing programmes (see Hockenhull 2015b), achieved critical acclaim.

Another wartime filmmaker who created Home Front propaganda cinema was Australian-born Margaret Thomson (1910–2005). Thomson began her career making nature films for Gaumont-British Instructional and worked in Britain for most of her life. She later progressed to making short food flashes for the Second World War campaign, including *Making a Compost Heap* (1942), *Clamping Potatoes* (1942), *Hedging* (1942), *Clean Milk* (1943) and *The Signs and Stages of Anaesthesia* (1944). Thomson continued working in post-war Britain with films about children including *Children Learning by Experience* (1946) and *Children Growing Up with Other People* (1947) as part of the Ministry of Education's efforts during the period of reconstruction. *Prevention of Cross Infection: Respiratory Tract Infection in Children's Wards* (1953), which is a Ministry of Health sponsored film demonstrating hospital practices and hygiene, advocates a means of protection against the spread of bacteria. Her films are 'all characterised by their visual simplicity and their ability to communicate complex information in a clear, unpatronising way' (Anon. 2006). Thomson later directed *Child's Play* in 1954 for the government-backed feature unit, Group 3.

By the end of the Second World War, there were fewer opportunities for women, and directors such as Craigie and Box struggled to stay in the system, although Box had married into the industry and was therefore more easily able to secure funding. She continued to direct a variety of 'women's films' post-war, including *Street Corner* (1953), *The Truth about Women* (1958) and *The Passionate Stranger* (1957). She also made 'social realist films like *Too Young to Love* (1959), a film which ran into trouble with the censor for presenting facts about prostitution and venereal disease' (Merz 1991: 90) and *Rattle of a Simple Man* in 1964, which mocks a chauvinist northern working-class male group. Box remained an outspoken critic of the sexism that she experienced within the British film industry until her death in 1991 (McFarlane 2003: 77), however, as Caroline Merz points out, 'None of them found it easy to sustain the momentum of their work after the war, or to find their way into commercial production' (1991: 88).[23]

One filmmaker to continue working post-war was Kay Mander (1915–2013). Prolific in her output, Mander directed nearly 50 films, including the award-winning French-language feature *La Famille Martin* (1948), created as a French teaching aid. Her final work, *The Kid from*

Canada (1957), was made for the CFF, but thereafter she abandoned a career in directing, deciding that she no longer wanted to be associated with children's films. By the 1960s she had moved into continuity editing, working on Vincent Minnelli's *Four Horsemen of the Apocalypse* (1961), François Truffaut's *Fahrenheit 451* (1966) and *Tommy* (Russell 1974) among others.

By the 1950s, women mainly directed children's films (Harper 2000: 192), although comedy was also a staple in the industry into which category Wendy Toye's (1917–2010) work falls. Originally trained as a ballet dancer who formed her own dance company in 1947, Toye moved into directing in 1952 with her 23-minute film, *The Stranger Left No Card*, which won Best Short Fictional Film at the 1953 Cannes Film Festival. For Merz, 'Toye's films fall into two broad categories: whimsical fantasy (mainly the short films) and light comedy (mainly the feature films)' (1991: 92). They do, however, have one theme in common: 'the failings of men and the hollowness of patriarchy' (Merz 1991: 92). Toye also favoured musicals, drawing on her own training background for inspiration. Subsequent to *Raising a Riot* (1955), which analyses male vulnerability, Toye's directing career continued into the 1960s, even though her output consisted of only 'five successful but unremarkable British studio features and [she] contributed the most chilling episode to the horror omnibus *Three Cases of Murder* (1955)' (Botting 2015: 23). Her final film for Rank was *True as a Turtle* (1957), a film demonstrating divisions of gender, and, while 'not essentially subversive [her films] are a sophisticated riposte to extremism of all kinds' (Harper 2000: 199). Toye ended her career in the 1960s with *We Joined the Navy* (1962), an unsuccessful comedy, and afterwards returned to theatre and ballet work.[24]

Apart from a small number of experimental films, the 1960s saw a dramatic decline in women directors with only a handful of films on release during the entire decade. Indian-born, Sarah Erulkar (1923–2015) directed the children's film, *The Hunch*, in 1967 and Jan Darnley-Smith (1932–96) *A Ghost of a Chance* in 1968. Erulkar originally started at the Shell Film Unit, scripting and editing *Aircraft Today and Tomorrow* in 1946, and in the same year she directed *Lord Siva Danced*, followed by *Flight for Tomorrow* in 1947. *Lord Siva Danced* charts a trip to India with her father to participate in Indian independence celebrations and is mostly shot in Bombay. The film received theatrical release, premiering at the Academy Cinema in London's West End, Erulkar's aim here to 'promote her homeland and wave two fingers at the British' (Cranston and McGahan 2010: 232). Her subsequent *Steps of the Dance* (1948) is a three-reel Crown Film Unit production on British ballet, introducing dancers from the Sadler's Wells and Covent Garden companies. Features such as *New Detergents* (1949), *Night Hop* (1950) and *The History of the Helicopter* (1951) ensued. Following her marriage to assistant director, Peter de Normanville, Erulkar left Shell, chiefly because the manager, Arthur Elton, advised that it was now her job 'to put out Peter's slippers' (Cranston and McGahan 2010: 233), a comment made despite the fact that Erulkar was her husband's senior and in a better paid job.[25] She continued to direct freelance, making films for the Central Office of Information with the aim of promoting Britain to its overseas audiences, before eventually joining the National Coal Board Unit.

Some of Erulkar's 80 films follow women's themes and human interest stories, including the Samaritan/Basic Films co-production, *Birthright* (1958), which centres on the work of the Family Planning Association. However, in this film, 'much of the actual content is liberal and supportive of women who wish to spread the births of their children, of infertile couples, and of those forced into illegal abortions, for example. But throughout, there is a nagging air of deference to middle-class values and to doctors and senior professional figures' (Boon 2010: 23). Another of her works, *The Smoking Machine* (1963), is the first ever anti-smoking campaign film directed at children. Made by the Realist Film Unit, it was followed by *Ready for the Road* (1970) about cycling proficiency and the safety film *Never Go with Strangers* (1971). *Something Nice to Eat* (1967) is an award-winning Gas Council sponsored production and celebrates the art of cooking, and *Picture to Post* (1969) is 'one of Erulkar's most widely seen works' (Davidson 2010: 69). She uses Technicolor and montages to follow three graphic artists, David Gentleman, Arnold Machin and Jeffery Matthews, working on stamp designs. MGM released the film in ABC cinemas on a broad scale as a supporting feature for *Alfred the Great* (Donner 1969), dubbing it where appropriate, and it went on to win the Best Short Film at the BAFTAs. In sum, Erulkar's output was diverse, reflecting her belief that creative freedom was on offer for women after the war (in Cranston and McGahan 2010: 236).

Despite Erulkar's output, the 1960s was otherwise not a fertile period for women film directors. In 1962 Joan Littlewood's (1914–2002) comedy drama *Sparrows Can't Sing* was produced by the Associated British Picture Corporation, a company which also owned its own group of cinemas, thus providing a distribution outlet for the film. Initially, Littlewood had formed her own theatre company in Stratford, East London, producing the successful *A Taste of Honey* (1958) before it was directed by Tony Richardson for the screen. In a similar vein, *Sparrows Can't Sing* was a Theatre Workshop production written by Stephen Lewis, but this time Littlewood decided to take control and direct it for cinema herself, although she had no prior experience in this field. A humorous film centred on Cockney life, *Sparrows Can't Sing* was the first British film to be released in America with subtitles because of the dialect.

The 1970s proved a more prolific period for women, who now pursued an avant-garde and feminist trajectory. Subsequent to Jennie Lee's[26] White Paper entitled A Policy for the Arts: The First Steps (1965; see Gardner 2015), encouragement was given for the growth of the voluntary Regional Arts Associations and, in 1966, the British Film Institute (BFI) Experimental Film Fund was renamed the BFI Production Board. Michael Balcon retired as Board Chair in 1972, and a younger and more responsive team took over 'eager to implement the new policy of funding innovative low-budget feature films' (Dupin 2012: 204). With the formation of the Independent Filmmakers' Association and the Association of Independent Producers in the 1970s, a considerable number of avant-garde films and political documentaries were produced, the majority of which were from left-wing and feminist collectives. The London Film-makers' Co-op included Annabel Nicolson, Lis Rhodes, Sandra Lahire and Sally Potter and, as Harper points out, during this period, 'A number of production, exhibition and distribution networks were built up which privileged or specialized in films directed by women: among them were the London Film-makers' Co-op, Cinema of Women, the Berwick St Collective and The Other Cinema' (2000: 200). Others include the Leeds Animation Workshop, Sheffield Film Co-op, Red Flannel, Twentieth-Century Vixen and Amber Films. With comparatively large individual grants of up to £20,000 available, a significant number of films with a feminist agenda were created on subjects such as abortion, female oppression and equal pay.

During this period one of the main issues for the BFI Production Division was its attempts to find a wider audience for British cinema. Carol Myer was made chief of the Film Promotion Unit and, via film festival participation, retrospectives and promotional work, she was instrumental in marketing British cinema through an expansion programme, both in the UK and abroad. In 1972 the Edinburgh Film Festival included a women's section for the first time and, as Harper maintains, 'The 1970s represented a high-water mark in terms of formal innovation for women film-makers' (2000: 206), who were operating outside the mainstream in terms of both funding and style. At this point, the BFI Production Board was committed to funding avant-garde projects typical of British independent cinema.

A strong voice in the 1970s was the aforementioned Claire Johnston, who was part of the London Women's Film Group. Her comments on the position of women in the film industry are insightful regarding this period. As she relates:

> The film industry in this country reflects the American industry: it's extremely hierarchically structured and in a state of tremendous crisis ... Women obviously have a marginal role. They tend to exist in ghetto jobs – in continuity and in television, as production assistants. There are no camerawomen and virtually no sound women. Whole areas are closed, so there was, and is, a need for women to actually start making films, acquiring and sharing skills. (in Kaplan 1977: 396)

Those women making films included Johnston herself, Linda Myles and Laura Mulvey, who were all involved in the 1972 Edinburgh Film Festival's Women's Film Festival, showing 20 feature films in all. The London Women's Film Group's first collective film consisted of interviews with miners' wives, resulting in *Bettshanger, Kent 72* (1972) about the Bettshanger miners' strike. Esther Ronay, another group member, who had been refused an interview at the National Film School, directed *Women Against the Bill*, also in 1972, which dealt with issues of equal pay, and *Women of the Rhondda* (1973). The London Women's Film Group output was not generally shown outside film festivals, although schools, colleges, women's groups and conferences exhibited their work, often accompanied by talks from the director.[27]

If the 1970s was a decade of experimental cinema then the 1980s, with the advent of Channel 4 and its commitment to film funding, witnessed further disquiet in terms of the numbers of women employed in certain roles within the industry, resulting in a number of changes. This commenced in 1979 when a group of women convened to discuss how the new channel might aid the female position in broadcasting. Subsequently they moved on to form the organisation, the Women's Fourth Channel Lobby, afterwards renamed the Women's Broadcasting and Film Lobby, which not only highlighted a lack of women in governing and senior administrative positions but also a shortage of women involved in television programming; their remit included a call for an improvement in employment and training opportunities.

In summary, women directors worked in the British film industry during the twentieth century, but there was by no means a proliferation, and this under-representation persists to the present day, a situation not restricted to the UK.[28] Indeed, various reports from other countries observe the same problem (see Renée 2013). For instance, Danielle Cliche (2005) notes that although female directors in Austria, Finland, Germany and Portugal are on the increase, they remain in a minority.[29] Similar trends can be observed throughout Europe, even if some countries fare better than others.[30] Conversely, by the beginning of the twenty-first century, the USA showed a stark decrease, with women directors accounting for merely 6.4% of Hollywood films between 2013 and 2014 (Child 2015).[31]

Thus, the percentage of women directors continues to run counter to other trends in employment internationally, although it is beyond the scope of this study to produce an exhaustive examination of global issues at play.[32] Also outside of the remit of this study is an in-depth discussion of female screenplay writers. This has been the focus of a number of debates in terms of equal opportunities and, again, sees some overlap with women in other above-the-line professions in the industry. In fact, many women film directors also write the screenplays for their own films. Instances include director, Lynne Ramsay, who wrote the screenplay for *Ratcatcher* (1999) and *Morvern Callar* (2002), and the screenplay adaptation for *We Need to Talk About Kevin* (2011), and Andrea Arnold who wrote the screenplays for both *Red Road* (2006) and *Fish Tank*, and the screenplay adaptation for *Wuthering Heights* (2011). According to Stephen Armstrong, in almost every genre, British women screenwriters outperform their male counterparts at the box office:

> From 2010 to 2012, the UK produced 372 independent films – movies made purely with British money. According to the BFI figures, women wrote or co-wrote only 16% of them. If you remove short films and low budget debuts, the numbers look a little better: about 18% of films with a budget of at least £1m … had female writers … looking at the 20 best performing films across the same three year period, however, you find the male/female ratio is very different. Fully 50% of the top 20 movies employed women writers … nine of the top 12 films were either exclusively female written or had a female writer attached. In other words, men outnumber women in the screenwriting game by a ratio of 4:1, but when it comes to writing successful movies, women greatly outperform men. (2013: 14)

Even so, while it is acknowledged that there is a scarcity of women working in screenwriting and other above-the-line positions, it is not possible to discuss this here, although the role of the creative team producing the films will sometimes be examined.

The principal content of this book, as the title suggests, is film, although I acknowledge that directing also includes television. Given the growing convergence of media, it would be beneficial to consider both film and television in this analysis, and, where appropriate, women television directors will form part of the discussion, particularly where the work of film directors intersects with their television directing careers or provides contrast and comparison.

I have chosen the year 2000 as a watershed because it not only represents the contemporary situation, it also incorporates the era of the founding of the UKFC through to its demise in 2011. The UKFC was a public body that existed for over ten years, and significantly, in 2003, instigated a diversity report leading to policy, thereby triggering a dramatic increase in female film directors during its final years.[33] Conversely, while the UKFC was instrumental in providing funding for a large number of films, not all women filmmakers benefited from financial aid. In fact, many raised finance through other methods, including private sponsorship and television channel funding, mainly Channel 4 and the BBC (although this was often in conjunction with the UKFC).

British Women Directors in the New Millennium commences by discussing the industry and the various funding opportunities available since the start of the new millennium, explicitly referencing the UKFC's policies in equality and diversity. In order to situate the developments achieved after 2000, I also include a broad historical overview of the funding opportunities available to filmmakers before the new millennium. Chap. 2, therefore, briefly considers the policies of Channel 4, and the women's workshops and collectives, referencing the variety of ways in which finance was made available. The founding of the UKFC and its resultant strategies are discussed, including the various specific funds available. This is later taken into account when I note how women have fared in acquiring financial backing, their funding sources and the production companies and organisations involved in the making of their films. In addition, where appropriate, I explore distribution patterns and other outlets utilised by women to exhibit their work.

While the first part of the book documents UKFC policy and funding, the subsequent chapters offer critical perspectives on women's practices within the considerable variety of genres and cinematic traditions of British cinema, and through an industry framework.[34] A contention is that the women filmmakers discussed here offer a significant female voice, not solely in terms of authorship, but also in content, and they are not restricted to working within one specific genre. In the main, and due to the financial constraints of filmmaking in general, documentaries have formed the major part of female film production in Britain; these are often written and shot by the directors themselves either from a feminist standpoint or focusing on issues that raise concerns for and about women. Indeed, in its early stages, feminist film study was largely a critique of dominant cinema and paid little attention to documentary film. However, as Janet Walker and Diane Waldman argue, female-directed documentary films represent 'the images and voices of women who are not professional actors and whose documentary representation seeks to build consensus with actual women for the audiences of these films' (1999: 12). The films discussed in Chap. 3 are predominantly observational, women seeming to prefer this mode of address, rather than participatory. Furthermore, on analysis they are largely focused on concerns about climate change and ecology or on the problems women encounter as a result of male oppression because of their culture, or both. In order to situate these films within a broader context, the director's background, qualifications and aesthetic style are also explored, as well as their distribution strategies and exhibition outlets.

The second key area that British women directors work in is low-budget fiction films: these are often centred upon a troubled pivotal female protagonist and reflect significant socio-political situations. Film directors such as Andrea Arnold, Lynne Ramsay and Clio Barnard successfully compete with their male counterparts, having something to say for and about the position of men, women and children in contemporary society. This category of filmmaking is frequently referred to as 'social realism' and, although such films which convey societal anxieties existed prior to the new millennium, in terms of female-directed films, this style came to prominence in the early 2000s. Social realist filmmaking is viewed as a rich tradition in Britain (Lay 2002) and arguably a trajectory can be traced from the 1930s' documentary movement, with the work of filmmakers such as John Grierson and Harry Watt (1906–87) in their films for the Empire Marketing Board and the General Post Office, and on into the 1940s. Documentary filmmakers such as Humphrey Jennings (1907–50) investigated British leisure in *Spare Time* (1939), and later this fertile tradition was influential for filmmakers such as Karel Reisz (1926–2002),

Lindsay Anderson (1923–94) and Tony Richardson (1928–91) from the 1950s onwards, when British social realism came to the fore with the Free Cinema Movement.[35] This movement left a legacy in its commitment to the representation of the commonplace in British society, rejecting what was considered a stereotypical and inaccurate portrayal of the British working classes witnessed in the Ealing comedies of the 1950s. The filmmakers involved believed in personal expression and a commitment to a true depiction of social status. Filming took place on location, a practice which was a continuation of the working procedures of their European counterparts,[36] and the use of natural light enabled a new visual approach. The Free Cinema Movement led the way for a more experimental style of filmmaking in the 1960s known as the British New Wave, which challenged the dominant mainstream cinema and was identified with the work of individual directors rather than studio production. British New Wave focused on the working classes, but not in a superficial or misleading way. Instead, it addressed issues of masculinity, particularly masculinity in crisis in films such as *Saturday Night and Sunday Morning* (Reisz 1960), *The Loneliness of the Long Distance Runner* (Richardson 1962) and *A Kind of Loving* (Schlesinger 1962). While not particularly shocking by contemporary standards, these films gave voice to working-class people and explicitly discussed thorny issues such as teenage pregnancy, adultery, class disparities and upward mobility.

If British New Wave explored the lives of the working classes then, by the late 1990s, deindustrialisation and privatisation had led to a redefinition of social strata, and the term 'working class' became defined by consumption rather than production. The 1990s onwards, according to Claire Monk (2000a), witnessed the emergence in film of new types of character—from the underclass. Gone was the focus on the working class who strived for respectability through hard work and decency, to be replaced by a concern with drug and alcohol abuse and its effects on family and society at large.[37] Furthermore, like the British New Wave, these films pivoted around masculinity in crisis—a theme adopted in films such as *Raining Stones* (Loach 1993) and *The Full Monty* (Cattaneo 1997).

The term social realism is a problematic concept and is shaped by social and political circumstances. Samantha Lay makes some attempt to define this as a mode of expression demarcated by what it is not, rather than by its chief characteristics. As she says, these films are 'independent, low budget, directed towards either the art house circuit and/or the video and television marketplace, and they stand as texts in contrast to classical

Hollywood realist texts' (Lay 2002: 8). The setting up of Channel 4, which saw itself as a commissioner rather than producer, gave rise to a growth in the genre, its films addressing minority audiences and representing those generally marginalised in mainstream cinema—what Lay (2002: 79) terms 'the unrepresented'. Writing in 2000, John Hill argues that social realist films reflect the concerns and issues of society, and this was particularly evident during the Thatcher years when filmmakers such as Mike Leigh, Ken Loach and Stephen Frears confronted right wing policies and addressed youth unemployment, and familial and personal relations through their work.[38] However, the formal concerns which characterised these films and their forebears have given way to what Lay terms 'social surrealism and heightened realism' (2002: 89), particularly in the later work of Mike Leigh. Loach's films have straightforward narratives in order to identify societal problems within a credible environment, and usually dialogue is the key vehicle for facilitating the narrative. Whereas male directors dominated social realism prior to the new millennium, female film directors are now prominent within this genre and making films not only with a bias towards societal concerns, but also through a poetic optic. The latter might be attributed to the fact that many emanated from art schools, but it also chimes with what David Forrest (2010) claims is a new realist impulse prevalent across trends in European cinema.

At this juncture, it is worth noting that while documentary and socio-political films feature prominently in female output,[39] very few British women are engaged in making horror, even though the turn of the century saw an upturn in the production of this particular genre. In order to address this, the project Darklight: Women Direct Horror Films was set up in 2006 with funding from Skillset Film Skill's Fund, WarpX—a UK low-budget digital film studio established by the UKFC's New Cinema Fund and Film4 with partners EM Media, Screen Yorkshire, Optimum Releasing and Threshold Studios also involved. Its remit was to encourage women to develop horror film projects, and the first four directors selected were Juliet McKoen, Miranda Bowen, Smita Bhide and Corinna Faith, resulting in the following productions: *The Tantrik* (Bhide), *The Men's Room* (Bowen), *This Little Piggy* (Faith) and *2d4* (McKoen). Subsequently, another six female directors were chosen to participate in the programme, including Nichola Bruce, Finola Geraghty, Faye Gilbert, Toni Harman, Olivia Lory Kay and Amy Neil, the aim being to link this new talent with producers and distributors for worldwide theatrical release. The Darklight project provided appropriate extensive training for the ten directors, incorporating weekend workshops in story development, sound technology and cinematography. At the time of writing, *The Tantrik* is in production in India, and Bombay-born Bhide is now a successful writer and producer for television dramas such as *Hunted* (2015), a new prime-time thriller produced by the BBC and HBO. However, all the above-named projects have yet to be theatrically released and, therefore, this genre does not form part of the discussion here.[40]

While the contention here is that women directors are under-represented and their work is principally observed through realist and documentary filmmaking, there are nonetheless higher budget female-directed films. Indeed, Phyllida Lloyd's *Mamma Mia!* turned out to be a blockbuster, and Danish-born but UK based Lone Scherfig directed the British films *An Education* (2009) and *One Day* (2011), both of which achieved box office success. Sharon Maguire's UK/US/France co-production adaptation of Helen Fielding's novel *Bridget Jones's Diary* (1996) was also a hit, along with its follow-up, *Bridget Jones: The Edge of Reason*, both backed by Universal. Chap. 5 therefore considers the work of British female directors who direct more mainstream films, either in terms of production values or through their mode of narration. With both male and female British film directors, blockbusters are rare, hence this chapter not only refers to those films which have achieved box office success, use known stars and have huge post-release financial potential, but also popular films which engage a classic or traditional mode of narration. Again, on analysis, these loosely fall under the categories of bio-pics—films that depict the life of significant figures in history—or comedies that also deal with issues of race, class and gender.

Finally, Britain has a history of women's independent, avant-garde and experimental cinema rooted in the work of the collectives of the late 1970s and 1980s, and this is the subject of Chap. 6. There has been little consensus as to what is meant by avant-garde and experimental cinema, although a commonality is that it is often created by individuals and differs fundamentally from the mainstream in terms of narration. This chapter contains a variety of filmmakers whose work is diverse, and includes discussion of Potter's later films since 2000, along with that of documentary filmmakers such as Gillian Wearing, Sarah Turner and Sophie Fiennes.

My process of selection is not arbitrary, and to some extent is too ambitious in its attempt to encompass all women filmmakers currently working in Britain.[41] From those selected, it is not possible to consider all in depth. For this reason, I have chosen to incorporate and analyse the work of those filmmakers who have made a sizeable contribution to British cinema thus far, and those whose work shares common features with their contemporaries. Filmmakers not discussed in any detail are footnoted where appropriate, which may be relevant to other researchers in the field. Similarly, in general my film analysis is relatively short, and reference, where possible, is made to lengthier examinations of the films in journals and books.

Notes

1. The first film awards ceremony took place in 1949, although the Best Director category did not come into existence until 1969.
2. Lone Scherfig was also nominated in that year for the Best Film category with *An Education*.
3. Usually directors, actors, screenwriters and producers are considered above-the-line workers at fixed cost. The remainder are therefore below the line, for example, costume designers and make-up artists. Although these are all extremely important to consider in the creation of the film, it is beyond the scope of this work to discuss them in any depth.
4. However, even with such an increase, this statistic is undermined by the fact that, in the same year, 34% of the National Film and Television School (NFTS) graduates on the Directing course were women which raises the question: what happened to the remaining 17%? The NFTS was established by the government in 1970, and is supported by public and industry funding, whereas the London Film School, set up in 1957, is financially dependent on student fees. Both schools eventually established themselves with university status in order to qualify for funding from the Higher Education Funding Council of England. By 2000, the NFTS had established a number of degrees at MA level, which were validated by the Royal College of Art. As a result, the courses were reduced from three years to two, with the consequence that 'while the reduction had no serious implications for certain specialised areas such as documentary or animation production, it did have a detrimental effect on the fiction programme where students effectively no longer had the opportunity to develop and work on a longer piece of dramatic work' (Petrie 2012: 361). The London Film School also altered their two-year diploma course into an MA in Filmmaking, followed by a one-year MA in Screenwriting. When these courses were validated, the thrust changed from a practical

emphasis to greater stress on an academic component. This resulted in a critical journal with the opportunity for students to reflect on their practice.

5. I acknowledge that it is now problematic to discuss the term 'national cinema' when many films are co-productions, or are Hollywood sponsored but made in Britain. To clarify, the directors discussed here are either British born but practising abroad, practising in the UK, or born outside the UK but now working in Britain making British films. There also exists the difficult aspect of defining British cinema, and for the purposes of this study it is based on the nationality of the director or the fact that it is British funded. For further attempts at some definition see: http://homemcr.org/article/bfi-film-academy-studying-british-cinema/ (accessed 24 June 2016).
6. The second part assesses the work of women who contribute to the film industry in a variety of roles: directors such as Wendy Toye and Sally Potter, producers such as Betty Box, scriptwriters such as Clemence Dane and Muriel Box, costume designers such as Shirley Russell and Jocelyn Rickards, and a variety of female editors and art directors are all examined.
7. See also Jacqueline Levitin, Judith Plessis and Valerie Raoul (eds) (2003) in *Women Filmmakers: Refocusing*. However, apart from the sections on Sally Potter and Pratibha Parmar, they offer an international perspective on the film industry rather than centring on British cinema.
8. Significant work on women working in film and television is also being undertaken by Melanie Bell and Vicky Ball, including an Arts and Humanities Research Council project entitled Women's Work in British Film and Television, which assesses the various contributions women have made to film and television production in Britain during the period 1933–89. In addition, Christine Gledhill is compiling the UK entries for an international Women Film Pioneers Project Database on Lydia Hayward (scriptwriter), Dinah Shurey (producer/director), Billie Bristow (publicist), and Rosita Forbes (filmmaker), all working in the UK in the 1920s (albeit Hayward crosses over into the sound era, working in the industry up until 1942).
9. Early examples of directors are provided with dates of birth and death to give some idea of when they were actively working, but this practice is not continued in the remainder of the book.

10. The Court-Treatts were one of a number of husband and wife teams working together. Others included Alfred Hitchcock and Alma Reveille, Ronald and Jean Haines, Muriel and Sydney Box, and Jill Craigie and Jeffrey Dell. Jean Haines and her husband established British Foundation Pictures in 1937 and produced documentary shorts of Kenya.
11. British Instructional was a British film production company operating between 1919 and 1932. It later merged with British International Pictures.
12. While the contribution of amateur women filmmakers is not discounted it is beyond the scope of this book to include all filmmakers. However, a name worthy of note is celebrated amateur director, Rosie Newman (1896–1988).
13. Ethyle's career as a director commenced with *Peggy Gets Rid of the Baby* (1912), the first of five comedies in which Ernest and Ethyle's daughter Dorothy appeared as Peggy, the naughty girl of the film's title. Other films in the series included *Peggy Becomes a Boy Scout* (1912), and *Peggy as Peacemaker* (1913). For the most part, the Batley output fitted largely into the comedy genre, although *Through the Flames* (1913) was a 21-minute serious drama about a little girl actress who escapes a burning house. Ernest, Ethyle and Dorothy moved on to join British and Colonial Kinematograph Company (B&C), where Ethyle continued to write and direct. Together, she and Ernest made 110 films, although it appears that Ethyle was a victim of gender discrimination. Ethyle worked mainly with children, including her daughter Dorothy, and as a result her oeuvre was less varied than that of her husband. In 1913 she released *The Child Mother*, her longest film to date, which received commendable reviews. Other titles attributable to Ethyle included *The Artist* (1914), *There's Good in the Worst of Us* (1914), *Saved by a Dream* (1914), *Three Little Orphans* (1914), *A Child Shall Lead Them* (1914) and *The Old, Old, Story* (1914). Following the outbreak of war, the Batleys became part of the propaganda war effort, making films such as *An Englishman's Home* (1914), a story about the invasion of Britain. Gerry Turvey provides a fascinating insight into the couple's respective output and notes that 'Ethyle's productivity was greater than that of her husband' (2009: 362). For further reading see Turvey (2009). Lesser known filmmaker, Paula Hilburn Blackton (1881–1930) also initially worked as an actor

and directed only one film, *The Littlest Scout* (1919), which she also wrote and acted in, starring as the mother of her own children. For a comprehensive list of female film directors not included here see the website on Women and Silent British Cinema: https://womenandsilentbritishcinema.wordpress.com/ (accessed 2 October 2015).

14. The Association of Cinematograph Technicians (ACT) later became the Association of Cinematograph Television and Allied Technicians (ACTT).
15. For further reading on Glyn's collaboration with MGM as a screenwriter see Barnett (2007).
16. This series was dedicated, as the title suggests, specifically to science and images of nature, but Field eventually adapted her style to include wartime propaganda films on rationing and agriculture.
17. Between 1951 and 1982 the Children's Film Foundation (CFF) made films for children's Saturday matinees. Production was funded by a cinema ticket levy titled the British Film Production Fund (known as the Eady Levy), and set amounts were awarded to independent producers who signed over their rights to the films on completion. By 1969 a total of £3 million had been spent on production. Funding was eventually cut and the CFF was restructured as the Children's Film and Television Foundation (CFTF) in 1982. The Eady Levy was abolished in 1985 and the CFTF closed in 1987.
18. Fox (2013) challenges the notion that there were few women employed in the film industry prior to the Second World War. She explores the broader picture of female access to directorial roles and argues that increased demand for non-fiction information films meant more women in general were involved in filmmaking in the 1930s, and many took advantage of any opportunity to gain access to the industry, working first in secretarial and office jobs. Her examples include the various roles undertaken by both Box and Mander, which 'permitted an accumulation of experience, such as vetting and amending film scripts, and prompted a shift into production through continuity work, since the latter demanded secretarial skills in order to record filmic lapses' (Fox 2013: 588).
19. Christian names are deployed for Marion and Ruby Grierson to avoid confusion.
20. A Canadian, Evelyn Spice trained as a schoolteacher before studying journalism and, on meeting Marion Grierson, she travelled to

London in 1931 to work for the Empire Marketing Board. The first film she directed was *Spring on the Farm* (1933), which was narrated by a child. Spice's best known work, however, was *Weather Forecast* (1934), which offered a frank camera style, while incorporating an intricate soundtrack. In 1934 she moved back to her native Canada to make *Prairie Winter*, one of the first Canadian films to be exhibited theatrically in the UK. Returning to London, she directed *Calendar of the Year* (1936), *Around the Village Green* (1937; co-directed with Marion Grierson), *A Job in a Million* (1937) and *Behind the Scenes* (1938), which was an observation of London Zoo and the people and animals who make up its daily life. Other examples of Spice's work worth noting here include *Sheltered Waters* (1934), *Sydney Eastbound* (1938) and *Birth of the Year* (1938), all of which observe the daily working lives of women. Spice went on to direct 16 films (Fox 2013: 590). She married Lawrence Cherry in 1937 and, when war broke out, the couple returned to Canada where they made a number of films together.

21. However, she moved on to make promotional films while in charge of the Travel and Industrial Development Association (TIDA). Attached to the Empire Marketing Board, TIDA sponsored *Edinburgh* (1934), a silent travel film, and its sound equivalent, *The Key to Scotland*. Along with her husband, Donald Taylor, Marion directed *Britain's Countryside*, a silent short film, also for TIDA, which was described as having 'a pleasant eye for detail' (Low 1979: 76). Her first major directing project was an observation of British coastal resorts entitled *Beside the Seaside* (1935). In this, she recorded passing conversations with a voice-over commentary by W.H. Auden. In 1937, Marion co-produced and co-directed *Around the Village Green* with Spice, a film lasting 12 minutes and accompanied by music from Benjamin Britten. Charting the changes in village life, both socially and through mechanisation, the film proposed that the younger generation travel to work in the major towns to acquire a higher standard of living than their village-dwelling counterparts. Grierson and Spice employed a particular interviewing technique, whereby a group of men seated outside the village pub provide their views on rural life direct to camera. Shot in the Essex villages of Finchingfield, Great Bardfield and Steeple Bumpstead, the film is accompanied by a

commentary from John Watt about the structure of country living. This work chimes with much documentary filmmaking of the period, which had begun to see itself as more factual in its approach, and in 1935 the organisation, Associated Realist Film Producers was formed by Marion Grierson's husband, along with Paul Rotha, Edgar Anstey and Arthur Elton, with Marion herself operating as a consultant for the body to put sponsors in touch with filmmakers. In 1936 she became editor of *World Film News* which was a representative and voice for the documentary movement.

22. Ruby Grierson died in 1940 while filming the evacuation of British children to Canada when the liner they were travelling on was torpedoed.
23. Although Box continued directing into the early 1960s she eventually turned to writing. Indeed, many producers questioned her competence and she experienced much male prejudice. See Harper (2000).
24. As noted, many women discontinued their directing careers post-war or moved into experimental cinema. Margaret Tait (1918–99) was one such director. A filmmaker and a poet, she had spent time in the Far East during the Second World War before studying film in Rome. For most of her life, however, she lived in her native Orkneys where she founded Ancona Films, producing work inspired by the landscape. *A Portrait of Ga* (1952) is a 4-minute short, one of 32 that she made, along with *Hugh MacDiarmid: A Portrait* (1964) and *Place of Work* (1976), which is a film devoted to the depiction of her house and garden. Her later *Land Makar* (1981) 'works through imagery and the rhythm of editing rather than any correspondence to the external world' (Roddick 2015: 54). At the age of 74 she made her only feature, *Blue, Black, Permanent* (1992) which is an abstract semi-autobiography using the actors, Celia Imrie and Jack Shepherd in the film.
25. Shell's policy was not to employ married couples. See Cranston and McGahan (2010).
26. Britain's first arts minister.
27. The Other Cinema, set up in 1970 as a non-profit making distribution company, also provided outlets for films to be shown.
28. UK figures available from UKFC Group and Lottery Annual Reports and Financial Statements 2000–11, and BFI Statistical Yearbooks.

29. A recent report of German feature film directors finds that women are not adequately represented, with only 22% of films made between 2009 and 2013 female-directed. German statistics available from Study by the Institute for Media Research at University of Rostock (2015). See also Hockenhull (2015a).
30. The Nordic states are significant in attempting to increase the number of women in film production roles above the line through policy-making and regulation of the industry. Norway and Sweden in particular, are known for introducing various forms of gender quotas in order to balance the representation of men and women, not only in the public sector but sometimes also within corporate contexts. In line with this development, both the Swedish and the Norwegian Film Institutes have launched initiatives to improve gender equality in the film industry. Additionally, in Denmark a number of women have been remarkably successful as directors in the past decades; one example is Lone Scherfig. Scherfig is included in this book for her contribution to British filmmaking rather than as a British director. See Edström and Mølster (2014).
31. In response, Melissa Silverstein, who runs the Women and Hollywood blog and is co-founder of New York's Athena Film Festival, has organised a petition decrying the absence of female directors nominated for the Palme d'Or. Silverstein calls for 'transparency and equality at Cannes and other festivals … Look what happened to Lynne Ramsay. *We Need to Talk About Kevin* was at Cannes, it was well received, it went to Toronto. But along the way it lost momentum Which [sic] happens to a lot of women-directed films' (in Child 2012).
32. Although this analysis invariably overlaps with other national cinemas because there is often a wider context to British cinema through co-productions and the variety of funding opportunities available from a range of schemes and initiatives.
33. UKFC funding benefited both male and female film directors.
34. The author acknowledges that genre categorisation is movable, and some liberties have been taken in the groupings.
35. Between 1956 and 1959 a number of short documentaries were shown at the National Film Theatre which had a similarity of style, termed by Anderson 'Free Cinema', owing to their freedom from box office restraints. For further reading see Aitken (1993), Winston (2008) and Austin and de Jong (2008).

36. For example, the Italian neo-realist directors filmed on location immediately after the Second World War, and the French New Wave directors followed suit. See Shiel (2006) and Greene (2007).
37. The visual style associated with this movement and the topics examined were adopted by later filmmakers such as Ken Loach. However, social realism is much more complex than this. Loach, although renowned for his work in this genre, explored broader social issues and societal injustices in films such as his early BBC television drama *Cathy Come Home* (1966), and later films, including *Raining Stones* (1993), *Ladybird, Ladybird* (1994) and *Sweet Sixteen* (2002). Hill (2000), Monk (2000b) and Moya Luckett (2000) all argue that social realism is preoccupied with masculinity in crisis. Hill, in particular, identifies the two concepts of failure and utopianism in contemporary films, the former associated with Ray (Ray Winstone) in *Nil by Mouth* (1997), and the latter with male collective action and resolve in films such as *The Full Monty* (Cattaneo 1997) and *TwentyFourSeven* (Meadows 1997). See Hill (2000).
38. Julia Hallam and Margaret Marshment see the term 'social realism' as more discursive and suggest that it is generally used to describe characters and their milieu, even though they conclude that it shares a visual aesthetic which 'tends to be associated with an observational style of camerawork that emphasises situation and events and an episodic narrative structure, creating "kitchen sink" dramas and "gritty" character studies of the underbelly of urban life' (2000: 185). For them, there are thematic groups associated with this mode of expression, such as alienated youth and the dysfunctional family, filmed with a lack of artifice favouring, at times, a documentary aesthetic. Further, as they argue, social realism's mode of expression enables an understanding of the 'broader social mechanisms that generate conflict between individual desire and what can be achieved within a given situation' (2000: 194). Although interest in character is paramount, the spectator is also privileged to what John Urry (1990) terms 'the tourist gaze'—whereby observation of difference allows spectacle and distance, or 'the aestheticism of urban squalor' (Lay 2002: 63).
39. Whereas social realism and documentary films dominate female output, their male counterparts produce more action and horror cinema. For example, between 2007 and 2009 Neil Thompson directed the violent film *Clubbed* (2008) and Marcus Warren

directed *The Heavy* (2009), one of a number of gangster films to appear in the new millennium. The period also saw a large number of horror films such as Marek Losey's *The Hide* (2008), Johnny Kervorkian's *The Disappeared* (2008) and Mark Tonderai's UKFC and Channel 4 thriller *Hush* (2008).

40. Another genre to receive little attention by female directors is the gangster/crime film. An exception is Sally El Hosaini's *My Brother the Devil* (2012), an urban drama about two brothers involved in criminal activity, and gay gangsters. Prior to this, El Hosaini made two shorts, *The Fifth Bowl* (2008) and *Henna Nights* (2009). In addition, women animators are not discussed in this book, but one significant director to consider is Sally Pearce. She graduated from the NFTS with a degree in Animation Direction, and her graduation film, *Elephants*, is a fiction story for children, mixing live action with traditional paint on glass animation and 2D digital compositing. The film screened at over 70 festivals and won the Welsh Short Film BAFTA and over 20 other awards around the world. It was also selected for the show reel of British shorts presented by the UKFC at Cannes in 2009, and by the British Council at Anim'est Festival, Bucharest, as part of a show reel of outstanding British animation, and shortlisted for the British Animation Awards. In 2011 Pearce produced a short mixed media UKFC and Welsh Arts Council funded film entitled *Hally* which premiered at Chicago International Children's Film Festival and was awarded second place in the Academy Award qualifying Adult Jury Live Action Short Films section.
41. It is beyond the scope of this book to include all female filmmakers here. Others worthy of note are Sara Sugarman, Maeve Murphy and Gaby Dellal. Following training at RADA, Sugarman went on to make shorts before her debut feature film, an adaptation of Kathy Lette's novel *Mad Cows* (1999). *Very Annie Mary* (2001) and *Confessions of a Drama Queen* (2004) followed, and her more recent *Vinyl* (2013) is a US/UK comedy. Maeve Murphy wrote and directed *Beyond the Fire* in 2009 and *Taking Stock* in 2015, a comedy made with the assistance of Northern Ireland Screen. Gaby Dellal's film *On a Clear Day* (2005) opened the Galway Film Fleadh in July 2005. The film is about childhood and children, and her subsequent Canada/UK release *Angel's Crest* (2011) also concerns a three-year-old child who disappears in the settlement of Angel's Crest.

CHAPTER 2

Women and British Cinema Funding: From the UKFC to Creative England

The1997 general election, when New Labour was elected and formed the government, was a significant moment for women in general, first, because the party returned a record number of female MPs (101) as a result of All Women Shortlists in the selection of candidates, and 44% of women voted for Tony Blair's party. As Claire Annesley and Francesca Gains note, 'what we can observe is an awareness on the part of New Labour of the significance of women as political and social citizens who have agency ... the increase of the number of women in Parliament is a crucial way to improve the opportunity for a feminisation of politics and policy' (2007: 4–5). Second, Gordon Brown's policy initiatives sought to erode gender inequalities in modes that the previous Conservative government had not. According to David Coates and Sarah Oettinger, the government 'designed macro-economic policy in ways that were sensitive to the changing gender divisions in the new economy, and to the disproportionate burden of poverty carried by women at the bottom of the society whose economy it was managing' (2007: 122). With its increased representation of women and awareness of women's issues, New Labour became involved in public policy across an array of topics from equal pay to childcare and development policy, and further saw fit to support female appointments to significant positions.[1]

Not only did New Labour introduce vital changes for women, but the party also extended funding policies within the British film industry, making the year 2000 an important turning point in British cinema finance

S. Hockenhull, *British Women Film Directors in the New Millennium*, DOI 10.1057/978-1-137-48992-0_2

because it marked a period which saw the initiation of the UKFC under the chairmanship of Alan Parker. A government quango originally entitled the Film Council, the UKFC was a public body set up by New Labour under Chief Executive John Woodward to direct lottery funding into filmmaking. Its remit was to finance British-made films which would entertain and be shown in multiplex cinemas across the country, in other words to 'facilitate the production of popular British theatrical films which are profitable and attract significant audiences at home and abroad' (James 2000: 16).[2]

The formation of the UKFC replaced or absorbed the functions of the existing structures of the Arts Council England Lottery Film Department, British Screen and the British Film Commission, and succeeded in marginalising the BFI until its demise. Outlining its purpose in its launch document, *Towards a Sustainable UK Film Industry* (UKFC 2000), the suggestion was to impose a limit of £1 million per film, and to create a coherent umbrella structure for the industry, whether on the production side or in terms of finance. The UKFC set up nine Regional Screen Agencies, all committed to improving levels of inclusion, diversity, opportunity and access, and created three separate funds: the Premiere Fund, the Development Fund and the New Cinema Fund. Through these, the UKFC proved instrumental in providing sponsorship for a large number of new projects, and the period 2000 to 2011 saw financial support for British cinema, and consequently an increase in British film production. This rise was not without precedent. Writing in 2012, Sean Perkins notes a general trend towards the expansion of film production in the UK over the previous 25 years,[3] but a noteworthy aspect of the UKFC was that it initiated a study which included the paucity of women in the industry. The period from 2000 onwards thus saw efforts to address this, resulting in an increase in female directors that reached its zenith in 2009.

The UKFC was not the first funding body to subsidise film. In 1981, a co-production agreement was negotiated between Channel 4 and the BFI Production Board through which the former took first option on broadcast rights on BFI supported films for an annual sum. Channel 4 was launched on 2 November 1982, and its remit was either to purchase or commission work from independent production companies. Channel 4's policy of devoting a quarter of its viewing hours to feature films had resulted in an increase in independent filmmakers supplying them with low-budget productions. More significantly, it sought to invest in films intended initially for theatrical release. In its first 12 years, it invested over £90 million in 264 films, and this idea was emulated in part by the BBC and a number of ITV companies. Enacting a policy to support British talent, by 1990 Channel 4 had partially funded 170 films, including Sally Potter's *The Gold Diggers* (1983) and her later *The Tango Lesson* (1997).

Channel 4 subsidies continued into the 1990s, backing, along with the BFI, NFTS graduate Carine Adler's *Under the Skin* (1997), which was a feminist depiction of the grief of two women, Iris (Samantha Morton) and Rose (Claire Rushbrook). The New Directors scheme was established by Channel 4 in 1987 as a place for nurturing future feature filmmakers. This was originally supported by a fund of £50,000 increasing to £200,000, with the scheme's responsibility being to finance short projects, experimental films, documentaries, fiction or animation projects on video, 8mm and 16 mm film up to a limit of £20,000 per project (Dupin 2012). Arguably, the New Directors scheme was attractive to female filmmakers, who were encouraged to make documentaries because they were inexpensive and the cameras lightweight. It also provided impetus for fresh talent, guaranteeing them a theatrical showcase with Channel 4, and afforded an opening for low-budget features such as Adler's film. Adler had some history with Channel 4: along with the BFI, the New Directors scheme had earlier commissioned her to write and direct a short film, *Fever* (1994), and at that time these bodies were especially committed to giving women opportunities. As Kate Ogborn notes, in the mid 1990s, 'the BFI and Channel Four were actively looking for women writers and directors for their joint development fund, having decided to address proactively the lack of women feature film-makers in the UK' (2000: 64). Adler's directing career was short-lived, being limited to the above-mentioned films, apart from an episode of the television series *Shooting Gallery* (1995) and directing *Stray* in 2005. However, as she points out, '96 or 97 was apparently "women's year" in film for the BFI. I think they decided there wasn't enough being made by women, and this year was set aside as being almost exclusively female funding ... if it hadn't been for positive discrimination I may well not have made *Under the Skin* at all' (in Fowler 1998).[4]

Channel 4 was and is committed to projects on diversity and social issues, and, as a result, another director to receive their support was Nigerian-born Ngozi Onwurah. First studying at the NFTS, Onwurah was keen to explore racism in the UK, and she successfully expressed the problems she encountered on her arrival in Britain in her film *Coffee Coloured Children* (1988) as well as in her later *The Body Beautiful* (1990). Her feature film debut, *Welcome II the Terror Dome* (1995) is a comment on police brutality, and received sponsorship from Channel 4 which, at this time, also supported Hettie MacDonald to make *Beautiful Thing* (1995), a social realist low-budget film starring Meera Syal,[5] and Andrea Weiss's documentary entitled *A Bit of Scarlet* (1996). In the same year, Coky Giedroyć was awarded Arts Council lottery funding derived from regional incentive money (Brunsdon 2000), Channel 4 subsidy, and sponsorship from the BFI for her first feature-length film, the hard-hitting drama, *Stella Does Tricks* (1996). Inspired by a documentary series on homelessness, the film focuses on a teenage prostitute played by Kelly Macdonald, and uses 'fragmented close-ups and hand-held camera wobbles [to] emphasise her subjectivity' (McGrath 1998: 50). Later in the decade, the benefits of lottery funding were evident in films such as *Amy Foster* (Kidron 1997) and Lynne Ramsay's *Ratcatcher* (1999).

Writing in 2000, Ogborn, who was executive producer of the BFI and Channel 4's New Directors scheme (also producing Samantha Morton's *The Unloved* in 2009), notes that this commenced in 1987 as a kick-start for new names in the field to develop their career: both the BFI and Channel 4,

> shared a strong interest in supporting and developing voices from the margins and exploring what the medium of film could do. It is significant, though, that the New Directors scheme was initiated at a time when Channel Four was withdrawing most of the funding it had provided to the independent workshop sector, an indication of the switch away from infrastructure funding for production financing for one-off films. (Ogborn 2000: 61)

Other figures to emerge during this period and to benefit from TV sponsorship include American-born but British-based Nancy Meckler. Meckler comes from a theatrical background and has two directing credits: *Sister My Sister* (1994), a Film Four International and British Screen production, and *Alive and Kicking* (1996), the latter a film about a dancer with AIDS which was funded by Channel 4 and distributed by Film Four Distributors. New Zealand-born Anna Campion was based in the UK during this period when she directed *Loaded* (1997)—a film set in southern England. Sponsored by the BFI, Channel 4 and the New Zealand Film Commission, *Loaded* was originally titled *Bloody Weekend* and explores early 1990s' youth culture.[6]

As well as Channel 4's commitment to the film industry, additional encouragement came in May 1991 with the establishment of a British Film Commission; subsequent to the 1992 general election, a new government department, the Department of National Heritage, recognised the cultural significance of film by backing a small tax relief for British film production. Whereas initially the Arts Council of England had been responsible for the distribution of lottery funds, it was replaced by the UKFC, which absorbed British Screen Finance[7] and the British Film Commission (Minns 2000) in the process. Initially, it was envisaged that the BFI would be assimilated into this new body, but that was not what happened. In fact, as John Hill later pointed out, the situation was paradoxical given that the BFI is now responsible for lottery distribution, and 'It is, therefore, something of a historical irony that it survived to subsume its short-lived parent organisation' (2012: 336).

Although the responsibility of Channel 4 was to finance independent productions, these were not the only types of films to receive its sponsorship and benefit women. As mentioned, the film workshops obtained support and the first regionally based workshop, Amber Films, was formed in 1968 in Newcastle upon Tyne. In the early 1980s Amber Workshops negotiated the Workshop Declaration permitting cross-grade working and an equal wage structure under trade union conditions. The declaration ruled out status issues and, subsequently, in 1982, Channel 4 made a commitment to support such groups. This period turned out to be relatively prolific for female-only workshops and, as Antonia Lant suggests, '[i]ts work represents an aspect of British eighties' film culture that usually escapes both academic discussion and international distribution, despite the fact that it is a highly successful cinema in its own right' (1993: 163–4). Moreover, the workshop filmmakers all possessed a 'desire to work outside the political, aesthetic and economic constraints of the mainstream film and television industries' (Petley 1989: 6) and, further, they continued the British documentary film tradition, offering women an opportunity to work on films in a variety of capacities.

The period from the late 1960s to the late 1980s witnessed a flourishing of these workshops, which benefited from financial aid. Originally based near Regent's Park, the first, the London Film-makers' Co-op, was set up in 1966. Eventually moving to Camden, it functioned equally as a workshop and an educational resource, attempting to combine screenings, writing and performance in addition to distribution, and was autonomous from the BFI and the Arts Council. The London Film-makers' Co-op facilitated the process of working with the physical material of the film, and filmmakers could distribute their work in-house. Aiding a new innovative generation of artist/filmmakers who were 'nurtured by the Arts

Council and the British Film Institute, which channelled small amounts of funding towards experimental time-based media' (Phoca 2010: 7), it merged in 1999 with London Video Arts to form LUX.[8]

Another of these workshops, the Sheffield Film Co-op, was formed in 1973 and was set up by women's rights activist, Christine Bellamy. It deliberately left out the word 'Women' from its title, although the group consisted entirely of women (albeit they also had male collaborators), and was comprised of documentary film lecturers from Sheffield City Polytechnic (now Sheffield Hallam University). Producing a variety of documentary programmes for television, and engaged in raising consciousness concerning issues that women faced in their daily lives, the group disseminated feminist ideology. After realising the limitations of television, the Sheffield Film Co-op moved into the medium of film with a production about abortion choices entitled *A Woman Like You* (1976) using a documentary drama format. It was followed a year later by *That's No Lady*. Another female-only women's film collective, Leeds Animation Workshop (LAW), was originally formed in 1976 (formally established in 1978) by a group of friends. The BFI Production Board had continued its interest in non-feature and non-commercial projects throughout the 1980s, including regional workshops and collectives, and under pressure from the ACTT and the Independent Filmmakers Association, agreed to instigate a Regional Production Fund which, in turn, offered support for the administration, management and remuneration of a number of workshops including the LAW. LAW is still in existence, and is the only female animation workshop in Britain, if not the world (Lant 1993). Their first film entitled *Who Needs Nurseries?—We Do!* (1978) was produced entirely by women from the initial research stages through to final distribution. The BFI Production Board also financed a number of feature films including the aforementioned *The Gold Diggers* and Laura Mulvey and Peter Wollen's *Crystal Gazing* (1982) which arguably 'fitted to some extent the art cinema format (length, increased production values, non-rejection of narrative) yet retained a number of aesthetic and political concerns of 1970s independent film-making' (Dupin 2012: 210).

By 1990, Channel Four and then the BFI withdrew support for the workshops, aiming instead to commission more commercially viable productions from independent producers rather than investing in the long-term running of an organisation. Many of them disappeared, but some, like Amber, managed to survive, adapting to the new economic context. Such evolutionary processes worked in favour of the later establishment of small production companies which benefited from lottery funding. As Jack Newsinger affirms:

> There is a direct continuity between the film organizations that can be grouped under the workshop umbrella during the 1970s and 1980s and the structure of film funding and production as it developed up to 2000 with the formation of the UKFC and the RSAs [regional screen agencies], and this is shown in the transition from independent film workshops to open access workshops to small media production companies exploiting the influx of production finance for short and, to a lesser extent, feature films. (2009: 46)[9]

Towards the turn of the new millennium, the 1990s witnessed big industry changes, with a shift to casual and short contract labour which had a significant effect on women.[10] This altered towards the end of the decade when New Labour came to power and adopted the concept of 'Creative Industries', a term originally articulated by a group of Australian academics in Brisbane and identified by Blair as playing a part in the future for Britain in terms of jobs generated through creativity. As Petrie observes, such a policy appealed to a certain sector of society, and 'hence the clear attractiveness of this sector for a government that was particularly keen to appear trendy and youthful while at the same time demonstrating a sound management of the economy and enthusiastic support for business and enterprise' (2012: 364). The implications of this were that emphasis was placed on the marketplace, particularly in terms of film production and film education and training. In addition, a report entitled *A Bigger Future* (Till 2003), published by Skillset and the UKFC, noted the need for greater diversity. As a consequence, a five-year strategy enabled the setting up of a number of Skillset Academies[11] to respond to the needs of the industry, resulting in an increase in funding channelled through National Lottery grants. This allowed scholarships for home students to be introduced and, furthermore, through the way the strategy was worded, encouraged greater diversity and social inclusion.[12]

This emphasis on the marketplace meant that a commitment was made to a more commercial stance in the UKFC, which was to be directed through its attendant funds. The Development Fund, under its director Jenny Borgars, formerly head of British Screen, saw its sphere of activity as piloting films from their very early stages. Funding for script development was therefore a priority, following what were perceived as the disasters of the preceding decade, when accusations had been made concerning quality, particularly in the scriptwriting stage.[13] Therefore, the Development Fund became important in terms of supporting and guiding projects from their commencement and was advantageous in providing a start for filmmakers.[14] In fact there are a number of directors who are able to make one debut film but, if this fails commercially, find it more difficult to obtain funding second time around. Jenny Borgars terms this 'second film syndrome. It is something we have all been aware of: there are a number of brilliant debut voices who are taking a long time to get their second features made' (in Macnab 2005b: 10). Therefore, a later aim of the Development Fund was to support ingenuity and ambition 'in an industry which is often both unwelcoming and daunting. Recognising that filmmakers can benefit from our support at every stage of their career, there are two distinct funding streams to allow us to engage with both emerging filmmakers and those with a demonstrable track record' (Woodward 2009: 6). While this does not obviously reference women, it might be a circuitous allusion to those under-represented and, indeed, Woodward moves on to comment specifically on the list of female directors that the Development Fund supported. As he notes, 'Filmmakers such as Andrea Arnold, Jane Campion, Gurinder Chadha, Lynne Ramsay and Sam Taylor-Wood have all benefited from the Development Fund, with some of their projects already taken forward with the backing of our production funds' (Woodward 2009: 6).

An important component of the UKFC was the New Cinema Fund run by Dutch-born film and television producer, Paul Trijbits. The remit of this scheme was to nurture filmmakers with original and inventive ideas, offering a training ground for innovative directors in order that they might further receive funding from the Premiere Fund. It was never anticipated that the New Cinema Fund should have the same commercial interests as its more prestigious counterpart, the Premiere Fund, and its aims were considerably lower, with the expectation of assisting novel rather than mainstream features. The Premiere Fund, on the other hand, was led by Robert Jones, a former film distributor and producer, and was seen as 'the UKFC's flagship national funding scheme, concentrating simply on the production of popular mainstream British films' (Newsinger 2009: 44). This is explained by Gillian Doyle, who suggests that:

> The creation of the Premiere and Development Funds signalled a marked shift in the emphasis of film support towards fostering a more business-minded and market-led approach to new production ... At the same time, the estab-

> lishment of a New Cinema Fund whose purpose was to back radical and innovative film-making showed that the new body was also committed to the wider and more culturally based remit surrounding public support for film. (2014: 135)

The UKFC policy documents pledged to support a diverse range of films and, more significantly, expressed as part of its responsibility an assurance that it would redress the gender balance. As a result, in 2003 the UKFC stated a commitment to equal opportunities in terms of gender, ethnicity and disability, and set up a working group entitled Leadership on Diversity in Film chaired by the co-chair of Working Title Films, Tim Bevan,[15] subsequently publishing its findings. Described 'as a paper for consultation' it acknowledged that:

> Contemporary British society today is simply not reflected in the industry's current workforce or in on-screen content and portrayal. Although under-representation, say, for women, minority ethnic groups or disabled people, has been recognised and discussed by the film industry over a number of years, very little has been done to change the situation. We all acknowledge a deep sense of frustration at the slow pace of progress in this area over the years. (Bevan 2003: 2)

Moreover, the paper noted that there are 'formidable barriers' to getting into the profession regardless of ethnicity and gender, and that the profile of the workforce ultimately impacts 'on the stories that are told, the way they are told on screen, the levels of access to film for potential audiences and, in terms of content and portrayal, the images of Britain and the concepts of "Britishness" around the globe' (Bevan 2003: 5).

If the committee's aim was to achieve a more diverse workforce 'behind, and in front of, the camera across the film sector value chain (development, production, post-production, distribution and exhibition)' (Bevan 2003: 6), then it also noted the scarcity of women in certain grades. Despite the fact that women accounted for a large percentage of the staff, particularly in cinema exhibition and areas such as wardrobe and costume, there remained a disproportion in terms of female film directors, the report noting that 'Last November, the *bfi* counted only eight films directed by women out of a total of 350 that were made in the UK' (Bevan 2003: 9). The stated aims of the committee in terms of gender were to monitor progress carefully, and examine future fiscal policy and the advantage of co-production treaties for potential benefits. Apart from sponsoring a number of films by black and Asian directors as part of its strategy, the UKFC funded the Women in Film and Television Awards, the largest annual event in the UK to celebrate women in the industry.

The diversity report's stated aims also encompassed distribution and exhibition, particularly their Specialised Films Print and Advertising initiative to 'embrace films that are specialised because of their ethnicity, sexuality, or disability related subject matter, or because of the identities of the filmmakers' (Bevan 2003: 15). In addition, and in line with New Labour's approach, the working group sought to redress the balance in the film industry through greater compliancy by 'developing flexible working and remote access policies and potentially a flexible benefits package' (Bevan 2003: 15). In September 2003, after a period of discussion, Skillset and the UKFC published a national film skills training policy entitled *A Bigger Future* 'to ensure that the UK industry is able to compete successfully in the European and global marketplace on the basis of world beating skills' (Till 2003: 9). This report also noted the requirement for a more socially and culturally diverse workforce.

In 2002, the UKFC had appointed a Head of Diversity, Marcia Williams, to administer the development and implementation of these later published concerns, including funding. Her influence in this area was noted early in her term of office when disquiet was also expressed over the disparity between the films on release and the cultural diversity of the British population, the former not being representative of the latter. In the UKFC annual reports for year ending 2004, under the heading 'Success through Diversity and Inclusion', it was expressly stated that the UKFC was committed to:

> improving diversity and inclusion across the industry ... we are now working with the industry to help change attitudes and working practices. Our aim is to deliver an industry workforce that more accurately reflects the makeup of the UK population and ultimately we aim to ensure that a more diverse range of British films is offered to audiences across the UK. (Woodward 2004: 7)

In response to this, the Development Fund in that year supported the work of a number of women, including Emily Young with *Kiss of Life* and Amma Asante's *A Way of Life*.[16] In the same year the New Cinema Fund backed Sarah Gavron's (also BBC funded) *This Little Life* and Sally

Potter's *Yes*. Amma Asante benefited from the New Cinema Fund as well, through the financing of a training course at the NFTS. As mentioned, the Premiere Fund's remit was to invest in big-budget, commercially successful films, yet this appeared to deter women directors. In fact, those helped in 2004 included male directed films such as *The Constant Gardener* (Meirelles), *Vera Drake* (Leigh), *The Merchant of Venice* (Radford) and *Ladies in Lavender* (Dance).

By 2005, the UKFC finalised its diversity policies and also sponsored Breakthrough Brits, an event in Los Angeles, to promote British female filmmakers in the film industry which 'aimed to raise the profile of British female filmmaking talent by honouring 13 British women from various film disciplines who are tipped for mainstream success. New contacts were made and at least one job has been secured as a direct result of the event' (Woodward 2006: 9).

In sum, whereas in its early stages UKFC policy made little or no mention of gender inequalities, towards the mid period of its existence it sought to redress any disparity and in its *Annual Report and Financial Statements* for 2006/7, under the heading of 'Diversity and Inclusion', its aims were more explicitly stated. Indeed, it announced its intention to 'help achieve a more diverse and inclusive workforce and film culture, and ensure that the funds meet their diversity targets for women, black and minority ethnic groups, disabled people and regional applicants as well as overall content or portrayal targets' (Woodward 2007: 9). In an earlier report, special mention had been made of the then promising newcomer, Andrea Arnold: as Chairman, Stewart Till, commented, the year had witnessed quality 'innovative and thought provoking cinema ... [including] Andrea Arnold whose work bodes so well for the future of our film culture' (2006: 6). At this juncture, the BBC also committed to increase investment in British film production and acquisition in order to 'drive innovation and awareness of film, and to further support British talent, training and development' (Woodward 2006: 12).

In February 2006, the UKFC signed a Memorandum of Understanding for collaborative projects with identified schemes such as the Digital Screen Network to enable filmmakers greater access to screens throughout the country. Also, the support of script development continued 'through its £4 million a year Development Fund, the largest source of such public finance within Europe' (Woodward 2006: 8). Those women's schemes to benefit included Andrea Arnold's Advance Party Films Ltd, which received £10,963 for her film *Red Road* from the Development Fund and £436,144 from the New Cinema Fund. In this year, the Development Fund also assisted Annie Griffin's Pirate Productions film, *Festival* with £2,494. Advance Party Ltd again received funding for *Red Road* with £90,000 for Prints and Advertising, rewarding its backers by winning the Prix du Jury at Cannes, gaining a screening at the Toronto International Film Festival and being nominated for the US Golden Globe award.

The 2006 report also commented on the success of British cinema, which accounted for 33% of the UK box office share, and, in particular, its promotion of equal opportunities through its new diversity policy, noting that:

> real progress is now being made on really embedding diversity in the film industry … to promote equal opportunities and good practice, and tackle issues of access, training and presentation, both behind the camera and on screen. In addition, the UK Film Council hosted Breakthrough Brits, a showcase programme in Hollywood, celebrating the work of a new generation of British female talent, including a writer and cinematographer, as well as actresses, directors, producers and composers. (Woodward 2006: 9)

The remainder of the report discussed policy with the aim of promoting 'social inclusion and [to] celebrate diversity so that every citizen in the UK has access to film culture and barriers to working in the industry are reduced' (Woodward 2006: 11). Films directed by women to benefit from the New Cinema Fund in 2006 included *Brick Lane*, an adaptation of Monica Ali's novel by Sarah Gavron, whose company, Seven Seas (SL) Ltd received £650,000 (UKFC 2006/7 end of year report). *Brick Lane* was also awarded £200,000 towards distribution and exhibition through the company Optimum Releasing. In this year Premiere Fund Awards granted £179,830 to the production company, Pont Neuf Ltd for film rights to Jackie Oudney's *French Film*, and to Young Pirate Films Ltd for *The Festival* (gross award £700,000). New Cinema Fund Awards were also released for Jane Campion's *Bright Star* (£600,000) and to Ruby Films Ltd, Alison Owen's independent production company, for *Brick Lane* (£25,000). *Dear Frankie* (Auerbach 2004) received £900,000. Concurrently, Woodward claimed an economic upturn in the statistical report for 2006 'which trumpeted how the [film] industry contributed over £4 billion to the economy (up 39% on 2004) and noted the UK share of worldwide box-office takings was 8.5%' (Leggott 2008: 7). This meant that low-budget films (up to £20 million) benefited by 20% net and higher budget films (over £20 million) gained 16% net tax relief. In terms of support for female directors, further Development Fund Awards were made to Modern Films Ltd for Carine Adler's *Under the Skin* (£111,949) and Sally Potter Films Ltd for Actor-Based development projects (£48,000). At this point Sally Caplan was in charge of the Premiere Fund, and Jenny Borgars was head of the Development Fund.

In March 2007 the Secretary of State for Culture Media and Sport announced an increase of a further £675 million in lottery contribution for the Olympics. As a result, in February 2008 a statute was passed allowing a substantial transfer of money from the National Lottery Distribution Fund for the forthcoming 2012 games. The UKFC committed to contribute £21.8 million between February 2009 and July 2012 but this impacted on future planning and complaints were made over this funding liability. Nonetheless, the period still saw a large number of film productions, possibly as a result of the new tax reliefs and the 'cultural test', which had been in place for 18 months; this 'provided a welcome boost to the confidence of the UK film industry and its international partners. In 2007, 60 UK features went into production, up from 55 in 2006 with a UK production value of £141 million' (Woodward 2008: 6). In this year, a beneficiary of the Development Fund was Polly Stenham's adaptation of her play *That Face*, although there were no women granted Premiere Award Funding. The New Cinema Fund, on the other hand, 'continues to encourage unique ideas, innovative approaches and new voices by funding an eclectic mix of films that connect with a range of UK audiences' (Woodward 2008: 6). Films in receipt included Morag McKinnon's *Rounding Up Donkeys* (2010), Jane Campion's *Bright Star* (2009) and Andrea Arnold's film, *Fish Tank* (2009).

Again the UKFC expressed its commitment to equal opportunities suggesting that:

> We are continuing to promote long-term diversity in the film industry workforce through a range of sponsorship and awards. Together with Skillset we are leading a £1.4 million project funded by the European Commission's EQUAL programme to create new pathways into film for people from diverse or excluded groups. Initiatives such as our Breakthrough Brits programme continuing to champion our diverse creative talent to the industry at an international level. (Woodward 2008: 8)[17]

Woodward also reiterated the significance of script development, appointing Tanya Seghatchian as the new head of the Development Fund:

> After a strategy of investing in script development at every budget level, the Development Fund has refocused its support for talent and screenplays with the launch of two distinctive funding channels under its new head Tanya Seghatchian. The first aimed at emerging filmmakers who have not had a feature film or who have not yet had a feature film released theatrically or broadcast on UK television, while the second is aimed at filmmakers and production companies with a demonstrable track record in feature filmmaking. The fund will continue, however, to support world renowned British talent through a discretionary signature awards scheme. Films backed by the fund include Polly Stenham's adaptation of her own critically acclaimed play *That Face*, Bruce Robinson's *The Peculiar Memories of Thomas Penman* and Patrick Marber's *Don Juan in Soho*. (2008: 6)

Notably, at this juncture, and in line with New Labour's ethos, the Board of Directors comprised a number of women, including Sally Caplan, Tanya Seghatchian, Jenny Borgars, Rachel Grant, Gail Egan, Elisabeth Murdoch, Rebecca O'Brien, Alison Owen (retired 19 October 2007), Heather Rabbatts and Amanda Walsh: as noted, Borgars and Seghatchian were both in charge of fund distribution.

The 2009 report makes special mention of the UKFC Diversity Unit, which it states 'creates and supports innovative projects that open doors to disabled people and filmmakers from ethnic minority backgrounds who might not otherwise have seen a career in film as an achievable goal. The Unit also nurtures female filmmakers who have found certain avenues in film closed to them' (Woodward 2009: 7). Again, it comments on the significance of the Development Fund for women film directors suggesting that, 'Filmmakers such as Andrea Arnold, Jane Campion, Gurinder Chadha, Lynne Ramsay and Sam Taylor-Wood have all benefited from the Development Fund with some of their projects already taken forward with the backing of our production funds' (Woodward 2009: 7).

The success of female directors continued and the UKFC 2010 end of year report made mention of two in particular, Sam Taylor-Wood and Clio Barnard, claiming their triumph was a result of UKFC funding. As Woodward suggests:

> Sam Taylor-Wood, James Marsh and Clio Barnard joined directors such as Paul Greengrass, Kevin Macdonald and Noel Clarke, whose film careers we helped launch and who have gone on to become internationally regarded

> filmmakers. In funding Sam Taylor-Wood's first feature, *Nowhere Boy*, an enormously talented artist has developed into an acclaimed film director. James Marsh's *Man on Wire* took two of the world's top film honours with the Oscar for Best Documentary and the Outstanding British Film BAFTA, while Clio Barnard was named Best New Documentary Filmmaker for *The Arbor* at tribeca ... Andrea Arnold, whose career we have supported from the beginning, won her second Cannes Jury Prize with *Fish Tank*, whilst Armando Iannucci's *In the Loop* and Jane Campion's *Bright Star*, both of which we helped develop and produce, were Oscar nominated ... Our continued investment in emerging filmmakers saw Esther Campbell's *September* win BAFTA's Short Film Award ... Looking ahead, we are pleased to have supported exciting and ambitious films such as *Another Year*, *Made in Dagenham*, *Brighton Rock*, *The King's Speech*, *Tamara Drewe* and *Wuthering Heights*. (2010: 5)

Indeed, the Premiere Fund supported Taylor-Wood's *Nowhere Boy* and, as Woodward noted, 'Helping creative and ambitious projects to take the leap into production is where the UK Film Council's Premiere Fund and New Cinema Fund come in' (2009: 7). Woodward's celebratory comments were not universally shared. As Sophie Phoca points out, the 'Film Council's seemingly alternative funding of Sam Taylor-Wood's *Nowhere Boy*, 2009, and Gillian Wearing's *Self Made*, 2010, was criticised for cynically cashing in on their yBa[18] celebrity status rather than nurturing and supporting lesser-known edgier artists' (2010: 9).[19]

In 2010 Woodward resigned, and his report commented on his last year as head of the UKFC. For him 2009/10 was a period of sustained financial unrest, 'and the UK film industry, like all sectors, was not immune' (Woodward 2010: 5). In this year, independent British films took an 8.5% share of the UK box office (2009), and Skillset supported more than 4,000 trainees. Even so, the UKFC annual reports for 2009/10, using research into Labour Market Intelligence, suggested that women at that time remained seriously under-represented in key roles, with six times the number of women than men leaving the sector in the three years leading up to 2009.

In December 2009, internal restructuring of the UKFC took place, merging the Premiere, New Cinema and Development Funds under one roof and, less than a year later, in April 2010, the UKFC created one unified Film Fund to support UK filmmakers, with an Innovation Fund to help UK film companies move into the digital world. Further, the Department of Culture Media and Sport announced a proposal to combine the UKFC and the BFI, and from this point on Tanya Seghatchian commenced a three-year contract as head of the Film Fund. The governing body of directors consisted of a 50/50 gender split, with a number of women prominent in the field of film: these included Barbara Broccoli (film producer), Pippa Cross (film director), Gail Egan (film director), Beeban Kidron (film director), Elisabeth Murdoch (film director), Rebecca O'Brien (film director), Heather Rabbatts and Amanda Walsh.

Thus, to summarise, the period between 2000 and 2011 witnessed greater concern for diversity within the film industry and a resultant change in film policy. The UKFC sponsored a number of female-directed films from a variety of funds, some of which went on to receive critical acclaim and various accolades: Andrea Arnold's *Red Road* won a BAFTA award for best newcomer, and her later film, *Fish Tank*, won best director in the 2009 British Independent Film Awards and the 2009 Jury Prize at the Cannes Film Festival. Esther Campbell's short film, *September* (2008), which won the BAFTA Short Film Award, also qualified for UKFC investment.

An important factor in the success of this latter film and others might be attributed to film producer Tanya Seghatchian, who, as noted, became the head of the UKFC's Development Fund and subsequently head of the Film Fund from 2010. Writing in *The Independent*, Rachel Millward, the founder/director of the women's film festival Birds Eye View (BEV), commented: 'Much has been made of the "three musketeers" of independent film finance – Christine Langan, the Creative Director of BBC films, Tessa Ross at Channel 4 films, and Tanya Seghatchian, who takes control of the UK Film Council's funding in April' (Millward 2010).

Tessa Ross succeeded to a role previously held by males (David Rose, David Aukin, and Paul Webster) when she was appointed Head of Drama in 2000 and Controller of Film and Drama for Film4 and Channel 4, a position she held between 2002 and 2014, before resigning from the post. Ross highlights the issues she encountered when she first took on the role, resulting in a decision to invest in a closer integration between programming and Film4. Her argument was based on a need for greater synergy and, as she proposes:

> it was about having Channel 4 want the films, and having the talent that comes into Channel 4 believing that film is a possibility for them as part of their livelihood, and as part of their ambition. And having Film4 addressing its relationship to the industry … They needed good stuff that gets their name out in the world, and makes them look like they mean who they are.

> And what do the talent want? They need a collaborative, supportive, public service, British home that understands its own audience and its role among whatever other public money is out there. (in Smith and Mayne 2014: 541)

Ross's aim was not for cinema hits necessarily, but for 'good stuff on telly' (in Smith and Mayne 2014: 541), and she too saw the need for more substantial investment in development, particularly at the script stage, perceiving that her remit was to be 'adventurous and [to] drive new talent, and be curious and at least edgier in some way ... there is a flavour we are injecting into the industry which definitely has a different energy' (in Smith and Mayne 2014: 543). Ross attributes much of the enthusiasm and success to her staff, especially Head of Development, Rose Garnett, and Katherine Butler, Deputy Head of Film.

Likewise, Seghatchian had overseen two major reorganisations: the merging of the UKFC's disparate development and production offices into a single unified Film Fund in early 2010 and, following the closure of the UKFC, the transfer of the Film Fund to the BFI in 2011. Described by *The Guardian* as 'the most powerful woman in the British film industry' (Dawtrey 2010), Seghatchian had access to both the Premiere Fund and the New Cinema Fund, which together constituted a sizeable budget that enabled her to support the production of both small- and large-scale projects and to look 'for creative excellence in the shape of great vision and good stories' (in Dams 2011). As she states, films such as Lynne Ramsay's *We Need to Talk About Kevin*, Arnold's *Wuthering Heights*, Barnard's *The Arbor* (2010) and *The Iron Lady* (Lloyd 2011), all 'currently show the breadth and ambition of our investments' (in Dams 2011). Langan, Ross and Seghatchian were responsible for heading film finance, and worked closely together, experiencing 'an easy collegiate relationship' (Curtis 2010). Although Seghatchian's interventions in the funding of female directors are not transparent in any documentation, this triumvirate authority was certainly advantageous[20] for directors such as Sam Taylor-Wood with *Nowhere Boy* (Channel 4 and UKFC) and Andrea Arnold with *Fish Tank* (UKFC New Cinema Fund and Development Fund in association with BBC Films).

While priority was given by the UKFC to first- and second-time filmmakers, and women appeared to benefit from policies that it put in place, particularly after the inception of its Diversity and Inclusion Policy, support was also provided for established figures such as Stephen Frears, Mike Leigh and Ken Loach. However, it may be no coincidence that the annual report for 2006/7, published in August 2007 (after Seghatchian's appointment, albeit Borgars had been in place earlier), indicated a firm commitment to women, and thereafter UKFC documentation called for greater equality in terms of gender.[21] Furthermore, the latter period of the UKFC saw an increased number of women directors in receipt of funding, for example, with Clio Barnard directing *The Arbor*, a low-budget documentary which received support from the UKFC Development Fund. This is one of several films displaying a raw and documentary realist style. Indeed, a whole array of UKFC funded documentary films emerged at this time, including Carol Morley's *Dreams of a Life* (2011), a disturbing account of a woman who died of natural causes and whose body lay undiscovered in her home for three years. By 2010/11 there was greater equity in terms of funding: 58% of the lottery funding was awarded to men and 42% to women, whereas the year before it was less evenly split with 70% of the funds awarded to men and 30% to women.

Following the general election and the formation of a Conservative-Liberal Democrat coalition government in 2010, a decision was made to abolish the UKFC. The Conservative side of the uneasy alliance was determined to get rid of the quangos associated with Labour and a public statement came in July 2010 from Jeremy Hunt, the new Secretary of State for Culture, Media and Sport, to this effect. Reassurances were made that lottery funding and the film tax credits would remain in place, and the BFI was to be given greater authority and artistic freedom. One of the criticisms was that the UKFC spent a quarter of its budget on salaries, albeit this was hotly disputed (Doyle et al. 2015: 164).[22] Whatever the truth, by the end of the UKFC's tenure, there was undeniably an increased awareness pertaining to female representation in the film industry.

Notwithstanding Seghatchian's influence within the UKFC, she was left little time to make a more significant impact before its closure, and she ultimately resigned her post in 2011. Subsequently, the Film Policy Review Panel published an independent report in January 2012 titled *A Future for Britain: It Begins with the Audience*. This consisted of an independent panel of film industry experts reviewing the government film policy which demonstrated the success of the UKFC suggesting that:

> British film is going through something of a golden period … The astonishing success of *The King's Speech*, of course, heads the list; but add to that the final *Harry Potter*, *The Inbetweeners*, *Tinker Tailor Soldier Spy*, *Shame*, *Wuthering Heights*, *We Need to Talk About Kevin*, *Johnny English Reborn*, and quite a few others, and it's an impressive picture. (UK Film Policy Review 2012: 2)

Unsurprisingly, the bulk of these films were UKFC funded, and two were made by female directors. In its place, the BFI has become the government's lead agency for film and, keen not to underplay the scarcity of women working within the industry, it notes that:

> the UK film industry has a tendency to over-representation of white males and under-representation of women and people from diverse groups ... There is also a deficit of female writers and directors. In 2010, only 12% of writers and 13% of directors of British films were female. This despite the fact that some of the most successful British films in recent years (eg *Harry Potter*, *Mamma Mia!*, *Nanny McPhee*, *StreetDance 3D*, *Kick-Ass*, *Bend It Like Beckham*, *Bridget Jones*) have been originated and/or written and/or directed by women. (UK Film Policy Review 2012: 69)

Yet the vestiges of UKFC support lingered on. Phyllida Lloyd released *The Iron Lady* in 2011, the bio-pic of Lady Thatcher and a UK/France co-production, and Sophie Fiennes's UK/Ireland documentary, *The Pervert's Guide to Ideology*, which had also received assistance from the UKFC, was released in 2012. *I Am Breathing* (2012) is Emma Davie's and Morag McKinnon's documentary about Neil Platt, the Scottish architect diagnosed with Motor Neurone Disease at the age of 33. The film follows his final months as he bravely documents his circumstances and experience, and the directors were fortunate in acquiring a number of sponsors from the Scottish Documentary Institute and Danish Documentary. It was also supported by Channel 4, the UKFC and the Wellcome Trust.[23]

However, Creative England has now taken over the mantle, providing what it terms 'bespoke support' for filmmakers. The organisation entered into a four-year deal with the BFI to provide funding for cinema releases, including Lynne Ramsay's short film titled *Swimmer* (2011), and *One Mile Away* (2012), the Edinburgh International Film Festival award-winning film by Penny Woolcock (discussed in Chap. 3), which was supported through Creative England's West Midlands Production Fund and Channel 4.

In 2011, Amanda Nevill became the head of the newly expanded BFI, with a directive to distribute lottery funding. Activities to be transferred from the UKFC included film development and production finance, film distribution and exhibition activity, films skills, training and education funding. The 2012 report, *A Future for British Film: It Begins with the Audience*, was closely followed by the BFI's revised policy, entitled *Film Forever: Supporting UK Film*, issued later that year, identifying its priorities as the expansion of education, learning opportunities and increasing audience choice in the UK. Further, its stated aims were to continue investing in film development, preservation and digitisation (Doyle et al. 2015: 172).

The success of the UKFC cannot be underestimated for women directors. The proportion of female directors in 2011 (15%) was the second highest since monitoring of the gap began in 2007, but the number of female directors was the same (21) as in 2009, which saw the highest proportion (17%) since 2007. Some of the female directors associated with UK films released in 2011[24] were: Andrea Arnold (*Wuthering Heights*), Sangeeta Datta (*Life Goes On*), Lynne Ramsay (*We Need to Talk About Kevin*) and Lone Scherfig (*One Day*). Both Datta and Ramsay also wrote their own screenplays.[25] The numbers remained fairly constant with films for 2012/13 including Clio Barnard's *The Selfish Giant*, the aforementioned Emma Davie's and Morag McKinnon's *I Am Breathing* and Sophie Fiennes's *The Pervert's Guide to Ideology*, Tina Gharavi's *I Am Nasrine* and Jacqui Morris's *McCullin*. Clio Barnard and Tina Gharavi both wrote the screenplays of their films as well as directing them.[26] Concern continues over this gap, and in November 2013 a BAFTA event was held which was chaired by Baroness Oona King and entitled Diversity in the UK Film and Television Industries with speakers Penny Woolcock, Gurinder Chadha and Sally El Hosaini expressing concern that women accounted for only 7.8% of all directors in 2012 (Wiseman 2013). Similarly, in 2014 *Screen International*, *Broadcast* and Creative Skillset, in response to Skillset's latest employment census,[27] hosted a cross-industry conference regarding the under-representation of women in UK film and television. At one of the panels at the event entitled Women in Film and TV, Ben Roberts, Director of the BFI Film Fund, claimed with some optimism that they are making positive moves towards female directors. As he suggests, 'I don't think that we, the Film Fund, are doing as badly in some areas as others. Our support for women filmmakers would probably earn us a B+' (2014: 16). Indeed, in this year the BFI Film Fund sponsored projects involving a number of women directors and writers, including Barnard's *The Selfish Giant*, *Second Coming* (tucker green),[28] *InRealLife* (Kidron), *The Falling* (Morley), *Exhibition* (Hogg), *Belle* (Asante and Sagay), *Posh* (Scherfig), *Gone Too Far* (Ekaragha and Agbaje) and *Suffragette* (Gavron and Morgan).

Greater inroads were made in 2015 when the BFI opened a Diversity Fund with a Three Ticks Scheme for all BFI lottery funded projects. The organisation commits to 'recognise and acknowledge the quality and value of difference' (Wiseman 2015; Wiseman 2016) in accordance with the BFI Diversity Standard, and the Diversity Fund is designed to subsidise under-represented groups on screen, and to address diversity in race, disability, gender, age, sexual orientation and socioeconomic status. The fund is managed by Deborah Williams. Applicants must tick a minimum of two areas of the four categories to succeed. These include On-screen Representation, Themes and Narratives; Creative Practitioners and Artistic Leadership; Industry Access and Opportunities; Opportunities for Audience Development—the latter a grouping for festivals and distribution funds and funded audience activities. Gurinder Chadha's *Viceroy's House*, Amma Asante's *A United Kingdom* and Andrea Arnold's *American Honey* are examples that have qualified so far.[29]

More recent statistics released by the BFI show that, even though takings at the global box office for British films are high, female-directed films are rarely top-grossing or big-budget features. As Beryl Richards, Director and Chair of the Directors UK[30] Women's Working Group argues: 'Of the British films that were included in the top 200 grossing films worldwide between 2001 and 2012, only one was directed by a woman: the 2008 musical *Mamma Mia!*, which was directed by Phyllida Lloyd. Female-directed films took 4.5% of the $1.3 billion (£8.6 billion) earned by the top British films' (2013). The BFI Research and Statistics Unit published a report in 2013 tracking the under-representation of UK screenwriters and directors of UK films between 2010 and 2012 entitled *Succès de plume? Female Screenwriters and Directors of UK Films, 2010–2012.* Written by David Steele, this report acknowledged the lack of women directors, but highlighted successes in other areas:

> although the numbers of female writers and directors of UK films released are consistently low, recently higher proportions of women have been associated with successful films. Of the independent UK films released between 2010 and 2012, just 16% of the writers and 11% of the directors were women. However, for the top 20 UK independent films over the same period, women represented 37% of the writers and 18% of the directors. And for profitable UK independent films, 30% of the writers were women. Successful female writers and directors of independent UK films over this period include: Jane Goldman (*The Woman in Black* and *Kick-Ass*), Debbie Isitt (*Nativity 2: Danger in the Manger!*), Phyllida Lloyd and Abi Morgan (*The Iron Lady*), Dania Pasquini and Jane English (*StreetDance* and

> *StreetDance 2*) and Lucinda Whiteley (*Horrid Henry: The Movie*). In addition to independent UK films, a number of female writers and directors had success over the same period working on UK-USA studio titles. Examples include: Jane Goldman (*X-Men: First Class*), Lone Scherfig (*One Day*), Sarah Smith (*Arthur Christmas*), Susanna White and Emma Thompson (*Nanny McPhee and the Big Bang*). (Steele 2013)[31]

Summary

To conclude this chapter, pre the millennium Channel 4 and the BFI were instrumental in funding a number of films directed by women, specifically through its New Directors scheme, with the British film industry witnessing the emergence of some new names in the field. However, it was the late 1990s and the new millennium that saw substantial industry changes when New Labour came to power. Adopting the 'Creative Industries' concept, the party emphasised the need for greater workplace diversity, which was, in this instance, achieved through UKFC policy. Indeed, film funding at the chief institutions lay in the hands of women and, with low-budget fiction films in particular, a number of female film directors benefited.

Funding and diversity strategies in film production are of paramount importance to women directors and, taking this into account, in the next four chapters, I now move on to examine the output of a number of British women filmmakers, or female directors practising in the UK. Commencing with documentary cinema, a field in which women directors are more prolific than in any other genre, Chap. 3 analyses a number of examples, and explains how funding is secured, and the ways in which the films are distributed and exhibited. This section is not arranged in any hierarchical order, but grouped according to subject matter and visual style.

Notes

1. New Labour also championed a range of policies which impacted on the lives of lesbian and gay people, a point noted by Angela Wilson who suggests that, 'Without a doubt, New Labour has been the most lesbian-and-gay-friendly government in our history' (2007: 193).
2. While this statement indicates that large-budget Hollywood-style productions would be favoured over and above European lower

budget films, this point was denied by Woodward (see James 2000).

3. In feature films alone, the 1980s saw the release of 40 films, and 80 in the 1990s, with a jump to approximately 130 per annum since 2000. Whereas the UKFC tracking of releases tended to focus on large-budget features costing over £500,000, there is also an increase in the production of low-budget films (see Perkins 2012). These figures also include co-productions, although there were more co-productions released between 2001 and 2004 than later in the decade owing to a tightening in co-production certification requirements and new UK film production tax relief systems. See Perkins (2012).
4. Other film directors working at this time included Antonia Bird, who commenced her career in 1994 directing *Priest*, a film sponsored by the BBC and Miramax. Set in Liverpool, *Priest* follows a homosexual priest, Father Greg Pilkington (Linus Roache) who faces up to his celibacy and develops a relationship with Graham (Robert Carlyle). Following her later film *Face* (1997), Bird eventually moved into television, directing serials such as *A Passionate Woman* (2010) and *The Village* (2013), having also directed episodes of *EastEnders* (1985–6), *Casualty* (1986–7), *Morse* (1992), *Peak Practice* (1993) and *The Men's Room* (1991) among others prior to this period.
5. *Beautiful Thing* was adapted from Jonathan Harvey's play. This was her one and only film, although she moved on to direct for television, in particular *Dr Who* (2007 and 2015), *Fortitude* (2015–16) and *The Tunnel* (2013).
6. Other women backed by Channel 4 include Angela Pope, a prolific director with a number of TV and film credits to her name including *Captives* (1994), a BBC Films Production. Her first feature film, *A Man You Don't Meet Everyday* (1994), was followed by *Hollow Reed* (1996) and *Kansas in August* (1999). Fiona Cunningham Reid graduated from the London International Film School moving on to produce and direct *Thin Ice* in 1994 and a number of documentaries for Channel 4, whereas Mandie Fletcher's success came from her television direction, with numerous credits in both series and films. *Deadly Advice* (1993), described as a 'hodge-podge of sexual repression and Enid Blyton cuteness' (Anwar 1994: 41), is cited as Fletcher's feature debut. Alison de

Vere was a British animator and, in 1987, she directed *The Black Dog*. De Vere was unusual in that she was the first female animation director and *The Black Dog* was released when she was 60. Commissioned by Channel 4, the film follows a woman on a mission of self-discovery and was shot in Cornwall where she resided. *Psyche and Eros* followed in 1994, again commissioned by Channel 4. Other female directors to note are South African-born director, Elaine Proctor, who studied at the NFTS, directing *Friends* in 1993. Filmmakers operating outside of Channel 4 funding from the 1980s onwards include Christine Edzard, who founded Sands Films with her husband Peter Goodwin. Edzard built her reputation on films such as *Biddy* (1983) and *Little Dorritt* (1988), and, financed through private loans and Goodwin's money, Sands Films continued to provide an outlet for Edzard's career. *The Fool* (1990), based on Mayhew's *London Labour and the London Poor* (1851), and her contemporary version of *As You Like It* (1992), a modern adaptation of Shakespeare, comprised her directing career for the remainder of the decade until the release of *The Children's Midsummer Night's Dream* in 2001.

7. British Screen Finance's shareholders included United Artists Screen Entertainment, Channel 4, Granada and Rank. The organisation received £4 million per annum for its main fund and the European Co-production Fund.
8. In time, the Thatcher government began reducing support for mainstream structures in the arts, although regional funding bodies commenced grants and bursaries for production and exhibition which encouraged new artists such as Isaac Julien. Julien came from the black film collective, Sankofa, and was supported to develop independent productions such as *Young Soul Rebels* (1988). Similarly, John Akomfrah, director of the critically acclaimed *Handsworth Songs* (1986), set up the Black Audio Film Collective during this time. Regional film policy has its origins in the Regional Film Society movement of the 1950s and saw the establishment of regional film theatres (RFTs) set up by the BFI as a consequence of the devolution of their activities outside London. By 1970, there were 36 RFTs across the country, showing a variety of films drawn from European and Art House directors. RFTs not only developed exhibition on a larger scale, they also provided a regional cinema drawing on a diversity of cultures.

9. Towards the end of the decade, women filmmakers such as Kay Mellor were directing for TV, and she also had scriptwriting credits to her name. Her programmes and films were 'popular with audiences ... [and] accessible, finely crafted dramas, which winningly combined the character based concerns of soap opera with a salty dash of social realism' (Lawrenson 1999: 45). Mellor wrote for a variety of dramas such as *Brookside* (1982–2003), *Band of Gold* (1995), *Playing the Field* (1998), *Coronation Street* (1960–) and *Girls Night* (Hurran 1998), the latter a film supported by Granada television, which had followed Channel 4's lead on financing films for theatrical release. Mellor's film directorial career commenced with *Fanny and Elvis* in 1999, which was financed partly through the Film Consortium. She returned to television directing with *A Passionate Woman* (2010), *In the Club* (2014) and *The Syndicate* (2015). Others who should be mentioned include British-born Sue Clayton, who directed *The Disappearance of Finbar* in 1996 and went on to make documentary shorts, and Sandra Goldbacher, who directed *The Governess* in 1998, which was supported by the Arts Council, and *Me Without You* (2001) before she too moved into television directing with *The Hour* (2012) and *Endeavour* (2016).
10. For example, freelance workers were not entitled to maternity leave.
11. These included the NFTS, Screen Academy of the LFS, Bournemouth Screen and Media Academy, the Screen Academy at the London College of Communication and the Ealing Institute of Media, the Screen Academy Scotland, the Screen Academy Wales, the Film Business Academy at Cass Business School. A further 19 academies were also established from existing institutions.
12. The focus, however, was more on the training of writers and producers than directors.
13. See Peretti (2000) and Petley (2002). Various problems beset the UKFC at the outset, particularly in terms of controversy concerning what were perceived as non-commercial projects. The infamous *Sex Lives of the Potato Men* (Humphries 2003) received £1.6 million in lottery money but was vilified as an example of a British filmic disaster.
14. The UKFC's investment in script development had important repercussions for women as many, including Andrea Arnold,

Samantha Morton and Lynne Ramsay, write their own scripts. See Susan Rogers's (2007) report for the UKFC.

15. Later to become chair of the UKFC.
16. Others to benefit in 2004 included Danny Boyle's *Millions*, Dominic Savage's *Love and Hate* and Peter Richardson's *Finest Hour (Churchill)*.
17. As a result of the change in tax laws, the number of co-productions dropped dramatically.
18. Young British Artists—the name given to a group of visual artists who exhibited together from 1988 onwards and largely graduated from Goldsmiths in the late 1980s. These included Damien Hirst and Tracey Emin. Wearing and Taylor-Wood were graduates from the class of 1990.
19. Further lottery awards were made in this year to women directors as follows: Adventure Pictures (Rage) Ltd—£200,000, Adventure Pictures Ltd—untitled Sally Potter projects (£50,000), Artangel Trust Ltd Buttershaw aka Arbor (£25,000), Bend It Films Ltd (Untitled) Gurinder Chadha (£50,000), Blast Films Ltd, *One Day* (£8,850) and Catherine Shepherd *Like a Virgin* (£14,500) (figures from UKFC Group and Lottery *Annual Report and Financial Statements*).
20. Documentary filmmaker, Lucy Walker, recognises the contribution of the female TV heads of drama to support women, particularly Tessa Ross. As she argues, 'There was a recent season at the BFI, Made in Britain, curated by Clare Stewart that focused on female directors, myself included. There's an extra determination on the part of BBC films and Film4's Tessa Ross and Katherine Butler to stick with us and support us in a creative and solid way' (in Amelia Hill 2012: 42).
21. The 'Success through diversity and inclusion' report of 2003 presented an overview of Women in Film, but not specifically female directors. However, it did report that out of 350 films made during 2002, only eight were directed by women (See: http://industry.bfi.org.uk/media/pdf/3/r/Success_through_diversity_and_inclusion.pdf (accessed 16 December 2013).
22. While concern has been expressed about the disbanding of the UKFC, many commentators argue that its benefits were marginal. As Phoca points out, the UKFC 'sucked vital funding from bodies

such as the BFI, Arts Council and British Screen, hitting a diverse group of time-based practices. In effect, the cultural agenda pursued by the Arts Council and the BFI was overshadowed by grander political ambitions to promote British commercial cinema' (2010: 9).

23. For Emma Davie, the urge to make documentaries emerged from a desire to understand a bigger world. As she suggests, 'The type of documentary I love and aspire to recognises the filmmaker's own perspective and somehow allows us as an audience to participate in this process of seeing' (Davie 2003: 4).
24. Albeit three of these were in receipt of UKFC funding.
25. This has been the subject of two reports: *Scoping Study into the Lack of Women Screenwriters in the UK* (IES 2006) and *Writing British Films—Who Writes British Films and How They Are Recruited* (Susan Rogers, Royal Holloway and UKFC 2007). The combined conclusion of these reports is that female under-representation exists in screenwriting also, and that this is an aspect of a commissioning process that tends to recruit writers who:

   - are already known to the commissioning producers; and/or
   - are members of the Writers Guild of America; and/or
   - have American agents (even if they are British).

   At the time that these reports were commissioned, evidence suggested that around 10% of UK films had a female director and around 15% of UK films had a female writer. Of the 144 identified writers of UK films in 2010, 17 (12%) were women. The proportion of female writers in 2010 was the same as in 2007, but lower than in 2008 (17.3%) and 2009 (16.5%). Although the percentage of female writers was similar in 2010 to that in 2007, the absolute number of female writers associated with released UK films in 2010 was the lowest since the study of the numbers of female writers and directors began in 2006. Some of the female writers associated with UK films released in 2010 were: Moira Buffini (*Tamara Drewe*), Jane English (*StreetDance 3D*), Jane Goldman (*Kick-Ass*) and Emma Thompson (*Nanny McPhee and the Big Bang*). As well as being involved in the writing process, many of the female writers also directed or co-directed their films. See Rogers (2007).

26. Again, some of these films were in receipt of UKFC funding.
27. This demonstrated a decline of diversity in the workplace.
28. debbie tucker green uses lower case to spell her name.
29. Others to benefit included Peter Middleton and James Spinney's *Notes on Blindness*, Michael Lennox's *A Patch of Fog*, Andrew Steggall's *Departure*, Ben Wheatley's *Free Fire* and Colm McCarthy's *She Who Brings Gifts*.
30. The professional association for British directors working in the audio-visual sector.
31. Many of these female writers also directed their films. Statistically, the figures published by the BFI in 2014 suggest that in 2007 women directors amounted to 6%, in 2008 11.5%, in 2009 17.2%, in 2010 12.5%, in 2011 15% dropping to 7.8% in 2012 and rising to 14% in 2013. Female directors associated with UK films released 2011–2012 are: Debbie Isitt (*Nativity 2: Danger in the Manger!*), Phyllida Lloyd (*The Iron Lady*), Deepa Mehta (*Midnight's Children*) and Sally Potter (*Ginger & Rosa*).

CHAPTER 3

Women Directors and Documentary Cinema

In the domain of documentary filmmaking there is a wealth of female directors working in Britain in the new millennium whose films merit attention. Insofar as US cinema is concerned, Melissa Silverstein has remarked on the achievements of women in this genre, stating that 'female documentary filmmakers have achieved a level of success that has eluded women in the fiction film business' (2008).[1] According to Silverstein, part of their skill in documentary is that they take on large-scale topics and 'explore them through intimate, relatable stories' (2008). She attributes much of this to the low budgets required to make the films, and to the fact that there are a number of women in high positions giving the green light on broadcasting channels, and she uses the American cable and satellite television network HBO as an example. As mentioned, a similar situation exists in UK broadcasting, with female programmers in executive positions in the industry. Like their US counterparts, many of the British documentaries are relatively inexpensive to make and they consider international issues which are told in a detailed yet personal manner.[2]

Documentary cinema is comprised of a large variety of forms and styles and is a growth area since the turn of the millennium, in particular for women directors who, as Waldman and Walker note, 'don't shrink from difficult, multidimensional, and topical issues' (1999: 2). The films discussed below offer a distinct means of address in this field, dealing with these 'difficult, multidimensional, and topical issues', often from a feminist standpoint and certainly from a female perspective. Further, they often

S. Hockenhull, *British Women Film Directors in the New Millennium*, DOI 10.1057/978-1-137-48992-0_3

favour what Bill Nichols (1991) might term an observational style over an intrusive approach. Observational modes of address,[3] sometimes termed 'direct cinema' (Bruzzi 2000), suggest a lack of personal intervention by the director, and are typified by the use of long takes and synchronous sound to connote life surveyed rather than created through the camera. This notion of total objectivity through the apparent absence of the filmmaker from the process does not mean passivity on their part, as many of those discussed here are interventionist purely through their lack of interaction with their subjects. They are dedicated, and the conflation of observation and objectivity is not at the expense of their personal belief and commitment. In other words, the filmmakers are passionate about their projects and the subjects they explore. Other modes of address that women documentary makers pursue include the docu-drama or the performative documentary: a mode which manipulates or constructs a film around the subjects or actors. Such an approach is based on the assumption that drama can engage with contentious issues through non-fiction techniques. Rarely in this study do women documentary filmmakers 'act', or even appear on screen. Generally, they give a voice to the other and are decentred. Indeed, they function as mediators activating their subjects to provide explanations and to express feelings.

In terms of finance, documentary films are fairly inexpensive to make, yet, despite the fact that UKFC funding was more readily available from the start of the new millennium onwards, it was directed more at low-budget fiction films rather than, with a few exceptions, factual cinema. Thus many of the filmmakers discussed here operate independently, raising finance themselves rather than through lottery money. Regarding subject matter and style, the films of female documentary makers, and those discussed in this chapter, have shared themes and features. In the main they focus on climate change and ecological issues, or local and global cultural and societal concerns. Furthermore, and demonstrating a strong allegiance to these topics, the filmmakers frequently continue to campaign on these issues long after the release of their films.

Documentary Cinema: Ecological Issues and Climate Change

If female documentary directors seem to favour environmental topics, this is because, according to Christine Haigh and Bernadette Vallely, women are more likely to address these issues more actively than their male counterparts. In their study, based on a published document entitled *Women and the Climate Change Agenda*, they contend that women are more inclined to take effective action in the prevention of climate change, because they contribute less to it. Their report notes that the reasons for this are that:

> poverty – lower consumption roughly equates with lower greenhouse gas emissions – and their social roles – for example, women are less likely to fly for business reasons, and less likely to hold a driving licence or own a vehicle. It is also observed that women are more inclined towards pro-environmental behaviour, such as recycling and energy efficiency, taking part in citizen actions, and are more likely to favour policies that reduce greenhouse gas emissions, such as limiting airport expansion, or taxing activities with a large climate change impact. This report highlights the way in which the industries that are contributing most to climate change continue to be dominated by men in the most senior roles. It also finds evidence that the majority of those who continue to deny that climate change is a reality, or a problem that requires attention, are male. (Haigh and Vallely 2010: 5)

While much of this remains the subject of debate, it is the case that many female directors deal with the environment in their work. One such filmmaker is Franny Armstrong, whose company is financially independent, raising money from sources other than lottery funding and television. Armstrong, a former drummer in a band and a graduate in zoology from University College London, is an environmental activist with deep-seated beliefs about social inequality. She has strong convictions in the sphere of climate change which she successfully expresses through her work. Described as 'moving and ... received with great enthusiasm' (Kazimuddin and Young 2003: 392), her early film entitled *Drowned Out* (2002) is a low-budget documentary aimed at both a home and an international market. The film focuses on displaced tribal villagers in the Narmada Dam region of India, and the director gives insights into their lives and livelihoods. When filming, Armstrong demonstrated her allegiance to the project by immersing herself wholeheartedly in the lives of the villagers. She lived with them during the three years it took to make the film, which was produced by Armstrong's company, Spanner Films and distributed by Journeyman Pictures, a company that specialises in original and thought-provoking material, and therefore appropriate for this film.

Armstrong possesses an independence of spirit which is significant for her filmmaking, permitting her liberty and autonomy with the content and the marketing. In terms of *Drowned Out*, she suggests that it is helpful to be free of the financial constraints imposed by backers because:

> Clearly films like this appeal only to a limited market here in the UK – the trick is to combine the limited market here with that in Europe, Asia, America and the rest of the world. And, again, it helps not to have a commission. Well, it helps that the copyright is owned by a small production company obsessed with getting the story out and not too bothered about making money. (Armstrong 2002: 14)

After its first screening in London in 2002 *Drowned Out* was shown at a number of international film festivals to gain distribution, including—in line with her convictions—the Greek EcoFestival (2004), the New Zealand Aotearoa Human Rights Film Festival in 2006 and the Women Make Waves Film Festival in Taiwan in 2007, eventually selling to terrestrial TV.

Armstrong's concern for the environment continued with *Baked Alaska* (2003), an educational video explaining how global warming has affected the US state of Alaska. This film preceded her later inflammatory *McLibel*, tackling a 'large-scale topic', which touches on environmental issues, animal cruelty and advertising to children. *McLibel* focuses on a libel case[4] involving the food chain, McDonald's, an avenue that ultimately proved problematic for Armstrong because of the longevity of the court case. The content consists of 'a no-frills earnestness that combines interviews with the protagonists, commentary by supportive journalists ... and restrained re-enactments of the trial (the actors in these sequences are directed, with an appropriate lack of histrionics, by Ken Loach)' (Porton 2005: 80).[5] Distribution initially proved a problem for *McLibel*, but as the director points out, her independence in the film's production was beneficial to this aspect and:

> with a bit of creativity the films get out eventually. Our distributors, Journeyman Pictures, sell to terrestrial TV (*McLibel* was broadcast in 7 countries, but not the UK); then there's film festivals, VHS and DVD sales, streaming on our website, cable and satellite channels and so on. Because I own the copyright I can give it away at ridiculously low prices ... A few weeks back it went out on a satellite channel in the US called Worldlink. They paid a pittance, but another three million people watched it. And that's what counts. (in Gillett 2003: 47)

True to this statement, *McLibel* was shown at a number of US film festivals, and on cable and cinema screens in 23 countries. It gained theatrical release in Australia, and was made available on thousands of VHS copies, also appearing on BBC2's Storyville Classics series, where it attracted over 1 million viewers. Armstrong's controversial film was shown at the London Children's Film Festival in 2005, and the director again retained complete control by raising the finance herself to make the film. She used credit card and debt for its production, her self-reliance thus enabling her to commit fully to the project and, additionally, evidencing her conscience and desire to effect change. 'Unfashionable, I know, but I just can't stop believing in documentaries' (Armstrong 2002: 14), she states.

Her subsequent film, *The Age of Stupid* (2009) is part fiction/part documentary in style and was presented at Swansea's ninth film festival, Beyond TV, along with *McLibel*. *The Age of Stupid* is set in an apocalyptic future scenario in which an elderly man, played by Pete Postlethwaite, is the only survivor in the world. In documentary mode, Postlethwaite directly addresses the spectator, but as a fictional character, not himself. He explains the events that have led up to this disaster in order to draw the spectator into the awful potential realities of climate change and, to further dramatise the situation, a view of the now motionless landmark, the London Eye, set amid destruction and chaos and superimposed with the subtitle 'The Year 2055' to the left-hand side of the frame, initiates the film. The remainder of the surrounding landscape is presented as derelict, devoid of colour and life and, in a similar mode, littered with debris and rubbish; indeed, the River Thames appears foul and polluted, its grey water mirroring the cloudy sky. Through its use of *mise-en-scène*, Armstrong's film documents a bleak futuristic world wrought from human folly, and the film prophesies that, in less than 50 years' time, the world will be a barren dystopia.

To suggest the gravity of climate change, a number of different international scenarios are introduced in the ensuing montage sequence: actual footage of alpine areas fronted by derelict chairlifts where futile machinery no longer works is juxtaposed with desolate mountain villages which are inhabited by a mere handful of people who walk about aimlessly, inspecting the damage from the effects of global warming that the film imagines. On another continent, the Nevada Desert reveals a fabricated, abandoned, windswept Las Vegas, its garish neon signs lying dormant on the barren wastelands; the Sydney Opera House, viewed from a distance, yet unmistakable in its architectural splendour, is engulfed in flames, the resulting black acrid smoke veiling the city's skyscrapers, which are set against a lurid sky; a low-angle shot of the Taj Mahal in India reveals a scene of putrefaction, where vultures gnaw at human remains, and the magnificent building is now in ruins. Armstrong's cataclysmic account of myopic twenty-first-century activity is topical and, as with *Drowned Out*, the director demonstrates her unreserved commitment to the cause, spending years filming communities in various countries to obtain a picture of the future costs to society. By using poignant strategies in *The Age of Stupid* to engage the spectator, Armstrong focuses on the individual to promote viewer identification. In this film, she succeeds in foregrounding distinct time periods assembled by a person in a fictional future who is regretfully lamenting the past, and specifically the past human destruction and obliteration of nature. Although, as Bruzzi argues, to combine performance and non-fiction is 'an alienating, distancing device, not one which actively promotes identification and a straightforward response to a film's content' (2000: 154), the factual evidence of selected experts in the field combats this. *The Age of Stupid* introduces this element through the strategy of individuals talking to camera. Writing about this in terms of three examples, Philip Hammond and Hugh Ortega Breton suggest that,

> the public, political messages the films attempt to communicate become intertwined with personal sadness, longing, and moral judgements about the present ... The ostensible political 'message' is the necessity for change in the present, but the film's [*The Age of Stupid*] negative, dystopian vision works against this since ... it tends to undercut any potential for political agency. (2014: 308)[6]

Due to the use of different time frames, the emotions of remorse, nostalgia and sorrow are mobilised, and the film incites political action, not on risk, but on 'evocations of loss set in the present and past that as a result have the potential to produce emotional engagements' (Hammond and Ortega Breton 2014: 304). This is a moot point for Mark Lynas, who reviews the film as a 'real documentary ... The film is anything but a good guys-versus-bad guys polemic; it is angry but nuanced, despairing but also strangely motivating' (2008: 18). Indeed, what makes Armstrong's film powerful is her stories of human cost and futility told from both an individual and international perspective. The interviewees are real people and frequently viewed in close-up, and the spectator is enabled to empathise and understand the personal damage done to each. Moreover, Armstrong represents individual loss in association with climate change, which makes it more poignant than specifically scientific programmes on the subject that focus solely on environmental damage and related statistics. *The Age of Stupid* is significant in that it may be understood as restoring a sense of political purpose by holding to account the present age bracket by future generations. This, and other such films, have developed expressive rhetorical tactics such as hope, guilt, compassion and nostalgia to enable spectator engagement, which coincides with 'an increase in emotional expression … evident in politics and a number of media formats that foreground the human as an individual, emotional subject' (Hammond and Ortega Breton 2014: 303–4).

In terms of an industry perspective, the director was unable to acquire funding for *The Age of Stupid*, despite the fact that—or maybe because—the film delivers such a harsh message through striking visual imagery. As a result, she devised an innovative method of raising money through the web—a process termed crowdfunding.[7] Recognising that a film of this nature would attract an extensive audience, Armstrong sought out co-producer John Battsek, to lend 'more mainstream credibility to the project' (Nahra 2008: 4). Battsek has pioneered a number of documentaries in the cinema, such as *One Day in September* (Macdonald 1999), a film about the tragic events of the 1972 Olympic Games in Munich, and *Live Forever* (Dower 2003), about the rise and fall of Brit Pop. He and Armstrong worked on sponsorship for this project through a mixture of social events, mass mail pleas and website donations. Commencing by hiring a small venue and screening the earlier *McLibel* to a group of family and friends before pitching Armstrong's new idea to them, the duo were able to raise enough capital to make the film. Over 100 people signed up, each buying shares worth £500 per person, with the process described by Jan Goodey as follows:

> Aiming for a total budget of £465,000, Armstrong and producer Lizzie Gillett invited prospective backers to a London bar … they raised £50,000 in one night. 'It was quite frightening to stand up in Soho with a piece of paper and nothing to show,' says Gillett. 'With the £50,000 we said we'd make a trailer but ended up funding a year of filming with three of the characters.' In 2006, they sold 40 more shares of £5,000 each. The remaining £215,000 came in over the next two years. (Goodey 2008: 4)

That Armstrong sourced money through crowdfunding is attributable to the content of her film and, indeed, films sponsored through this method are usually tilted towards issues that people feel passionate about. This claim is discussed by Claire Fox, Director of the Institute of Ideas, who notes: 'I think it is important that films get made about things we have never heard about and crowdfunding is mostly about orthodoxy, so the films that the crowd will go for are the ones you would expect about climate change and child abuse, for example, and not the things you've never heard of' (in Bulkley 2010). While seeking out aid with the scientific content of the script, Armstrong aimed at aesthetic and financial autonomy, with a profit share to be divided between the investors, who were wide-ranging in location and whose names would appear on the credit roll. Thus the film had editorial freedom and, as the director herself suggests, 'There is no commissioning editor telling you to tone it down. You also have control of the distribution' (in Goodey 2008: 4).

Armstrong's film was screened for an All-Party Parliamentary Climate Change Group on 21 July 2008, with a view to influencing the Climate Change Bill. It also won the Best Green Documentary at the Sunny Side of the Doc in June 2008, and the same at the Sheffield Awards in October of the same year. Armstrong wanted autonomy over the distribution process as well, and to this end, formed a partnership with the Channel 4 Britdoc Foundation, Good Screenings, which specialises in distributing documentary films. She developed software to enable anyone in the world to buy a licence online to screen her films, which resulted in 1,300 community screenings of *The Age of Stupid*. Armstrong did eventually benefit from the UKFC through its Prints and Advertising Fund, which helped launch the film as the world's first 'eco-premiere' to be screened by satellite to over 60 UK cinemas.[8]

Armstrong's interest in climate change issues did not cease after the film's release. In 2009, she was nominated Best Newcomer at the Grierson Awards and won the ITV Achievement of the Year Award. She maintained her commitment to create awareness with a new campaign project entitled 10:10. This scheme aimed at cutting the UK's carbon emissions by 10% in 2010 and, as a result, the Bideford Sustainability Group in Devon was formed; Gordon Brown and the Shadow cabinet signed up but, as yet 'No conservative-run council has committed to 10:10' (Carrington and Carus 2009: 10).[9] Ultimately, her campaign was joined by thousands of businesses such as the Royal Mail, B&Q, Aviva, Microsoft and Pret a Manger, all of which pledged to reduce carbon emissions by 10%.[10]

Not all filmmakers working on issues of climate change are forced into crowdfunding to raise money for their projects. British-born film director

Lucy Walker produces work with lottery funding, but she mainly gains US backing. While studying English literature at Oxford, Walker began her career directing plays and making films. She graduated in 1992 and won a Fulbright scholarship to the New York University Film School 'by convincing them that they needed more female film directors' (Hoggard 2011: 32). The director admits she is indebted to this opportunity and 'credits the course with giving her the confidence to become a film-maker' (in Saner 2013: 16). She is vocal in her feelings about the film industry which she describes as 'shamelessly sexist' (in Sanderson and Blakely 2013: 7), and she is a self-described feminist, believing that it is imperative to learn the craft of filmmaking and to become confident in its technical aspects as well as directing. Acknowledging the lack of female directors, Walker argues that 'Hollywood is a sexist industry ... There are still people who have an issue working with a woman director' (in Saner 2013: 16), although she does note that the UK does better than Hollywood in this respect (in Amelia Hill 2012: 42).[11] Her films are intensely visual, a factor which incongruously is attributable to her own poor eyesight: 'I'm sure this is why I'm such a cinephile and visual artist fanatic, because everything visual became so precious and intriguing to me that I saw things with different eyes' (in Hoggard 2011: 32).

Walker's early work consists of directing episodes of Nickelodeon Productions' *Blues Clues* (1996–2006), for which she was nominated for two Emmy awards, before she moved on to make two films about life experiences. *The Devil's Playground* (2002) was originally inspired by *Witness* (Weir 1985), a fiction film about the Amish people, and, in a similar way to Armstrong, Walker demonstrates her perseverance and commitment to the project, spending months cultivating relationships with Amish youth to produce, what has been described as 'a compelling, bizarre, authoritative account of a youth culture uniquely situated at the juncture of family, community, modernity, and individuality' (Monserrate 2004: 85). The film is very much about outsiders and, while Walker admires the Amish people and their caring spirit, particularly with the elderly, she dislikes their attitudes to homosexuality and the lack of education available to their children beyond a certain age. The film was nominated for three Emmys, as well as for Best Documentary at the 2002 Independent Spirit Awards and it was an Official Selection at Sundance.

Blindsight (2006) followed and Walker was approached by UK producer Sybil Robson Orr, of Robson Entertainment, and New York-based executive producer Steven Haft, both of whom admired the director's work, particularly *The Devil's Playground*. This film too focuses on a group of teenagers, but in this instance they are blind Tibetans who climb the north face of Everest, led by American mountaineer Erik Weihenmayer. *Blindsight*'s concerns are to discover the experience of the teenagers as well as contrasting cultural imperatives and, to achieve this, the film opens in darkness with only the voices of the blind Tibetans audible; this blackout sequence showed the public the world from the young peoples' perspective. The film highlights challenges such as language barriers, the conflicts between Eastern and Western attitudes, and the physical illnesses of the youths. Once again, Walker demonstrates a deep-seated commitment to her work: *Blindsight* was shot over two trips to Tibet totalling three months in all, and she followed the filming herself, directing from the mountain, while using high definition cameras that were relatively portable. The film premiered at Toronto where it received a standing ovation and was screened at *The Times* BFI London Film Festival (LFF).

With a similar approach to Armstrong, Walker clearly feels a responsibility to expose ecological crises, and this is an aspect she pursues through the film *Waste Land* (2010). She won more than 30 awards for this work—aimed at raising awareness in the same vein as Al Gore's political vehicle, *An Inconvenient Truth* (Guggenheim 2006)—including the top Audience Prize at the Berlin and Sundance Film Festivals, and the Amnesty International Human Rights Film Award. It is what Kevin Corbett might term a 'post-issue/advocacy' documentary (2013: 128) and centres on the work of Brazilian artist Vik Muniz, who recycles rubbish using garbage pickers known as *catadores*. They collect the materials for him so that he can create recognisable famous art images from history, one example being Jacques Louis David's painting *The Death of Marat* (1793). Filmed on the outskirts of Rio de Janeiro, *Waste Land* shows the *catadores* picking through rubbish every day to survive, and they, in turn, provide Muniz with his art materials.

In the making of this film, Walker, as with all her work, demonstrates fortitude, determination and social commitment: indeed, filming for the project took nearly three years in extreme temperatures at Jardim Gramacho, the largest landfill site in the world. Brazilian company, O2 Filmes became interested in the scheme because it was classified as a social undertaking and therefore qualified for tax breaks from the Brazilian government. While filming *Waste Land*, the director and team risked kidnap as well as contagion from leprosy and dengue fever—Walker's aim being 'to give the ordinary person on the street a clearer grasp of the issues' (Hoggard 2011: 32). Undeniably the director ennobles the *catadores*, each giving their personal story on camera, although she is accused of glossing over 'the economic and political conditions that are as much a part of these people's lives as the garbage they work in [ignoring] the very real problem of excess consumption leading to environmental and human hazard' (Corbett 2013: 132–3). Rather than focusing attention on environmental and social issues, these points are addressed in the early part of the documentary so that Walker can concentrate on the art works.[12] The director therefore acknowledges that *Waste Land* is more about the artist than the excessive amount of waste produced, and the poverty of those who constitute the poorest sector of Brazilian society and who are forced to sift through its contents for a living. However, the question of whether art has the power to bring about positive change is constantly expressed. Despite its subject matter, the film was well received—a point noted by Liz Hoggard who suggests that, 'On paper, a film about pollution, waste management failures and the gap between rich and poor sounds painfully worthy. But in Walker's hands, it's a thrilling and uplifting journey' (2011: 31).

As mentioned earlier, Walker derives her funding mainly from American support, and her later *Countdown to Zero* (2010) was produced by Lawrence Bender and Participant Productions.[13] This is a company passionate about social and political issues, with a central premise that the threat of annihilation has increased since the Cold War through modern terrorist warfare. Its aims are to disseminate important facts to a wide section of the public through a variety of advertising campaigns. Further funding for the project was gained from the World Security Institute. A polemical film, *Countdown to Zero* sums up Walker's commitment to the Campaign for Nuclear Disarmament, and focuses on the destructive forces of nuclear weapons; she also exposes the near disaster that occurred when a Norwegian scientific research rocket was mistaken for a US attack on Russia. In interview she confides her fears in this direction, suggesting that:

> the goal is to avoid something bad happening by talking about it and making sure it doesn't happen ... That's exactly why I made the film. I don't want to be sitting around on the news shows when the nuclear accident happens, or when North Korea, or when the Saudis, or Israel or Iran decide to use nuclear weapons. (in Anon. 2011a: 4)

To create her argument, the film opens with a low-angle shot of a cloud of black smoke before a dissolve changes the colour to a rosy hue. A series of images ensue before a cut returns the spectator to the cloud, which is now exposed as the mushroom effect from an atomic explosion, then a male voice-over describes the splitting of the atom and Robert Oppenheimer's work in the creation of the first atomic bomb. The narrative moves forward to encapsulate a number of bomb attacks in countries such as Bali, Madrid, London and Riyadh, and a female voice-over suggests that, had these terrorists had nuclear weapons, they would not hesitate to use them. Various settings and landmarks are depicted in a romantic light to indicate the potential devastation to national monuments and the landscape: the Coliseum in Rome is viewed from an aerial shot, as is the River Thames and the Tower Bridge, the latter illuminated at night to create affect. This imagery is accompanied by a narrator who explains how easy it is to obtain the materials to create a nuclear bomb, and how numerous uranium thefts take place, thus signifying the possibilities of the destruction of such landmarks and beauty. Arrests have been made, we are informed, and the finger pointed at Russia as being to blame for the larceny. Specialists in the field talk to camera to add weight to her arguments, and Walker remains unseen.

Later in the film, people on the street are asked how many countries have nuclear weapons and their ignorance is palpable as they make their guesses. The director then reveals the extent of nuclear power, and signals the ways in which it has become a symbol of national pride in certain areas, using Karachi in Pakistan as an example. Again, various experts detail the ways in which a nuclear weapon can be built, and Walker provides a montage of images of methods of construction with those of terrorism.

Throughout *Countdown to Zero*, Walker mixes archive footage with hard facts, and various scaremongering scenarios are discussed, such as when a flock of geese was mistaken for a nuclear attack, and when a Norwegian research rocket presented a false alert. She uses archival interviews with prominent figures, for example Mikhail Gorbachev, Jimmy Carter, Pervez Musharraf and Tony Blair, on the threat of nuclear terrorism, and when demonstrating the damage wrought from attack, produces aerial shots of cities superimposed with circular fire motifs radiating out, all accompanied by Israel Kamakawiwo'ole's version of the song 'Somewhere Over the Rainbow' (1996) to create aural affect. Meanwhile, the narrator explains the powerful effects of the bomb while Walker shows young people celebrating Christmas, juxtaposed with images of the statue of Christ the Redeemer in Rio de Janeiro. This concrete edifice is shown in silhouette against a dark blue night sky, as though to signify a numinous and observing presence which portends human folly. Later, scenes of the devastation of Hiroshima are intercut with details of the measures which need to be taken to prevent errors.

Countdown to Zero is titled as such because Walker is campaigning for zero nuclear weapons globally, and passers-by on the street in various cities around the world are asked how many weapons they think we should have. The response they all give is 'zero' and the film ends with a number to text to 'Demand Zero'. Described by Walker as a 'non-fiction horror movie' (in Hoggard 2011: 32), the 90-minute production proved a box office success, grossing in excess of $271,000 only a few months after its release. The film was unveiled at Sundance at the same time as *Waste Land* and was screened at Cannes out of competition.

Despite working mainly in documentary, Walker has ambitions to operate between this format and fiction film (in Benzine 2014: 26), but nevertheless believes that women are doing significant work in this genre. Akin to Armstrong, Walker is keen on the idea of working in documentary format as it permits her greater autonomy and imagination: 'you're left on your own to get on with it' she states and adds: 'When I watch a fiction film now, it has to be very good in order for me not to get bored. I think we have become oversaturated with tired fictional narratives' (in Saner 2013: 16). In addition, whereas Walker makes films with a political agenda, she also expresses societal concerns through her work and attempts to effect change. From 2010 onwards she directed a number of shorts, followed by the 108-minute film, *The Crash Reel* (2013)—a substantial departure from the theme of climate change, its subject matter is health issues in society. *The Crash Reel* documents the Olympic snow board contestant, Kevin Pearce, who crashed prior to the 2012 event, suffering severe brain damage. While Pearce retained his sponsors, they failed to provide Walker with any funding for her film, which follows the techniques of cutting together archive footage in the same way as for *Senna* (2010), Asif Kapadia's documentary on the Formula One driver, Ayrton Senna. Walker's film is more preoccupied with Pearce and his family support rather than exposing the culpability of extreme-sport organisers and their commercial backers, and she permits the interviewees to speak for themselves throughout.

Walker has the distinction of premiering five films[14] at the Sundance Film Festival, including her recent *The Lion's Mouth Opens* (2014), which follows actress Marianna Palka as she is tested for the crippling neurodegenerative genetic disorder, Huntington's disease. This is only 15 minutes in length but, as Adam Benzine suggests, 'Rarely has a short film made such an impact' (2014: 26). Walker, on receiving a phone call from Palka, decided to make the film immediately with no funding; as she comments: 'I wanted to film before she got her result' (in Benzine 2014: 26). *The Lion's Mouth Opens* raised $100,000 towards Huntington's disease research, and the director speaks of the beneficial appeal of her work in interview:

> I know as a filmmaker that documentaries can be very helpful and can give purpose when you are suffering horribly; the idea that your pain somehow can benefit somebody, even if it's not you, is a tremendously consoling thought … My films are very much about showing people in emotional circumstances, digging deep and finding the kind of grace that you can only dream of … truly special people. (in Benzine 2014: 26)

Walker is currently, at the time of writing, working on a screenplay about Simone de Beauvoir and her lover Nelson Algren, and, as indicated, one of the key aspects of her oeuvre is that she permits her films' subjects a voice of their own. Whether the Tibetan teenagers, the *catadores*, or victims of debilitating diseases, the films are told from their perspectives. Indeed, her commitment to her documentary filmmaking is unequivocal. As she puts it:

> to be a great director and to have this nomination [Directors Guild of America Award, DGA] voted on by other directors is a validation about the craft of what I'm doing. I'm particularly thrilled because three of the five nominees in this DGA category … are female … I cannot think of another directing category in any other award competition where the majority of nominees are women. Females are doing some of the best documentary work and it's a real thrill to be part of this group … I think women have always made fantastic documentaries … Women are patient enough to persevere … I believe in the craft of filmmaking and striving for excellence. With every project I do, I learn more, I practice more which is what you need to do for your craft. (in Goldrich 2014: 25)

Documentary Cinema: Women Effect Social and Political Change

The directors discussed thus far have demonstrated a firm commitment to and belief in their projects, and a preference to work autonomously, many aiming to effect political change. Other filmmakers, such as Kim

Longinotto, document societal and cultural practices. Longinotto is a long-time filmmaker who has been working in film since the 1970s. In line with the notion of direct address, she argues that her work documents transformation that is already happening rather than advocating for change (Basu 2008: 102). She thus adopts an observational and inquiring mode of documentary practice to inculcate a feminist politics (Lin Tay 2009: 62). Longinotto favours an aesthetic where the filmmaker merely surveys the events that occur rather than intervening or shaping the material that unfolds before her. Studying at the NFTS in the early 1970s under the tutelage of Colin Young, a man who believed in the inner direction of a student rather than an industry-led one (see Petrie 2004), Longinotto then became a documentary film practitioner of transnational feminism, and her films certainly eschew over-preparation, the director preferring events to reveal themselves as she shoots. This distinctive style was developed in her early years of filmmaking when, in 1976, she directed (with Dorothy Gazidis), and was also the cinematographer on, *Pride of Place*, a critical observation of her childhood boarding school.[15] *Theatre Girls* (1978) followed and this was the first of many films to celebrate the place of women in society. Longinotto's observational or direct process has continued throughout her illustrious career, and she has always demonstrated a commitment to women, focusing on various ethnicities on the brink of independence or change. Mainly based in non-English-speaking countries such as Japan, Africa and the Middle East, her films are often identifiable as ethnographic and are distributed in the UK by the Royal Anthropological Institute (RAI). Nonetheless, Longinotto does not necessarily perceive her work in this vein,[16] and she is often regarded as 'one of the least visible' contemporary documentary filmmakers (Wood 2008: 156).

To set in context the director's work, Longinotto's early films, made in collaboration with Jano Williams and Claire Hunt,[17] focus on Japanese culture, specifically that of female performers and gender roles; these include *Eat the Kimono* (1989), a film about entertainer and lecturer Hanayagi Genshu, who presents her feminist beliefs as performance for her audiences. *Hidden Faces* (co-directed with Claire Hunt [1990]) concentrates on the Egyptian feminist writer and activist Nawal El Saadawi, and *The Good Wife of Tokyo* (1992) centres on the concerns of Japanese women. The later *Dream Girls* (co-directed with Jano Williams [1993]) features the complex world of the all-women Takarazuka theatre group, and *Shinjuku Boys* (1995) concerns Gaish, Tatsu and Kazuki, biological women who live as men and work as hosts at a Tokyo nightclub. Her final film in the Japanese series is *Gaea Girls* (2000), which follows the world of Japanese women's professional wrestling.

Longinotto's *Divorce Iranian Style* (1998) offers something of a departure from the above and is co-directed with Ziba Mir-Hosseini, a UK-based Iranian expert on the Tehran family courts. Filmed in a Tehran courtroom, the film follows a series of representations of women seeking divorce:

> [i]n an attempt to remain unobtrusive, the camera takes us into the very small physical (six by four meters) *and* symbolic space within which women struggle for limited rights. Although the process of filming is not foregrounded, most of the individuals captured on film acknowledge the presence of the camera and the film crew in the courtroom [original italics]. (Rahimieh 2009: 101)

It took Longinotto two years to raise money for this film, which concerns women's rights within Sharia or Islamic law processes where there are few ways to petition for divorce. By juxtaposing images of the court room with those of the mosque at prayer time, and posters of the late Ayatollah Khomeini, she links 'religion, politics, the law, and patriarchal dominance' (Moore 2005: 24), accompanied by a female English voice-over, which, only where necessary, gives the backgrounds of the individuals involved and details of the court's legal procedures. In addition, to avoid intrusion, Longinotto places the camera on the presiding judge's desk in order that the women's requests and stories are directed straight to camera.

Runaway (2001) is Longinotto's second film based in Iran, and again is the result of her collaboration with fellow filmmaker Mir-Hosseini. The film centres on a shelter for women and young girls who have fled either their homes or marriages because of domestic abuse, forced prostitution and rape. Operated by women, the refuge advocates autonomy for the absconders, yet this situation is often unsustainable within Islamic law. Again, the directors remain off-screen thus permitting the subjects' personalities to surface. As Mir-Hosseini points out, 'we wanted to let women speak, to show them as individuals going through a difficult phase in their lives and to communicate the pain – and the humor – involved in the breakdown of a marriage' (in Smaill 2009: 51–2). For effect, the directors mix sensation with truth in *Runaway*, a point noted by Belinda Smaill who argues that the film blurs generic boundaries: 'In these narrative moments, the exaggerated emotions of the women push against the bounds of documentary realism. At points, *Runaway* and *Divorce Iranian Style* share something with the themes and conventions of the fictional genre of melodrama' (2009: 52).

Longinotto claims that she wanted to make a film in Iran because she deemed that there is a 'demonized view of Iranian people in England' (in Teasley 2000: 17). In this film particularly, she believes that using an all-female crew was beneficial, creating a sense of togetherness with the women she was filming (in Teasley 2000). Also, by working with three times divorcee, Mir-Hosseini, Longinotto considered that her colleague's life experiences and expertise aided the project as she was able to offer first-hand knowledge and advice to the women seeking divorce.

In the subsequent and shocking, *The Day I Will Never Forget* (2002), Longinotto documents, in vivid detail, female circumcision and polygamy in Kenya and Somalia. The film was made for Channel 4, which, Longinotto claims, required more of a campaigning content than she intended, the director preferring to inform the viewer from a more positive perspective. Tracking the story of two girls in Kenya who took their parents to court over female genital mutilation (FGM) and won, the film is intended as an example of female empowerment rather than being specifically about FGM: 'I see it as a film about girls changing their lives, a film about change and rebellion really' (in Fowler 2010: 103), Longinotto explains. She planned to end on this note, providing authority to the women and a female voice, rather than suggesting patriarchal domination. Unusually, however, whereas most of Longinotto's films are about women against authority, *The Day I Will Never Forget* focuses on the women in Kenya and Somalia who perpetuate FGM to comply with male control.

The film employs observational techniques, and is interspersed with interviews and minimal voice-over, and the characters are permitted to develop without a back story, this style forging a strong relationship of trust between Longinotto and the women and girls who have been abused. At one point in the film, and as a shocking method of documenting change as it transpires, Longinotto films an actual circumcision taking place. She was expressly informed that she must not protest before or during the operation otherwise it would later be performed illegally, and with subsequent health repercussions. As the female self-styled doctor conducting the surgery says, 'If you find it difficult, you'll just have to leave because the work that I'm doing depends on good relationships in the community' (in Nahra 2004: 8). Longinotto acknowledges that she did find it harrowing, especially with the second girl to be operated on, who screamed and hung on to her leg. However, had she objected and stopped the procedure, the girls would have had to endure it the following day without the same amount of hygiene and care. That Longinotto here acted as co-participant is crucial in any ethics debate, yet she makes inroads via this work in an effort to ameliorate the injustices that she witnesses. Rather than specifically engaging with the political and cultural debates surrounding the practice of FGM, Longinotto attempts to ascertain the differing approaches adopted by the various members of society, in particular the pressure exerted on the girls by other women within the tribe (while also not intervening in the situation).

For maximum impact, Longinotto's aim was to give *The Day I Will Never Forget* back to Kenya following its Channel 4 screening, and eventually it was seen by over 2,000 people in the town of Fespacho, the director working to campaign against FGM by showing the film in a number of other villages as well. It was also screened at the LFF, and a group of Kenyan women occupied the front rows with the intention of protesting about their cultural rights. However, they soon realised that their objections were indefensible, thus further reinforcing the director's belief that she documents change that is already happening, in other words, the changing attitudes of FGM advocates (Basu 2008: 102).

Longinotto worked with film school graduate Florence Ayisi, on her later film, *Sisters in Law* (2005). A story about female lawyers and judges in the Kumba district of Western Cameroon, *Sisters in Law* had a fairly high-budget for a documentary (£160,000), and was commissioned and funded by Channel 4's Peter Dale. Shot on film, Longinotto extols the virtues of the medium: 'When you're filming on film you watch everything and just film the bits that need to be filmed; with video you're watching through shooting' (in Mitchell 2006a: 13). She and Ayisi researched the content together on a trip to Cameroon, and it became the only documentary to appear in the Director's fortnight at Cannes, and was subsequently awarded the Prix Art et Essai for artistic merit and innovation. Made by Longinotto's long established company, Twentieth-Century Vixen, which she formed in 1986 with Claire Hunt, and distributed by Women Make Movies, *Sisters in Law* is not immediately hard-hitting, its narrative evolving organically to create impact. Also, the directing duo avoid voice-over commentary and any contextualisation: for them, their work is not about customs, traditions or the notion of otherness often associated with Africa; instead, the concerns of this and other non Western stories are universal problems and agendas with international commonalities. Ayisi is keen for the film to 'make people think differently about Africa because it presents a rare viewpoint that is absent from Western media' (in Price 2005: 21). Specifically, *Sisters in Law* follows the various issues that the women deal with, including domestic and child abuse, and ones that Longinotto and Ayisi feel strongly about. As Waldman and Walker might argue, 'Documentaries initiated by ... people and filmmakers coming together to tell common stories must be appreciated as at least potentially radical ... Many documentary films and videos spring from deep convictions held jointly by filmmakers and subjects' (1999: 17).

Longinotto's and Ayisi's principles are demonstrated throughout. For example, in one sequence in the film they introduce a Kumba village courtroom with a young woman whose child has been kidnapped by her estranged husband, who was aided in this by the woman's own father. The two men appear in front of a judge and as they are admonished by Vera Ngassa, the state prosecutor of the area, the camera frames each person in turn, monitoring their various views on the subject through close-ups of their faces. This female victim is permitted a lengthy speech and attack on her spouse who, it transpires, she married under duress and according to the 'country ways' of Cameroon; hence in the eyes of the law they are not legally married. Ngassa accuses the girl's father of using his daughter as merchandise and, at this juncture, the camera focuses on the young girl's face as she confronts her abusers and states in an accusatory tone: 'The way you people play in the villages. The way you play with women and children.' No comment ensues from the filmmakers.

Shots of the various Cameroon towns from a vehicle window are interspersed with an assortment of cases heard in the courtroom and, as with her other films, *Sisters in Law* lacks a voice-over, a stylistic device which makes it even more powerful because the spectator is asked to engage directly with the legal team. Furthermore, the directors see it as important that the characters' personalities emerge through their own dialogue. As Longinotto points out, 'I want you to feel that you're there, standing where I am and going through the emotional experience ... I like it when a documentary has the same constraints as fiction, when it doesn't have to give you a lesson to teach you what to think and is just an emotional experience' (in Pidd 2006: 23).

In a later sequence, a young girl named Sonita reports that she has been raped by a neighbour. The state prosecutor interrogates her in a direct manner, and again the directors remain off-screen, the camera observing the girl's face as she explains the horrors of the experience as she is forced to give evidence against her attacker, who is also in the same room. The discomfort experienced by the girl is similarly mobilised for the spectator, as both victim and perpetrator appear in the frame together; Longinotto passes no comment throughout. As Lin Tay argues:

> Longinotto's films about Africa broach issues about the ways in which, for instance, a feminist discourse might be inscribed into the law, and what might actually change when women's participation and a feminist perspective is taken for granted as an intrinsic part of public discourse. (2009: 80–1)

Sisters in Law continues with a particularly harrowing hearing of a 6-year-old child, Manka, who has been badly beaten by her aunt—her body bearing numerous scars to support her claim—and an acrimonious divorce case between an abusive husband and his wife. The camera then moves to a classroom situation where a session entitled Women and the Law is being taught. Ngassa addresses the group and, as she speaks, the camera swiftly swivels round to show the class, comprised of an assemblage of teenagers, Longinotto observing their learning processes and realisations about the iniquitous society in which they live. That *Sisters in Law* was screened at the Human Rights Watch International Film Festival is testament to the directors' commitment to transformative filmmaking, and the role of Westernised legal systems in Africa is a central feature. Ayisi and Longinotto's techniques in this film permit the spectator to encounter such knowledge as it surfaces, albeit 'knowledge of the event is registered in one way for those present and in another way for the viewer. The film … interpellates the viewer into the process of "knowing" in ways that position the viewer as the subject of knowledge' (Smaill 2009: 58).

Longinotto's and Ayisi's work is tied in with the conventions of observational documentary which mobilises the closest approximation of the spectator's gaze. In other words, the spectator's encounter is simultaneous with that of the camera, and context provides further knowledge. That Ayisi wanted the film to demonstrate strong and positive images of women in Cameroon (in Price 2005: 21) suggests that female strength emerges despite social constraints in some African countries. Dissatisfied with the patriarchal system of filmmaking which favours male leads, Longinotto wants to reinforce this element and, as she points out, 'In most films you see, the heroes are men. And I love the fact that we can have women heroes. I love celebrating women. So-called ordinary women who end up being extraordinary' (in Patterson 2009: 84). *Sisters in Law* received limited UK theatrical release and was screened at the Wales One World Film Festival, which simultaneously showcased a number of films by female directors from Mozambique, Burkina Faso and Vietnam.

Whereas, in general, Longinotto's films have largely focused on foreign countries where locals must learn to trust her and her judgement, a departure from this is *Hold Me Tight: Let Me Go* (2007), a feature documentary set in the Mulberry Bush boarding school in Oxford, an establishment founded by Barbara Dockar-Drysdale. The Mulberry Bush is a last resort institution for children with behavioural problems, where they remain for three years. Longinotto stayed there for one year, and the film documents the children's daily activities, as well as their behaviour and the traumas that created their problems in the first place. *Hold Me Tight* won a number of awards, including the Special Jury Prize at the International Documentary Festival Amsterdam (IDFA), Best British Feature Documentary at Britdoc, and Best Documentary at Birds Eye View and Britspotting British & Irish Film Festival, Berlin.

Longinotto's later *Rough Aunties* (2008) returns to her mission to offer a female voice to events. A 2009 Grand Jury Prize winner at Sundance Film Festival, the film was shown at the ICA (Institute of Contemporary Arts) as part of the Birds Eye View Festival and focuses on a group of South African women who work for the charity Operation Bobbi Bear, based in Durban, South Africa. This is a community project to protect abused and neglected children, as well as to bring child rapists and paedophiles to justice. The women in *Rough Aunties* 'are ordinary people living transformative lives' (Cochrane 2010: 18) and, in a similar way to Longinotto's other documentaries, this film favours a straightforward filming style, deploying lengthy scenes that unfold without interruption in real time (Fig. 3.1).

Following her work on women and law in a number of African countries, Longinotto moves her focus to India in *Pink Saris* (2010) (previously named *A Girl's Life*). Longinotto's fifteenth film, *Pink Saris* was fully funded by Channel 4 and concerns a group of women named the Gulabi Gang who live in Uttar Pradesh, India. Led by Sampat Pal, a women's rights activist, they wear the distinguishing pink saris of the title and travel the country protecting the powerless. Pal, an extremely charismatic character, was married off as a young girl, and subsequently beaten and made to work hard. Hence her mission is to aid the female communities around issues such as gender inequality. As Longinotto points out, 'She's very damaged – how could she

Fig. 3.1 Ordinary people living transformative lives, *Rough Aunties*, 2008

not be? ... She was married at eight and had a terrible life before becoming an activist. That's more interesting than a perfect person' (in Curtis 2010: 31). However, although Pal understands the communities and their problems well, what really emerges from the film is her acknowledgement of a newly acquired status that is realised in front of the camera. As Longinotto maintains, 'Audiences seem comfortable with the fact that they're not following the story of a one-dimensional hero but a damaged, rather desperate, person' (in Anon. 2011b: 61).

In *Pink Saris*, Longinotto operates in her usual bystander mode, rather than constructing an artificial scenario. Indeed, the director encourages the characters in the film to speak for themselves and what emerges is 'a deeply human portrait of activism which reveals the flaws in Sampat's character, as well as her heroic bravery' (Anon. 2011b: 61). Longinotto's film notes the contrasts in India between city and rural life, thus focusing the work as much on society as on women. Her profound sympathy with human rights is exemplified when, at one point in the film, she records a girl who is about to kill herself. The director films her, while simultaneously also isolating a young man running away as a result, it transpires, of his final acknowledgement that he cannot marry his sweetheart because of the rigidity of the caste system.

Critical of the distribution system in the UK, and noting that we have no equivalent to the US film promotion and distribution organisation Women Make Movies,[18] Longinotto handled this aspect herself, reaching agreements with all the distributors. As she points out, 'We make great music and TV in the UK, but we haven't got anything like ... Women Make Movies. They have a network that makes films last for a long time, schools and colleges [sic]. That's what we need' (in Curtis 2010: 33).[19]

Longinotto's latest film, *Dreamcatcher* (2015), also contributes to her feminist oeuvre and offers another example of her own individual stamp. The film follows charismatic Chicago ex-sex worker Brenda Myers-Powell and Stephanie Daniels-Wilson driving around the city handing out condoms to prostitutes for the duo's organisation, the Dreamcatcher Foundation. Described as harrowing through its 'harshness, brutalization, neglect and violence' (ML 2015b: 35) and by Mark Kermode as 'powerful, honest and empowering' (2015: 23), the film again demonstrates its director's commitment and willingness to acknowledge that change is always possible, particularly through female intervention. The film commences with Longinotto travelling in the back of Myers-Powell and Daniels-Wilson's car as they tour the prostitute district of Chicago; she remains unobtrusive as always, thus enabling the women to undertake their work without her interference. In fact, despite the use of close-ups, the participants seem oblivious to the camera; the women are immersed only in their own pain. At one juncture, Myers-Powell and Daniels-Wilson visit a prison and talk to the women inmates who are comprised of mainly sex workers. Longinotto's camera roves around the group, all of whom fix their attention on the Dreamcatcher women, seemingly unaware that they are being filmed. Only at strategic points in *Dreamcatcher* does the director ask questions, usually in the absence of Myers-Powell: this occurs just twice in the film when she interviews the pimps. Throughout, various sex workers are approached by Myers-Powell and Daniels-Wilson, and all openly divulge their heartbreaking stories. One particularly poignant moment occurs when Myers-Powell and Daniels-Wilson visit a school. It is a girls-only gathering and, seen in close-up, the teenagers inform the women of the sexual violence and rape that has occurred in their lives, often from a young age. Myers-Powell operates as a counsellor, providing information and advice, and the narrative of the film is driven by the women's agency, and their deeds and actions. Longinotto inconspicuously records the reactions of the girls and, by showing the female protagonists in their home environments, as well as at formal events, conferences

Fig. 3.2 Hope of social mobility, *Dreamcatcher*, 2015

and school workshops, makes 'the hope of social mobility explicit for the young students who seem trapped in an abusive cycle' (Mayer 2015a: 64) (Fig. 3.2).

In sum, Longinotto's films concentrate on subjects that might usually be considered destabilising cultural others, and to achieve this she deploys particularised conspiratorial practices with individual persons or groups within the long-standing tradition of feminist non-fiction film. As Smaill points out:

> Constituting a more contemporary phase of feminist practice, her work employs the conventions of realist documentary to seek a renewed understanding of the structuring of social relations, the dynamics of transformation, and the different ways that women across cultures are finding to function in this dynamic. (2009: 44)

The director is a bystander in her methods of representing female subjectivity and women as agents of change, presenting those 'who are struggling with the inter-relationship between long-standing custom … and the Westernized legal system of the nation-state' (Smaill 2009: 47). Throughout her career Longinotto has relied on private funding and money from Channel 4. Both the BBC and ITV refused funding for *Dreamcatcher*,[20] and the film was eventually supported by the non-profit foundation and women documentary producers, Chicken & Egg.

Just as Longinotto worked with film school graduate Florence Ayisi on *Sisters in Law*, subsequently Ayisi directed *Zanzibar Soccer Queens* (2007) with Catalin Brylla. A film about the empowerment of a group of Muslim women through the game of football, *Zanzibar Soccer Queens* conveys the story of their hopes and achievements and, as Ayisi says, it 'tells how Muslim women's passion for football helps them to transcend their expected roles and status in life' (in Anon. 2007c: 19). Ayisi, a lecturer at the International Film School Wales, and Brylla, a lecturer at the University of West London, forged links between Cardiff City Ladies Football Club and a women's football team from Zanzibar, the former now supporting their counterparts by donating kit and equipment. *Zanzibar Soccer Queens* constructs the women as individual and active members of the community, and the aim is to show them as empowered human beings rather than subjugated through an imperialistic gaze.

Ayisi's and Brylla's approach adheres to the criteria laid out by Murray Smith (1994), who presents a line of reasoning in terms of how films use narrative and aesthetic cues to construct character identification, which occurs specifically through close-ups of the women's faces, hands, skin and clothes.[21] Also, instead of dubbing the film, the women speak in Swahili, and the directors insert subtitles, thereby supporting their cultural identity. In line with Smith's taxonomy, access to the individual's emotions is enabled, and *Zanzibar Soccer Queens* sets out to document, in a positive way, Tanzanian women's lived experiences through a combination of extreme wide shots and close-ups; the wide shots afford an understanding of the geography of the objective space, and the close-ups recreate the bodily space of the characters (Ayisi and Brylla 2013: 130).

The female coach of the team, which is named Women Fighters, informs the interviewer that they earned the name because when they started to play they were bullied by the local boys, who called them 'hooligans', 'abnormal' and suggested that 'they will never marry'. Seen in close-up she talks direct to camera, and then a cut takes the spectator to meet the individual team members. The camera pans across a photograph of all the women players, and a further cut takes us to the soccer pitch, where the directors expose male prejudice as men explain that women revealing their bodies are temptresses; interviews with a number of key Muslim figures verify this. Ayisi and Brylla's film succeeds in bringing to the fore the struggles these women experience, and one team player confirms this, explaining that since the film they have become well known and people are taking notice of the team in a positive way. A screening of the film in

Zanzibar shows a packed cinema and the spectator is informed that the team are now more accepted by the male population.

Themes in *Zanzibar Soccer Queens* and the later *Art of this Place: Women Artists in Cameroon* (2010) include:

> the search for and expression of, identity, freedom, and social acceptance. The women in these two films express a strong sense of collective dynamism, survival strategies, and their desire to assume other identities outside their traditionally defined roles as wife, mother, cook, and caregiver. (Ayisi and Brylla 2013: 131)

Further, *Zanzibar Soccer Queens* and *Art of this Place: Women Artists in Cameroon* facilitate their female participants to establish an individual identity through their performances. Unlike fiction cinema, however, in documentary their performance is more a collaboration between them and the filmmakers, providing them with their own agency. In these two films, therefore, the camera becomes not only a mechanism for recording but also an egalitarian device for the women. The filmmakers avoid interference in their subjects' responses, with the women being given autonomy to contribute their own accounts, and their respective performances corresponding with their personalities. Through their cinematography, they facilitate a way for them to surmount their conventional societal roles as housewives and mothers and afford them the opportunity to stand for something else. Thus, *Zanzibar Soccer Queens* achieves 'this real-life empowerment into filmic form by empowering the women's screen personas through subjective points of views, constructing visible identities, and sharing authorship with them' (Ayisi and Brylla 2013: 134–5). In terms of their themes and narrative structures, these two films succeed in demystifying the women, and representing them as not invisible, but as familiar, ordinary and known.

The films set out to document Tanzanian women's lives and challenge the one-dimensional representations of life and society and the often 'reductive and even offensive' (Ayisi and Brylla 2013: 125) representations of Africa in the media influenced by neocolonial relationships with the West. These usually comprise negative cultural stereotypes, with many countries in Africa represented as either Other to civilised Europe, or through condescending self-glorification. As Ayisi and Brylla argue, 'iconic images of war, famine, poverty, disease, misery, and exotic landscapes continue to dominate Western media outputs' (2013: 126). *Zanzibar Soccer*

Queens and *Art of this Place: Women Artists in Cameroon* therefore reverse these prevalent stereotypical representations, and contribute to feminism by presenting women from Tasmania and Cameroon in a constructive light. This is achieved by steering away from experimental techniques and instead following the practices of mainstream cinema, with the aim of reaching a wider audience through conventional exhibition outlets on the films' release: *Zanzibar Soccer Queens* was privately sponsored and premiered at the Gothenburg International Film Festival and *Art of this Place: Women Artists in Cameroon* (2013) was shown at the Zimbabwean Women's Film Festival.

Female empowerment in non-Western countries is the subject of London-based American director and editor, Liz Mermin's films. Mermin specialises in documentary features in which she too employs a visual style worthy of note, as demonstrated in *The Beauty Academy of Kabul* (2004).[22] This film centres on three American and three Afghan-American professional hairdressers who set up a school in Afghanistan to train local women in the business of hair and make-up. The aim is to support female workers in Afghanistan, a point explained by Patricia O'Connor, the Western women's services worker who volunteered the women in the first place: 'We really wanted to help the women and empower them – give them a chance to build a better life for themselves and their families' (in Stuart 2004: 6). Mermin represents the armed British and US soldiers in the streets in a series of edits intercut with the homemaking labours of the women, the film not only affording the latter a voice but also documenting their interest in make-up and appearance, a hitherto prohibited experience for them. *The Beauty Academy of Kabul* opens with a fashion show and young people dancing, although this sequence is set in the past, and is clearly not representative of present-day Kabul. An edit to a young woman having her hair curled in a post-Taliban world indicates the present day, along with the nature of the beauticians' work now taking place, albeit subtitles indicate that previously they had to work in secret.

Mermin intersperses archive film footage from the 1970s, showing the turmoil that the country has experienced through invasion and Taliban rule. It is now the present, and one returnee, Sima, who fled the country 23 years previously, is shocked by the devastation. Her voice-over records her thoughts as the camera pans over derelict buildings, old overturned cars and barefoot children playing in the ruins; she attended university at that time, she says, when the city was modern and progressive. Sima is visibly horrified by the destruction of Kabul, and the film becomes as much a social and political history lesson as the story of the salon. Close-ups of rifles are intercut with the opening ceremony of the beauty school, and then one of the Americans explains to the women why they are there. The camera frames her in close-up as she states her passion for helping oppressed women, and intercut throughout the film are shots of men either standing around carrying guns or sleeping in the shade. *The Beauty Academy of Kabul* tells the story of the lives of the women who have been recruited by the salon to train for three months, and each has a personal and sometimes harrowing tale to tell. Interior scenes show their babies sleeping in makeshift cots and children helping with the tasks while they attend classes. Here, Mermin succeeds in capturing the camaraderie of women in the workplace as she films them squirting each other with water, giggling, massaging each other and having fun. The salon eventually opens to the public and women queue outside the door for beauty treatment. In an emotional ending the trainees attend graduation with their husbands who appear completely bemused by the process.

Mermin's later *Office Tigers* (2006) was produced by Cactus Three (US), a small production company based in New York, and this preceded her 2007 release, *Shot in Bombay* about the making of the Bollywood movie, *Shootout at Lokhandwala* (Lakhia 2008). This film within a film explores not only *Shootout at Lokhandwala*'s production, but also the political agendas which surround it. The narrative of the film is a fictional account of a real-life gunfight between criminals and the police which took place in the early 1990s. However, during its actual filming it was revealed that the lead star, Sanjay Dutt, was involved in his own gangster activities, including illegally possessing firearms. Subsequently, Mermin follows the trial of Dutt, who was in and out of jail at the time, and in this she 'effectively encapsulates the ennui and frustration of waiting on an expensive set for an elusive star' (Ramachandran 2008: 80).

In the first place, Mermin wanted to make *Shot in Bombay* within a broader remit of Bollywood, but Dutt's trial dictated terms. To create impact, the film opens with actual footage of Dutt's arrest and a newsreader in voice-over explains the situation regarding the trial which has been under way since the event occurred. *Shot in Bombay* mixes footage of the court case with interviews with the police, who themselves also seem to perceive that they are on a movie set (one even aligning himself with Clint Eastwood and the *Dirty Harry* films). For much of the filming of *Shootout at Lokhandwala*, Dutt is absent, and the director, Apoorva Lakla, is forced to rely on doubles. While awaiting sentence Dutt returns to work, and the camera observes his attempts at remembering his script, and the expressions of the frustrated Lakla, whose filming has been held up for months at a time. The camera focuses on Dutt through Lakla's video screen and close-ups, the framing within framing revealing the actor's anxiety. To create effect, Mermin compares the occurrences of the film with real-life footage, showing contemporary news articles and television clips about the case alongside sequences from *Shootout at Lokhandwala*.[23]

As the film progresses, Dutt appears more and more preoccupied, although Mermin adds no voice-over to enhance the drama. Instead, she sums up the film at the end in a trailer, and includes a critical reception of Lakla's film which, although panned by critics, fared well at the box office, much to the director's delight.[24] Making a political and social point, Mermin then cuts from Lakla's luxurious apartment, which is lined with photographs of him posing with Hollywood stars such as Robert de Niro, to a shot of chickens roaming the poverty-stricken streets of Mumbai, and then an apartment block in a shanty area of the city: the home of the parents of one of the criminals. Correlating with the work of a number of the directors discussed here, Mermin's style is to avoid commentary by adopting a 'fly-on-the-wall' technique and observing the subjects as they carry out their daily routines. Screened at the Mahindra Indo-American Arts Council Film Festival, *Shot in Bombay* was also shown on BBC4 as part of the Storyville series.

Mermin's later film, *Horses* (2009), was made for the Irish Film Board, BBC Storyville and RTE, and follows a year in the life of Irish racehorse trainer, Paul Nolan at his stables in County Wexford. Opening at the ICA in January 2010, it was eventually shown on BBC4 as *Storyville: Race Horses*. Her latest two documentaries are once more international, set in the Middle East and Eurasia. *Team Qatar* (2009) follows five wealthy teenagers to a competitive high school debate in Washington guided by two Oxford University students. This film is again low-key, and observational, while her later *Amazing Azerbaijan* (2012) simultaneously shows the rich nation's glittery façade alongside the human abuses which take place.

Different from those filmmakers discussed so far, whose work is mainly observational, some women use their own stories to express societal concerns in their work. Moreover, to achieve this, aesthetically they blur the boundaries between documentary and fiction. British screenwriter, producer and director Carol Morley operates in this mode. Morley graduated in 1993 from Central Saint Martins College of Art and Design with a degree in Fine Art Film, and it was here that she encountered the work of a number of experimental filmmakers including Maya Deren, Carolee Schneemann, Stan Brakhage and Lis Rhodes which influenced her style. Morley's work echoes her difficulties growing up (her father committed suicide when she was 11 resulting in unstable and irresponsible behaviour from her mother). She turned to alcohol at a young age following these disruptions, and her early films replay her personal conflicts and crises. *The Alcohol Years* (2000) is a BAFTA-nominated documentary (her first film) about her life between the ages of 16 and 21, growing up in Manchester. To construct the narrative, she placed an advert in a newspaper asking for people who knew her during her youth to provide information. Based on these memories, interviews and reconstructed footage, an image of Morley emerged in which she allowed herself to be seen as a promiscuous, manipulative drunk.[25]

Themes of loneliness and a troubled existence recur in the narrative of her later film, *Dreams of a Life*, which follows the finding of the decomposed body of 38-year-old Joyce Carol Vincent, who had lain undiscovered in her north London flat for two and a half years. Morley had first read about Vincent in the *Sun* newspaper while on the London Underground and, in a similar manner to *The Alcohol Years*, she focused on the life of Vincent over a period of five years, tracking, detective-style, people who knew her. She placed adverts in newspapers and on the internet, and a poster on the side of a black cab, while simultaneously researching in public records offices and libraries. This resulted in a film which 'announced Morley as part of a wave of British filmmakers, including Lynne Ramsay, Clio Barnard and Andrea Arnold, who are busy fraying the edges of documentary and social realism with the surreal, the erotic and the metaphysical' (Mayer 2015b: 29).

In *Dreams of a Life*, Morley attempts to reconstruct Vincent's life by interviewing the people who knew or remembered her, although those closest to her, the woman's family and her ex-fiancé, refused to participate. Morley acknowledges a correlation between her life and that of Vincent, a factor which intrigued her throughout the pre-production and production of the film. She and Vincent had lived on the same street; they were the same age; they had both wanted to be singers; and, finally, both had lost a parent at an early impressionable age. Sponsored by the BFI and Channel 4, *Dreams of a Life*, despite being a collage of interviews, carefully avoids speculation. Zawe Ashton[26] and Alix Luka-Cain play the parts of Vincent in her earlier and later years, respectively, and Morley worked with the interviewees carefully to build relationships with them rather than act as an interrogator, the director indicating that her technique is personal and intuitive:

> At the point of doing the interviews, I wanted to get [the interviewees'] best selves across – to show their characters as strongly as possible – so I wanted them to feel comfortable with me and the situation. So I had the camera in a very dark area of the room, and they couldn't see much but me. It was very intimate. And I really listened to them, and asked the same questions a lot. (in Nick Bradshaw 2012: 45)

The people who knew Vincent talk straight to camera, and Morley reconstructs the jigsaw puzzle through their comments in order to assemble a picture of the woman when she was alive.

The film commences with an extreme close-up of a map showing the location of Vincent's flat, and then a bird's eye view of the shopping centre where it is located. Morley positions the camera inside a reconstruction of the filthy apartment where the woman's body lay undiscovered, and films the front door, the image overlaid with the voices of the bailiffs who were called in because of unpaid bills. Alternating between Vincent's past, including reconstructed images of her as a child, and the present, and the forensics team and clean-up agents in the flat, *Dreams of a Life* continues in a self-reflexive manner. At times Morley interjects surreal imagery, the actor playing Vincent interacting with the interviewees who are shown on the diegetic television. The final sequences show Vincent wrapping the Christmas presents which were discovered on her death, the images accompanied aurally by the sound of Minnie Riperton singing 'Minnie's Lament' (1975), further indicating the woman's isolation. Such scenes lead Morley to admit that she 'realised it wasn't just about telling stories, but how stories are told, and so I became very interested in form, and how you construct films' (in Mayer 2015b: 31).

While predominantly a documentary filmmaker, Morley has more recently released a fiction film entitled *The Falling* (2014), which addresses female concerns using women protagonists. Renowned for her low-budget non-commercial work, Morley has a commitment to making films for and about women and, as she argues:

> If you don't write strong female roles then great female actors aren't going to get a chance. I am committed to telling stories about the female experience.

> For me, having a strong female presence on set is a political act. It changes the very nature of what a film set has come to be. (in Carpenter 2015)

Thus, although *The Falling* is not a documentary, having more of an alignment with fiction, it was originally designed as such (Brady 2015: 8). The film concerns mass hysteria, and Morley's interest in the subject stemmed from stories in various parts of the world. For example, in order to glean more information about the condition, she observed the YouTube posts of a New York group of female students in Le Roy who all simultaneously started twitching.[27] In addition, Morley discovered that in El Carmen de Bolivar, Colombia, a large proportion of pre-teen and teenage girls suffered fainting spells.[28] Additionally, she was particularly interested in a story she had heard about a medieval village in Britain where the villagers couldn't stop laughing, but found no concrete evidence of this in her internet searches. Eventually, she discovered a village in Tanzania whose population in 1962 had a laughing contagion, which was accompanied by other symptoms such as fainting, crying and agitation, and this fed into her research for the film. Her study of these symptoms continued when she consulted psychiatrist Simon Wessely for advice on the phenomenon. As a member of the Royal College of Psychiatrists, his investigation into mass hysteria spanned 25 years, and he confirmed that, for an outbreak to take place there is usually a stimulus, such as an emotional event or stress, which frequently occurs when a group of people (mostly adolescent females) are in a confined physical and social space. As he further explained, sometimes triggers are environmental, but usually originate from the mind. The point of this research for Morley was that she could thoroughly understand the occurrences. Her own exploration had begun ten years prior to making the film, poring over Wessely's articles in order to gain a comprehensive knowledge of the subject and process, which also dictated when the film was set. As she argues:

> I decided to set *The Falling* in the 1960s because much of the research I had carried out, certainly into mass psychogenic outbreaks at that time, suggested sexual guilt, or a preoccupation with sexual matters as a factor. I felt it would be an interesting way of looking at the complexity of young female identity and sexuality and the changing nature of sexual morality for women in particular, so the outbreaks could also be linked to cultural and social stresses. (Morley 2015a: 8)

Additionally, Morley prepared for her film by watching *The Devils* (Russell 1971), a British historical horror drama based on an Aldous Huxley novel, and Peter Weir's *Picnic at Hanging Rock* (1975) about the disappearance of a group of Australian schoolgirls during a picnic on St Valentine's day in 1900.[29]

In line with many of her contemporaries, Morley uses a predominantly female crew to tell the story of mass fainting at a rural Oxfordshire English girl's school set in 1969. Primarily about female friendship, the film focuses on the relationship between two schoolgirls, Lydia Lamont (Maisie Williams) and Abbie Mortimer (Florence Pugh). Abbie is promiscuous and believes that she is pregnant, Lydia is jealous because she is in love with her friend. Following an argument, Abbie experiences a seizure, and subsequently collapses and dies, and Lydia too later falls down in class, an incident that initiates a spate of fainting among the other girls in the school, as well as one teacher. The strength of the girls' relationship is demonstrated through the frequent shots of Lydia and Abbie as they exchange glances, thus intensifying the notion of female solidarity and revealing the affection they share—a theme later mirrored following Abbie's death. Subsequent enigmatic looks occur between the teachers and the girls inferring an exploration of adolescent female sexuality with its attendant repercussions.

Premiered at the BFI LFF in 2014, *The Falling* received a number of tweets about people fainting after watching the film. Morley's commitment to the subject is spelled out when she explains that:

> I filled up my own box file on mass psychogenic illness and I realise what kept me so committed to making the dreamed-about feature film that eventually became The Falling. It is the collective nature of an outbreak that has compelled me, the idea of a group of girls responding defiantly and resisting the world around them. While the experience of going through a mass psychogenic illness is a distressing one in most cases, I also liked the idea that you only get it if you identify with another person, if you feel empathy. (Morley 2015a: 8)

Described by Charlie Fox as containing 'a hint of gothic melodrama' (2015: 76), Morley's film was funded by the BFI's Film Fund and BBC Films. Agnès Godard was the director of photography,[30] Janey Levick the production designer and Tracey Thorn the composer. Thorn had previously formed an all-girl band, and only commenced the score after the editing process had begun. She created her soundtrack using the instruments played by the girls in the fictional school orchestra.

Morley returned to her Stockport roots for the Screen Stockport Film Festival,[31] which showed an exclusive clip from *The Falling* prior to its release. The film, in a similar mode to *Dreams of a Life*, suggests the director's capacity to research her subjects in depth, whether they are fiction or documentary, and, as a result, to produce work that has a strong female presence and tells stories about the female experience.

If Morley's work features conflicts and crises, and blurs the boundaries between drama and documentary, then Argentine-born Penny Woolcock too uses this hybrid format to pursue themes of isolation, abandonment and the outsider. Woolcock moved to Britain (via Spain), in 1970 when she enrolled in a filmmakers' workshop, and this saw the commencement of her career as a director in both film and television. Her early life was one of serious poverty as a child in a single-parent family yet, akin to Morley, the experience now enables her to identify with those less fortunate and her films often transgress generic boundaries. This is especially true of her series of films entitled the *Tina* trilogy, which use non-actors. *Tina Goes Shopping* (1999) is the first of the three, with a cast selected from a council estate in Leeds. *Tina Takes a Break* (2001) uses the same approach and is characterised by its realist aesthetics, except it opens with the disclaimer that it is a fictional drama based on real events and played by real people. Made for television, and told in the present tense, this docusoap follows the life of single mother (Kelly Hollis) and her two children, who are cared for by their father while Tina is in prison. The third in the trilogy is *Mischief Night* (2006).[32] This film was sponsored by Film4 and is a northern comedy tale of working-class life focusing on racial tension and Islamic terrorism. As stated, these films have a comedic undercurrent but deal with socio-political issues such as racism, poverty and unemployment. To make *Mischief Night*, Woolcock researched carefully, spending a lengthy period of time with Muslim groups in Yorkshire, and working long hours as a result. Furthermore, the fact that Film4 was involved suggests something about the nature of the film, as the channel favours more radical productions which appeal to a younger demographic and incorporate a multicultural diversity agenda. *Mischief Night* received its world premiere at *The Times* BFI LFF in 2006.

Woolcock's later film, *Exodus* (2007), is a modern-day story of Moses, a fictitious figure from an imaginary town named Dreamland. This film is included here as part of Woolcock's oeuvre although it pushes the boundaries of documentary drama by focusing on contemporary reality overlaid with myth. It was commissioned by Jan Younghusband at Channel 4 and produced by Artangel, a company which works with artists on site-specific projects, and Woolcock wrote the screenplay herself. The extras for the film were non-professionals and included a mix of street drinkers, asylum seekers, individuals with special needs and people from a variety of ethnic backgrounds. Filmed in Margate, a town replete with asylum seekers and the dispossessed, *Exodus* centres mainly on the biblical original, with the exception that the burning bush is transformed into a 25 metre Anthony Gormley sculpture of a man constructed of urban waste and discarded furniture, known as the Wasteman. In *Exodus*, Woolcock casts the Jews as the local marginalised people, and she sets out to make an epic, dystopian film on a small budget. The dispossessed live in Dreamland's shanty towns, and Woolcock had this area specially built out of waste materials, along with the sculpture. The effigy, which appears as a 'gesture of defiance from the unwanted to the people of the Promised land, warning of terrible violence unless poverty and injustice are addressed' (Woolcock 2007b: 49), is ritualistically burned. Shooting for this sequence took place all in one take and on one day, and accounted for 16 pages of Woolcock's screenplay. Although the film was scripted, Woolcock also relied on capturing events as she filmed. For example, on the day of the burning of the Wasteman, an event that was heralded in the film initially by the right-wing politician and People's Party Leader, Pharoah Mann (Bernard Hill), who takes centre stage to deliver a fascist speech, people turned up to watch, unaware of what was taking place as Woolcock filmed. The director was thus able to capture their surprised expressions.

Visually, Woolcock primarily drew on the Romantic painting *The Raft of the Medusa* (1818–19) by Théodore Géricault, which was based on a true story. Géricault paints an image of a shipwreck, its survivors clinging to a raft and resorting to cannibalism to escape death. Woolcock opens *Exodus*, which is initially set in the past, using a series of close-ups of the raft, and underwater images of a baby lost overboard. A man jumps into the sea and rescues the child as the driving rain batters the vessel, and the film cuts to a shot of Mann preaching to the populace about the scourge of immigrants. Subsequently, the *mise-en-scène* shows the police commencing an attack on the street beggars, drug users and ethnic population, rounding them up and imprisoning them in camps. Woolcock's use of hand-held camera creates a chaotic and realistic dimension of the narrative as people are dragged from their beds, children in arms, and hustled into Home Office vans. The story is told from Moses' (Daniel Percival) perspective; he is the adopted son of Pharaoh and Pharaoh's wife Batya (Ger Ryan), although it later transpires that the boy's mother is really a Romany gypsy who abandoned him on a beach to enable his escape from the concentration camp where the displaced are held. Twenty years on, the adult Moses becomes disenchanted with his father's policies and politics, questioning his actions. Following a visit to the camp as a tourist, he assaults a guard and is forced to flee, subsequently finding his true birth mother. As a result of his discovery, and due to his conscience, Moses leads the refugees in revolt, and symbolically climbs up Gormley's effigy before it is burned to the ground. As the effigy blazes, he receives a message from God and makes the quasi-biblical decision to lead the people to safety, a journey achieved through chemical warfare eventually enabling him to part the waves to open a pathway to freedom for the oppressed. By the end, the film moves full circle to reintroduce the raft scenes of the opening sequences.

Woolcock's next film, *1 Day* (2009), returns fully to her documentary mode. It is a low-budget feature about a day in the life of a UK city gang member. Set in present-day Birmingham, its plot is based on a mugging which Woolcock had experienced some years earlier while walking home one night. She was attacked after coming face-to-face with her assailant, and their eye contact made a marked impression on her before the man ran off with her belongings. The incident left her with concussion, yet also a desire to find out more about people who commit this type of crime although, as she says:

> I never hated my attacker. I wanted to know why someone who was not sadistic – he could have easily kicked me again for making it difficult for him – thought it was all right to punch and kick a lone woman for a few pounds … so I decided to make a film to try to answer that question: who are you? (Woolcock 2009: 36)

Woolcock deliberately chose Birmingham as the setting for *1 Day* owing to the city's multicultural vibrancy, and also because she believes that it is a place often ignored by filmmakers. Partly sponsored by Channel 4 and Screen West Midlands, and supported through the European Development Fund, as with all her films, *1 Day* is both written and directed by Woolcock. Though focusing on a day in the life of one particular gang member, the narrative revolves around city rivalry in the West Midlands, in this instance, the two main factions in Birmingham: the Burger Bar Boys and the Johnson Crew. Often related to one another, or even having attended the same schools, the gangs do not stray into one another's territories, as to do so would produce fatal results. Woolcock researched the subject and the people of Birmingham in great detail, eventually recreating the plot line as a rap musical. The cast was recruited from the locals through open audition, and the film follows the rival gangs, their drug-dealing lifestyles and gun crime. Keen to understand these communities and enable them to express their personal experiences, the director suggests, 'Just as spirituals and the blues were invented by people who were denied any voice to tell their stories, grime and hip-hop give a voice to young people to tell us what is going on in their lives' (Woolcock 2009: 36).

Premiering at the LFF in October 2009, *1 Day* was labelled '"Britain's first hip-hop musical", but don't expect lively song-and-dance numbers in the American mould' (Smith 2009: 77). Instead, the film's *mise-en-scène* is harsh and realist using a hand-held camera to convey this urban gangster drama with a rap soundtrack. Using indigenous residents from the Birmingham area resulted in authentic dialogue and colloquial accents, further enhancing the realism, albeit this was a perceived disadvantage because the film 'suffers from the inexperience of its street-cast performers' (Smith 2009: 77). The director does not rehearse; as she admits, the satisfaction derives from the observational:

> The pleasure of documentary ... is that you're not in control of what happens. Spontaneously something will happen in front of your eyes, or you'll turn up just after it's happened and you've missed it. If you're from a documentary background you welcome those surprises, whereas people who've only worked in fiction find it quite frightening. (in Romney 2004: 7)

Controversy followed *1 Day*'s release: the local Odeon and Cineworld cinemas decided not to screen it following advice from West Midlands' police, who officially approached the cinema chain, advocating that the film glamorised gang violence.[33]

For her next project,[34] and with the same degree of commitment, Woolcock moved on to spend eight months interviewing homeless people in central London in order to create *On the Streets* (2010), a television documentary on the UK destitute. Her later *From the Sea to the Land Beyond* (2012), however, offers a change of direction. This film is an evocative portrait of the British coastline, again devoid of commentary, and much of the film's footage was gleaned from the BFI archives, with the content ranging from that produced by filmmakers such as Mitchell and Kenyon, and John and Marion Grierson. Unlike Woolcock's previous *Tina* trilogy, which raised a number of social issues, this film contains archival images of the First World War, the fishing industry and, finally, Blackpool beach at the height of summer.

Woolcock's later *One Mile Away* (2013) returns to her previous subject matter of gang warfare, demonstrating the director's sense of responsibility. Filmed as a result of its earlier counterpart, *1 Day*, *One Mile Away* was instigated by the lead member of the Johnson Crew gang, Shabba, who contacted the director to ask her to set up a meeting with Dylan Duffus, the head of the rival group, the Burger Bar Boys from Handsworth. Woolcock's film traces the development and progress in attempts towards a peace process, this specific action taking place as a result of the deaths of innocent gun crime victims, Letisha Shakespeare and Charlene Ellis.[35] Although Woolcock's voice can be heard asking questions of the two gang members, she remains unseen by the spectator.[36] A final screen image informs that 'The Peace Process Continues' but this is not necessarily an optimistic viewpoint, and the problems continue between the men. Woolcock's technique is empathetic, permitting the actors or characters in her films to dictate the narrative to an extent, and the initiative in *One Mile Away* therefore came from Shabba and Dylan, the two lead gang members who were trying to bring an end to the gangs' hostilities. When discussing her reasoning behind the making of the film, Woolcock states that her ambition was never to make money, but to 'get this into areas where gang lifestyle is a real problem and get people listening to others' (in Clark 2013).

Woolcock's dedication to finding an answer to the ongoing warfare is suggested by her subsequent meeting with the former culture secretary, James Purnell, at a Britdoc event. He offered to produce the vilified film, which was experiencing problems such as the police requisitioning rushes and a Crown Court prosecution for refusal to hand them over. (She subsequently won the case and was awarded costs.) Critics, however, were positive—particularly in terms of the director's campaigning ability. As Philip Kemp observes, 'Woolcock has achieved something exceptional: her projects have not only created a vivid picture of the complex, vital, fraught street life of our cities but – with any luck – started to change it for the better' (2013: 99). Indeed, *One Mile Away* resulted in the establishment of the One Mile Social Enterprise, an organisation comprised of gang members who mentor children and work together on outreach programmes in primary schools and on the streets. Recent crime statistics now reveal that violent crime has fallen by 50% in one of the areas occupied by the gangs, and 30% in the other—and January 2013[37] was the first month for many years without a single firearms incident being recorded in the localities. *One Mile Away* received recognition, winning the Michael Powell Award at the Edinburgh International Film Festival (the first time a documentary has ever been a contender), and Woolcock dispatched it free of charge to inner-city areas. It had a limited theatrical release, showing at independent cinemas and venues such as the ICA, Rich Mix and some of the network chain Picturehouse Cinemas Ltd. Britdoc, however, applied for and received funding from the Bertha Foundation to enable the film to be provided free of charge on DVD and distributed in inner-city areas. The film, while being observational, is not voyeuristic, but is instead transformative, and Woolcock has since retained her connections with the One Mile Away Social Enterprise Group.

If the above directors are primarily concerned with problems in society, then Beeban Kidron is no exception. Better known for her 2004 adaptation of the Helen Fielding novel, *Bridget Jones: The Edge of Reason* (1999) (discussed in Chap. 5), Kidron has also directed a number of documentary films, her later work focusing on societal issues. The director has only more recently turned to cinema, with two television programmes: in 2007 she made *Anthony Gormley: Making Space* and in 2011 *Storyville: Sex, Death and the Gods*. The former is a one-off documentary and is a personal portrait of Gormley examining the artist's motivation, the latter a shoestring production about lower caste prostitutes in India. In 2013 she released *InRealLife*, which was sponsored by the BFI Film Fund and Sky as part of the Sky Atlantic documentary season. The film investigates the lure of the smartphone for British teenagers and uses the interface between the filmmaker and the participants in what Nichols might term an interactive documentary style which 'stresses images of testimony or verbal exchange … textual authority shifts towards the social actors recruited … various forms of monologue and dialogue (real or apparent) predominate' (1991: 44).

InRealLife attempts to discover why young people spend so much time on their phones, and Kidron interviews not only contemporary youths, but also American media academics and psychologists in an attempt to determine the reasons why. Rather than take a back seat to merely observe their behaviour, Kidron opens the film with a narration to express her feelings before a number of disturbing tales unfold. These include those of two amiable young men with an addiction to pornography, one teenage girl who consented to sexual favours to retrieve her phone from her assailants, and the harrowing story of a young teenager's suicide as a result of internet bullying. Kidron does not intervene in the replies she receives to her questions, yet she gently interrogates to gain a full understanding of their addiction. Interspersed in these interviews are the views of various psychologists, psychoanalysts and internet experts attempting to explain the phenomenon.

At one point in the film, Kidron introduces Page, a young black girl, who explains her relationship with the internet and her phone. In a series of uncomfortable extreme close-ups and lengthy takes, Kidron shows her applying eye and face make-up, at which juncture the images adopt an almost abstract opaque quality to suggest the girl's confusion and disengagement from the real world. It transpires that Page had consensual gang sex with five boys in order to reclaim her phone from them, a point that Kidron emphasises to demonstrate youth's obsession with technology. As the girl says, 'I kind of put my phone first', which is explained away by a psychologist who refers to chemical changes that occur in the body to justify this behaviour. Kidron elicits such personal stories from her interviewees who, as a result, produce shocking facts, and her message is that the internet and social media have a massive impact on teenagers in very personal ways.

In a similar mode to Woolcock, Kidron's interest in young people led her to try to effect change through her work. She is the co-founder of FilmClub, a highly successful charity providing education through film screenings, and she perceives this mode of address as an important educative device, offering:

> a fear-free way to discuss everything from form and language to history and social issues, and [which] creates a richness of experience from all over the world that, in the words of one teacher, 'breeds interest and enquiry'. At FilmClub we are glowing with pride and pleasure at the growing evidence that watching then reviewing films has a measurable effect on literacy. (Kidron 2011: 25)

Continuing with her theme of youth, Kidron compares the young people she interviewed and observed in India in the making of her film *Storyville: Sex, Death and the Gods* about the Devadasi (young girls married to God in childhood, and sold for sex in puberty) with the education of British schoolchildren. Commenting on social injustice she explains, 'I was asked by the UK Film Council to look at other organisations that use film as a tool for learning in schools and assess the outcome ... In the year that I spent in English schools and Indian villages and brothels, I was struck again and again by the contrast' (Kidron 2011: 25).

Just as Woolcock, Morley and Kidron are concerned with the problems that young people face, so too is filmmaker, Louise Osmond, who investigates unemployment, but from a different angle. Commencing her career in the ITN news journalism graduate trainee programme, and covering stories in Europe and Africa before moving into documentaries, her film, *Dark Horse: The True Story of Dream Alliance* (2015) was shortlisted from 50 applicants for BFI funding. This was in 2013, when the BFI Film Fund held the first of its twice yearly pitching sessions for documentary filmmakers at the world's leading documentary film festival, Doc/Fest in Sheffield. Applicants were invited to stand in front of their peers and make a five-minute pitch followed by a short questions and answers session. The reason for this approach was that the number of applications for documentary funding was rising, and, as the director of the BFI Film Fund, Ben Roberts, comments, 'we weren't making clear decisions in the way that we do for fiction material' (2013: 16). Roberts blamed the diversity of the applications submitted, along with the proliferation of television documentaries currently on-screen, and also the requirement to appeal to cinema audiences. Favoured films were what he terms 'genre docs' 'that seem to be having the strongest pull on cinema audiences' (Roberts 2013: 16). The judging panel consisted of Roberts, Lizzie Francke, the Senior Production and Development Executive of the BFI Film Fund, Clare Binns from Picturehouse Cinemas, and SXSW Interactive Festival programming executive Janet Pierson. Osmond had previously collaborated with Film4 on the critically acclaimed *Deep Water* (2006), about the yachtsman, Donald Crowhurst and his single-handed race around the world, and she recently directed *Richard III: The King in the Car Park* (2013), the highest rated specialist factual documentary on Channel 4 about the quest to find the body of King Richard, so had a good track record and, in this instance, they chose her film.

The story of Dream Alliance concerns a racehorse that was acquired by a syndicate of Welsh ex-miners and working-class villagers. Central character, Jan Vokes, then a barmaid, but now a supermarket worker, whose idea it was to breed and own a racehorse had always loved animals, and it was a casual conversation about horseracing at the working men's club where she worked that decided her. Consequently, in 2000 she bought a mare for £300 and mated her with an ageing stallion to produce Dream Alliance. Vokes and her husband Brian convinced 23 of their friends in the former mining town of Cefn Fforest to put in £10 a week to pay for the horse's food and training. One difficulty in the making of the film was that the only material documenting Dream Alliance's story—apart from any races that were televised—was some home movie fragments, photographs and newspaper cuttings. Osmond uses documentary footage to show the horse being tended to in various places, including an allotment. Another perceived problem was that of an animal as a central protagonist:

> who doesn't speak. We knew we needed to dramatise the documentary at various points, so we decided to let Dream play himself – and he proved the perfect gentleman. We also asked the villagers to help us recreate those days when Dream was competing and they couldn't have been kinder or more helpful. No professional extras were used in making Dark Horse, human or animal. (in Jones 2015)

In fact, though, as much as it is a story about horses, *Dark Horse* is also about the breaking down of financial and class barriers and introducing hope into a depressed area of Wales. Not only did the film recount a fairytale, it emphasised a strong cooperative spirit and, as Vokes herself states, 'it's never been about money; it's always been about the horse and the friendships' (in Jones 2015). As Osmond acknowledges:

> If Dream was racing, the whole community would turn out to support him and watch in the local bar. It's that sense of one of your own, out there on the big stage, getting to Aintree. When we went down there and met them, you really started to realise how much it had meant to all of the community. It wasn't really about the racing or the winning at all. It was like the light bulb that went on and lit up the whole village, breathing life back into a place where unemployment is at one of the highest levels in Britain. (in Jones 2015)

Dark Horse has been positively described by many commentators as the filmic equine equivalent of *Rocky* and the British answer to *Seabiscuit* (Jones 2015) and, as the director states, 'It's also part Billy Elliot, The Full Monty, underdog-makes-good' (in Jones 2015). The film won an award at the Sundance Film Festival, which is the largest independent film festival in America and a showcase for filmmakers to distribute their work, and it was one of two Welsh-funded films being screened that year, giving a taste of what life is like in the Welsh Valleys.

Film4 matched the BFI funding for *Dark Horse* and one of their conditions was that a distributor should be secured at the start: Picturehouse Entertainment, an independent cinema chain agreed, along with Protagonist Pictures, which had represented the documentaries *The Imposter* (Layton 2012) and *Searching for Sugar Man* (Bendjelloul 2012).

Summary

The above are examples of the divergent work in documentary cinema produced by British women directors. From environmental activism to documenting societal and cultural change, to controversial takes on inner-city life, the work described in this chapter demonstrates a wealth of capacity in the field. These filmmakers reinforce their allegiance to their beliefs by acquiring sponsorship for their work from private sources, although a few are more successful in their financial arrangements, with the UKFC and the BFI providing funding as well as broadcasting stations such as the BBC and Channel 4. The stories that they tell are simultaneously global and local, often dealing with immense and seemingly insurmountable problems, yet they relate them in a personal way to enable spectator empathy and identification. Those women who direct films about climate change and environmental issues do so from personal conviction, sometimes, as with Armstrong, continuing to carry out their pledge to create awareness, or similarly, as in Woolcock's mentoring enterprise, maintaining support for their projects. My examples of filmmakers who document change, where possible, adopt an observational and objective mode of address to enable spectator identification with the subjects and key issues at stake. Both Longinotto and Ayisi/Brylla represent the women they observe as individual and empowered, and as their own agents of change. When women filmmakers produce drama documentaries, the result is often based on their own personal experiences, or serves as a means of exposing societal inadequacies; in Woolcock's case, it is a way of finding an answer. In all the examples discussed, the directors demonstrate a dedication and obligation to their projects through careful and in-depth research, often living and operating for lengthy periods of time in hardship. Nonetheless, despite the fact that documentary seems to be the mainstay of women directors in the UK, they are also productive in other areas of filmmaking, and this is the subject of the next chapter, which reviews the second most prolific form of filmmaking by British women directors: low-budget fiction films which deal with inequitable societies through a poetic optic.[38]

Notes

1. In the USA, for example, they make up at least 50% of the directors in the documentary community.
2. This is not to suggest that women are new to this type of filmmaking. As early as the 1930s and the Second World War the British documentary movement provided the chance for a number of women to enter the industry in non-directorial roles. Indeed, although there was a limited number of women film directors prior to this period, by the 1940s more had moved into above-the-line positions, largely through the government sponsorship of propaganda films. See Chapman (2015).
3. Although the notion of observational is problematic. See Bruzzi (2000).
4. The McLibel Trial is the infamous lengthy and embarrassing British court case between McDonald's and environmental activists, Helen Steel and Dave Morris. It ran for two and a half years and became the longest ever English trial. The defendants were denied legal aid and their right to a jury, so the whole trial was heard by a single judge, Mr Justice Bell. The verdict delivered in 1997 ruled that McDonald's 'exploit children' with their advertising, produce 'misleading' advertising, are 'culpably responsible' for cruelty to animals, are 'antipathetic' to unionisation and pay their workers low wages. But Steel and Morris failed to prove all the points and so the judge ruled that they had libelled McDonald's and should pay £60,000 damages. They refused but McDonald's did not pursue it. In March 1999 the Court of Appeal made further rulings that it was fair comment to say that McDonald's employees worldwide fared badly and a high diet of McDonald's food was detrimental to the body. For further reading see John Vidal (1997).
5. Armstrong eventually called upon fellow director Ken Loach to interject a drama documentary aspect to the film.
6. For a more extensive analysis of this film see Hockenhull (2013a).
7. For further reading see Kate Bulkley (2010).

8. Similarly, and also without access to lottery funding, Emily James made *Just Do It: A Tale of Modern Day Outlaws* in 2011, a UK/US production, the director raising money through crowdfunding. Emily James was the executive producer for *The Age of Stupid*, and, in a similar vein to Armstrong, expressed the same dedication to documenting climate change issues in *Just Do It*, a feature-length documentary which observes climate activism and those individuals who are actively campaigning. Filming took place over one year, and follows militants as they blockade factories, attack coal power stations and glue themselves to the trading floors of international banks. The film delves behind the scenes on activists who are prepared to take extreme measures to effect change as her website says:

   > Just Do It is a totally independent, grassroots project that has been made possible thanks to the generosity of over 100 volunteers, 447 crowd funders and a handful of foundation grants. This film could not have been made without your help. Now we need your help to make sure as many people as possible – the world over – get to see the film. Let's give Just Do It the release it deserves.

   James was further supported through grants and private donations including the Bertha Foundation, a charity which aids film distribution and supports activism, and one that also assisted Penny Woolcock's *One Mile Away* (2012). Cinereach, whose aim it is to facilitate under-represented projects to reach large audiences, helped with sponsorship, and James managed all the funding herself, being generally critical of UK funding institutions. See http://justdoitfilm.com/ (accessed 13 May 2015).
9. Armstrong suggests that her inspiration for this scheme came as she was walking to a debate with the then Secretary of State for Energy and Climate Change, Ed Miliband (Saner 2011: 11).
10. Notable individuals such as Sara Cox, Ian McEwan, Kevin McCloud, Colin Firth and Delia Smith (Clark 2009: 21; Anon. 2010d: 14) also made a similar commitment. Further, MBDA Missile Systems, a UK based arms manufacturer, pledged to meet the 10% campaign too, although 10:10 rejected a Manchester Airport application for moral reasons, on the grounds that it

planned to double passenger numbers over the next 20 years (Hickman 2009: 21).

11. However, commenting on the all-male Palme d'Or line-up at Cannes in 2012 she suggests that 'the bigger problem is that there are not enough films being made by women because they are frequently perceived as too difficult to work with ... In the same way, male directors can behave abysmally but it's hard to imagine how bad they'd have to behave before they were described as too difficult to work with, which is an excuse commonly used against female directors' (in Hill 2012: 42).
12. We are informed that the pickers extract 200 tons of recyclable materials every day produced by Rio de Janeiro's population of 400,000.
13. Lawrence Bender and Participant Productions were also the team responsible for *An Inconvenient Truth*.
14. These include *Cherry Blossom* (2012) and *The Tsunami* (2012).
15. For most of her films, Longinotto acts as both the director and cinematographer. Exceptions are *The Good Wife of Tokyo* (1992) and *Love is All* (2014).
16. Though *Divorce Iranian Style* (1998) won the RAI Film Prize at the seventh RAI International Festival of Ethnographic Film. *Sisters in Law* (2005) won the Audience Prize and received a special commendation for the Basil Wright film prize at the ninth RAI International Festival of Ethnographic Film. In fact, although Longinotto's position is one of observer, she does collaborate with the individuals in her films, leading her to explain her approach as more participatory than observational (in Basu 2008: 101). On the other hand, the fact that she does not appear in them, always preferring to remain behind the camera, means that she does not influence responses through interview; her techniques, therefore, reject ethnographic conventions, and avoid voice-over commentaries.
17. Longinotto always uses an all-female crew.
18. In 1979 the feminist film distributor, Cinema of Women (COW) was established in the UK but is no longer in operation.
19. Longinotto's later *Love is All* (2014) was sponsored by the BFI and Sheffield Doc/Fest for the BBC, and distributed by Dogwoof. The film is a feminist take on love, based on an assemblage of found footage acquired from the BFI, Yorkshire Film, National

Fairground and North East Film Archives. Longinotto intersperses clips from narrative films such as *The Hindle Wakes* (Elvey 1927) with shots of female wrestlers and stories of prostitution and sexually transmitted diseases. Again, she makes no intervention in the film, and underscores the images with music from Richard Hawley, which was not specifically composed for *Love is All* but provided 'another method of recontextualising the footage that goes beyond any comparative cutting, helping to make the images more accessible to a contemporary audience' (Lucca 2015: 82).

20. The film was turned down by the BBC, according to Longinotto, because the corporation didn't want to fund 'another film about prostitutes' (in Mayer 2015a: 64).
21. These include: recognition, alignment, allegiance. See Smith (1994: 39).
22. Also a book entitled *The Kabul Beauty School* by Deborah Rodriguez.
23. Dutt was eventually sentenced to six years' imprisonment in 2007, but released on bail. In 2013 he was sentenced to five years' imprisonment.
24. Lakla acted as co-director with Mermin on *Shot in Bombay*, but the two experienced difficulties working together because they deployed different filmmaking practices. See Sauma (2008: 81).
25. *The Alcohol Years* was eventually shown at BFI regional cinemas.
26. Zawe Ashton is about to direct her own first film but complains about the paucity of roles on offer for black women actors. See Seymour (2013).
27. The *New York Times* featured a cover story about the outbreak of a mass psychogenic illness where 18 high school girls, many of them cheerleaders, suffered twitching, seizures and fainting.
28. This was believed to be as a result of side effects from a vaccine, Gardasil, administered as a protection against human papilloma virus. While the 240 girls affected protested, President Juan Manuel Santos argued that it was a matter of collective suggestion and a case of mass hysteria.
29. *The Falling* was not her first film to examine strange behaviours. In 2006 she made a short fiction film, *The Madness of the Dance*, about a series of dancing manias in Europe between the thirteenth and seventeenth centuries. The obsession involved hundreds, sometimes thousands, of people dancing in strange ways. *The*

Madness of the Dance featured Maxine Peake as a psychology professor. It was screened at the Freud Museum alongside a video entitled *Programme* (Squires 2006), which investigated the nineteenth-century work of Jean-Martin Charcot and his treatment of hysteria in a women's hospital in Paris.

30. Morley wanted an experienced crew and Godard fitted the bill. She had more knowledge of working in fiction films than the director (she has over 50 credits as Director of Photography), working in the industry for more than 40 years on a number of French films.
31. Set up in 2011 by Joe Barratt, Screen Stockport Film Festival is supported by IMDb and is one of the leading festivals in the north-west which encourages short films by students and independent filmmakers. Morley previewed a sequence from the film prior to its general release the following year.
32. Woolcock's films are politically motivated and it was with *The Principles of Lust* (Woolcock 2003) that she made her cinema debut. Sponsored by Film4 (one of the last of its productions) and the European Regional Development Fund, the film centres on various activities such as bare-knuckle boxing, drug abuse and unconventional sexual lifestyles. In this instance, although this subject matter might suggest a realist aesthetic style, the film also deploys a documentary approach to fiction, using a hand-held camera in real locations rather than studio sets. Elements of eroticism and surrealism prevail, and the characters within read *Story of the Eye* (1928), the sensual Georges Bataille novel. *The Principles of Lust* was shot in Sheffield in a short space of time, enabling Woolcock to move on to her next project, *The Death of Klinghoffer* (2003). Commissioned by Channel 4 and costing £1.8 million to make, the film is an opera by John Adams based on the hijacking of the Italian cruise ship, the *Achille Lauro*, by members of the Palestine Liberation Organisation. Taking a similar non-rehearsed approach to Woolcock's earlier work, it was mostly shot on a chartered cruise ship, and American baritone, Sanford Sylvan, who had originally played Leon Klinghoffer in the opera's 1991 world premiere, returned to the same part for the film. Although it was called a docuopera (Price 2003: 15), for this film Woolcock adopted a cinematic approach, introducing a contemporary improvisational style of film-making to the genre. She worked closely with the

composer and the cast lived on the ship for the ten days of shooting.

33. In one report, Woolcock comments that they were finding it hard to obtain bookings in Birmingham cinemas because they had been scared off by the police. In response, West Midlands Police produced a statement suggesting that they have 'no powers to prevent cinema managers from showing films, and, indeed, would never seek to act as a censor' (Anon. 2009a). See http://www.telegraph.co.uk/culture/film/film-news/6462775/1-DAY-gang-culture-film-dropped-from-cinemas-in-Birmingham.html (accessed 5 July 2015).
34. Woolcock is passionate about music and theatre. In between, in 2008, she directed *Doctor Atomic*, John Adams's 2005 opera about the creation of the atom bomb at the Metropolitan Opera House, New York. Prior to this she made the feature film entitled *The Death of Klinghoffer* (2003). More recently, she directed Bizet's opera *The Pearl Fishers* at the Coliseum in London. Her interest in this latter project developed partly as a result of her concern about climate change. As she suggests, the story is set in a poor village in Ceylon, and focuses on 'the human element, and the sheer poverty of these people who are subject to the power of the sea' (in Higgins 2010a: 22).
35. Two young women, Letisha Shakespeare aged 17, and Charlene Ellis aged 18, were shot in a gang-related killing outside a hair salon in Birchfield Road, Birmingham as they were leaving a party in the early hours of 2 January 2003. This was part of a feud between the two Birmingham gangster groups.
36. The filming of *One Mile Away* attracted controversy when the police contacted Channel 4, who had funded the film along with Creative England, to demand surrender of all the film footage that had been shot.
37. For more up-to-date statistics see: http://www.ukcrimestats.com/Neighbourhood/West_Midlands_Police/Birmingham_City_Centre (accessed 9 February 2016).
38. Other laudable filmmakers who receive funding yet retain freedom of expression are Jane Pollard and Iain Forsyth. The two met at Goldsmiths while studying in the 1990s and went on to form a collaborative partnership, releasing their first feature documentary/fiction film, *20,000 Days on Earth*, in 2014. This focuses on

musician and writer Nick Cave, and charts his life up to his 20,000th day on earth. Sponsored by Film4 and the BFI Film Fund, *20,000 Days on Earth* shows footage of Cave at home, in his studio and on stage. The multi-faceted Cave is a rock icon, yet the filmmakers present him as an ordinary person with the same commitments as everyone else as he discusses his work and thoughts. The film integrates archive footage and found objects with sessions with his therapist. Forsyth and Pollard's background is more associated with installations and sound, and their interest in performance is previously evidenced in *A Rock n' Roll Suicide* (1998), for which actors restaged David Bowie's farewell concert as Ziggy Stardust at the Hammersmith Odeon. Having worked with Cave before, the pair felt confident in their approach. Pollard and Forsyth wanted the film to be motivating 'but inspire people very particularly: with the feeling that Nick inspires in us' (in Wakefield 2014: 28). Favouring the close-up to capture Cave's performance, they remain passive during the filmmaking process, choosing improvisation and permitting Cave to freely express himself. Sound was a priority for the duo, which they used to create affect, stretching and distorting musical notes to suit. Prior to *20,000 Days on Earth*, Pollard and Forsyth created a number of installations and DVD shorts, including a series of 14 entitled *Do You Love Me Like I Love You?* (2009–11). In 2015 Pollard and Forsyth released *Who Is Gil Scott Heron?* a portrait of the dead musician seen through the eyes of his family and friends. Other female documentary filmmakers to include here, albeit in brief, are Polish-born Katarzyna Klimkiewicz with her low-budget drama, *Flying Blind* (2012), made with support from Bristol City Council, South West Screen and BBC films. Additionally, in 2013, James Erskine and Zara Hayes released *Battle of the Sexes*, a documentary about the match between tennis player Billie Jean King and Bobby Riggs, which was staged at the Houston Astrodome in Texas in front of over 30,000 spectators. The sibling team, Jacqui Morris and David Morris wrote the screenplay for, and directed *McCullin* in 2012, a documentary about Don McCullin, the war photographer.

CHAPTER 4

Women Directors and Poetic Realism

> Surveying the most recent examples of films with some claim to realism, two aspects are immediately apparent. Firstly, the masculinist bias of much British social realist cinema has been challenged by a proliferation of films centring upon female characters, very often from the perspective of a female writer or director. (Leggott 2008: 72)

In the above quote, James Leggott observes that a number of women writers and directors are working in social realism in the new millennium, and these often create a central female protagonist[1] who is either not given a voice or else is marginalised and subordinate to the demands of society. Struggling to survive in an inequitable world, they are forced to abandon their children, subsist through prostitution, or behave immorally and dishonestly. On the other hand, many social realist films concentrate on deprived childhood and impoverished youth. Indeed, since the start of the new millennium, children have become centralised in this genre, arguably because they are emotive subjects and illustrative of societal concerns.[2] Frequently, either as a result of poverty, lack of extended family or moral deprivation, they are presented narratively and visually as troublesome and socially outcast. This exposure is partly because the post-2000 period witnessed a surfeit of child-centred government Acts, as well as campaigns by non-governmental organisations for social justice. For example, in March 1999, Prime Minister Tony Blair announced a commitment to eliminate child poverty in the UK by the year 2020 (see Kennedy 2014). This target

S. Hockenhull, *British Women Film Directors in the New Millennium*, DOI 10.1057/978-1-137-48992-0_4

was to be met by initially reducing child privation by a quarter between 1999 and 2004/5, with total eradication by the year 2020.[3]

Additionally, in June 2009 the Child Poverty Bill was introduced and the Child Poverty Act was passed in 2010, with appropriate targets to be met by 2020/1, including new strategies for childcare and an emphasis on consultation with children or organisations working with children. Ongoing concern was expressed in May 2014 over poor nutrition, housing, emotional well-being, cognitive development and educational attainment as resulting from child poverty, culminating in a published report from Save the Children entitled *A Fair Start for Every Child: Why We Must Act Now to Tackle Child Poverty in the UK* (Kothari et al. 2014). In June 2014, the government published its second Child Poverty Strategy, to encompass the period 2014–17, a policy which set out to confront the causes of 'child poverty by assisting families into work with increased earnings' and 'raising educational outcomes of poor children' (Kennedy 2014: 1).

Thus, while pre-2000 social realist film plots were generally motivated by adult protagonists (one notable exception is *Kes* [Loach 1969]), with few female filmmakers working in this field,[4] since 2000, and arguably in direct response to these concerns, a number of British filmmakers, both male and female, have indirectly responded to these various Acts, representing childhood and youth as other and dispossessed. Such portrayals tend to appear in films that focus on the working or underclass of society, and that embrace social issues usually of a domestic nature. They are typically grounded in the contemporary scene and, as Samantha Lay suggests, 'tend to extend the range of characters and topics to include marginal or previously under-represented groups and issues in society' (2002: 9). Lay also attributes this refocus to the fact that children are now provided with greater societal prominence through a variety of media, such as television chat shows and teen magazines which offer counselling and listen to their problems. Correspondingly, since the start of the new millennium, a plethora of films have been produced which focus on societal concerns such as paedophilia, neglect, violence, school truancy, under-achievement, drug-related poverty and the issues that arise from growing up in a single-parent family.

Furthermore, if realist films in the new millennium demonstrate a concern with childhood and youth, they are arguably less focused on the political, placing greater emphasis on a poetic visual aesthetic. As

David Forrest (2010) contends, this not only provides them with a more international feel, but also uses the landscape as temporary reprieve from societal inequity and to emphasise the loss and isolation of the characters. Forrest notes the emergence of a different form of realism from its earlier counterparts. According to him, film directors such as Duane Hopkins, Pawel Pawlikowski, Shane Meadows, Andrea Arnold and Lynne Ramsay move away from the style of filmmakers such as Loach and Leigh to produce what he terms 'new realism' (2010: 31). Forrest perceives a radical transformation in contemporary realism with 'a more thematically diverse, expressive, ambiguous and author-driven address ... that ha[s] challenged the dominance of Ken Loach and Mike Leigh' (2010: 31–2). As a result, the films use social and political agendas as a backdrop, but deploy 'a poetic and aesthetically bold approach to their subject matter, which merges traditional thematic concerns with expressive art cinema templates' (Forrest 2010: 32). Forrest argues that there are similarities between the work of some 1960s British directors and that of a number of contemporary filmmakers such as Arnold, who 'share with the New Wave practitioners a grounding in a philosophy that identifies cinema as an artistically vital medium first, and a facilitator of socio-political substance second' (2010: 36). For him, landscape is at the forefront of this new realism, and 'the organization of foregrounded images and the realization of their figurative potentials act as the main conveyors of meaning within [t]his aesthetic approach' (Forrest 2010: 42). For Forrest, the changes result in a lyrical style particularly associated with the work of both Ramsay and Arnold. Indeed, as he observes, many of these new millennium films 'are imbued with a freshness by their grounding in, and subsequent reassessment of, the traditional platforms of realist cinema' (2010: 33).

New realism remains low budget, and many of the films produced attracted UKFC funding or, later, BFI support. This chapter analyses examples from filmmakers such as Andrea Arnold, Lynne Ramsay, Samantha Morton, Amma Asante and Clio Barnard, whose output not only reflects on social inequality and poverty but is also invested with a poeticism hitherto less discernible in British social realist cinema.[5] The final section examines the work of Joanna Hogg, whose films I have chosen to include here rather than elsewhere in the book because they fall into what David Forrest describes as a 'middle-class realist' style (2014).

Andrea Arnold

A key figure in British cinema, and one who has benefited from UKFC funding for this type of production is Andrea Arnold. Arnold left school when she was 16 and began her career in television as a children's TV presenter and actress. From writing stories she moved into film directing, studying at the American Film Institute in LA. Preferring to work in a filmmaking mode which is 'small, intense and heartfelt' (Mullen 2009: 19), and on a low budget, her films are visually and narratively taxing, presented in an observational style. Arnold's oeuvre focuses on female isolation and adversity, and one of her first short films, *Wasp* (2003), supported by the UKFC and Channel 4, features a poverty-stricken young mother, Zoe (Natalie Press), who is struggling to cope. In an attempt to experience some excitement, she leaves her four young children outside a pub to go on a date with old flame, Dave (Danny Dyer). The narrative centres as much on the children as it does on the two central characters and reveals the problems of single parenthood, deprivation and human emotion. Yet, despite its tough plot, its elegiac visuals resulted in a large number of awards, including an Oscar for Best Short Film,[6] with Director of Photography Robbie Ryan[7] using a hand-held camera throughout to create spontaneous documentary-style imagery.

Red Road is Arnold's feature debut, and her first to receive UKFC funding. An Advance Party[8] three-film concept resulting from a co-production agreement between the Glasgow film company Sigma Films, in conjunction with a Danish counterpart Zentropa, the initiative entailed presenting three different film directors with the same group of characters for which each would develop their own script. All of the films would shoot for the same time in the same city. Arnold was chosen for the project, along with filmmakers Morag McKinnon and Mikkel Noergaard, and the characters, developed by Lone Scherfig and Anders Thomas Jensen, were the starting point for the ensuing script.

Arnold's interest in personality meant that she subsequently fleshed out the characters, and then created a means of bringing them together. The producer brief was that the film be shot in Glasgow over a period of six weeks, and all three films would use the same actors chosen from a pool: Tony Curran and Kate Dickie were selected, and Arnold used improvisation practice sessions to work with them and then incorporated this into the script. This approach appropriated a specific type of realism and enabled the actors to immerse themselves in their roles. Indeed, Dickie became so involved that 'it took about a month after filming finished for her to completely let go of Jackie and recover from the psychological ordeal' (Verve Pictures *Red Road*: 16).[9] Curran also worked well with the director, understanding her requirements. As he commented, Arnold 'has a real instinct and sensitivity, she has an eye for detail about all the small things in life … I felt I could trust what she was wanting. I said to myself "Right if she wants to do these things then let's make it as truthful and real as possible"' (Verve Pictures *Red Road*: 12).

Red Road is based in the tough Glasgow housing estate of the film's title. The narrative is dark and follows Jackie Morrison (Kate Dickie), who works in a surveillance centre monitoring CCTV cameras on the Red Road development. Although not immediately clear at the outset, it later transpires that her husband and only child have been killed in a drink driving incident and the perpetrator, Clyde Henderson (Tony Curran), now out of prison, is espied by Jackie through her surveillance work. Jackie sets out to take revenge by seducing him and then pretending that he has raped her: an incident which she subsequently reports to the police. However, while visually the film shares a considerable number of traits with realist cinema there is resolution at the end when Jackie comes to terms with the past, and her husband's parents from whom she is estranged. She also forgives her nemesis, Clyde, for his crime in the process.

In this film, Arnold uses 'an impressionist-realist style via wandering hand-held camerawork and shifting focal planes' (Fuller 2007: 71) to offer the spectator a British version of *film noir*. Jackie operates as a transgressive predatory female determined to trap Clyde in a web of deceit by pretending that he has committed a crime when, instead, they have consensual sex. Jackie is an outsider looking in. She has closed herself off from the family (her dead husband's parents and sister), and her life is conducted from the interior of the CCTV surveillance room where she works. Her character fits into what Charlotte Brunsdon (2012) describes as, the 'desperate girls' category, commencing with Stella (Kelly MacDonald) in *Stella Does Tricks* and Iris (Samantha Morton) in *Under the Skin*. As Brunsdon claims, the 1990s consisted of:

> desperate girls. Since then, strikingly, their ranks have been increased, to considerable critical acclaim, by the eponymous heroine of Lynne Ramsay's second feature, *Morvern Callar* (2002), Jackie and Mia in Andrea Arnold's two features, *Red Road* and *Fish Tank* (2009), and Clio Barnard's Artangel-produced dramatisation of the life of Andrea Dunbar, *The Arbor* (2010).

> What is notable is that so many talented female directors working in the cinema are leading their work with 'fucked-up' heroines. (2012: 462)

Brunsdon draws a correlation between televisual and cinematic representations of women in the 1990s and argues that, while the former offered more space for strong women, the latter produced the opposite.[10]

Arnold won two Jury prizes at the Cannes International Film Festival for *Red Road*, a film which reflected her belief in an instinctive style. Yet she is single minded in her approach, as displayed when she cast Heathcliff as black in her 2011 adaptation of Emily Brontë's novel *Wuthering Heights* (1845–6): in her words, 'No one was going to stop me doing what I wanted to do, but eyebrows were raised' (in Fuller 2012b: 78). In terms of authorial control, Arnold acted as both director and writer of the script, believing that it is important to be in command of both 'because you understand the script so well and you can change things as you go, cut stuff that's not working and try to improve as you go. You know the material inside out and can be very instinctive when working' (Verve Pictures *Red Road*: 32). For Michael Stewart, the film is an example of European traductive realism,[11] which pushes narrative with 'no obligation to engage with specific questions or representations of the national' (Stewart 2012: 549), combined with melodrama. Indeed, Arnold uses the melodramatic tropes of narrative and character in script and direction to emphasise 'familialism and redemption; and the nomination of its central character as a woman and mother' (Stewart 2012: 548). Yet the film's traductive realism, for Stewart, pushes narrative realism closer to the avant-garde to approach abjection. According to him, *Red Road*'s melodramatic form is confirmed through the opening and closing sequences of the film, introducing the spectator to the ordinary lives of the film's protagonists at night, the ending offering positive closure and patterning in morning daylight. These aspects also arise from the film's use of innocence, utopia and nostalgia; as Stewart observes, the 'Photographs of her family surround Jackie when she returns at last to her in-laws' home and it is a 'photo of a cherished memory that provides her with a location for her daughter and husband's ashes' (2012b: 553). This provides one of many 'working-through' instances which recur in the film, along with the excessive moments typical of melodrama. One such example is the Clyde and Jackie scene in the bar when she engineers a meeting with him. The scene is followed by 'Jackie's noirish fatalism [which] is given its final performative flourish in Clyde's bathroom, where she becomes more crudely and calculatingly dangerous than at any point in the film: acting out in front of the mirror the final parts of her plan, lit in shadow and steely-cold blue-grey' (Stewart 2012: 555).

Stewart's description of *Red Road* as a woman's film of a moral tale, and Jackie as an icon of maternal suffering, is persuasive, yet the film more easily aligns itself with Forrest's notion of new realism. Indeed, *Red Road* is first artistic and second socio-politically motivated and, whereas dialogue is important to filmmakers such as Loach and Leigh, Arnold emphasises setting and privileges image over narrative. This is exemplified early in the film when Jackie journeys to a rendezvous with her married lover, Avery (Paul Higgins). They travel by car along a busy dual carriageway, engaged in an inane conversation about a mirror toy that dangles in front of the screen. When asked where it came from, Avery replies that his son gave it to him, making Jackie look downward because, the spectator later learns, she has lost her child in a drink driving accident. The camera is placed to the rear of the car, and hence Jackie is seen in close-up. Her inner turmoil, however, is perhaps better expressed in the surrounding *mise-en-scène*: at this juncture, Arnold cuts to the passing landscape. Dark trees fill the frame and, shown in silhouette, they are bare of leaves and create black outlines against the late afternoon's winter sky. The car speeds on, and the Scottish hills now overpower the image but the spectator is unclear whether this is from Jackie's point of view or not because the next shot of a tiny window looking out is from an interior perspective. A further edit reveals the couple seated in silence at a table of a pub followed by a shot of their vehicle parked up and shown from a distance.

Avery's dog, which has been let loose to wander, is depicted in silhouette and ventures towards the van, which is situated on the horizon. At this point, the colours are surprisingly pictorial, with the last rays of the setting sun casting a glow comprised of red and yellow hues onto the landscape. From this bucolic scene, Arnold returns to an interior shot of the van where the couple are having sex. Close-ups of Jackie's face pushed up against the glass of the window are intercut with extreme close-ups of Avery's rear as the two copulate until, finally, Avery leaves the vehicle to retrieve his dog, and he and Jackie return to the city. 'See you in two weeks then,' he states, and Jackie leaves the vehicle and stands alone in a car park. At this point, only her outline is visible, and Arnold creates a poetic affect as the sun sets behind her figure. Although this sequence remains rooted in reality, Arnold's *mise-en-scène* includes striking imagery, at times seemingly surplus to narrative requirements. The landscape is presented as an image-driven means of explaining and emphasising Jackie's loneliness without fully explicating it. This approach is aligned with Forrest's notion of landscape as being at the forefront of new realism, the composition of images becoming the main conveyors of meaning (Forrest 2010: 42). As he argues, this 'use of stylistic and image-led features, as opposed to orthodox naturalistic, observational aesthetics, shows the manner in which new realist cinema in Britain is signalling a changing of priorities where the depiction of reality – while still central – is increasingly open to a broader range of approaches' (2010: 41).

Red Road does not fit neatly into traditional concepts of social realism, yet it details female displacement and marginality using picturesque tropes to suggest Jackie's outsider and 'desperate' status. In a similar vein, Arnold's later *Fish Tank* defies many of the parameters set out by the genre's earlier counterparts, instead focusing on 'desperate girls' and dispossessed youth through an elegiac optic. The director again insisted on using hand-held cameras to uncover the raw side of life on an Essex housing estate,[12] using her usual cinematographer Robbie Ryan, and once again she stipulated that the footage and acting was to look as natural as possible (Creely 2009).[13] According to Ryan, Arnold does not do rehearsals. In fact, only the crew and the director had read the script beforehand, and the actors were not allowed to view it until the day before filming. As he says, 'So they were in the dark, basically. Andrea and I went for a meeting before the film was shot. We sat down and tried to think of a plan, an approach. And really … there is no approach' (in Creely 2009).

Fish Tank, is a tough and challenging story of teenager, Mia (Katie Jarvis), growing up with her neglectful and desperate single-parent mother. The girl has an ambition to become a dancer and she practises endlessly hoping to fulfil her dream. Tests of relationships are demonstrated with her mother's boyfriend, Conor (Michael Fassbender), with whom she has sex, and with a young traveller boy, Billy (Harry Treadaway). Mia does not fit in with friends or family and has become an interloper in her own home. After the sexual act with Conor takes place, he leaves immediately, presumably because Mia is underage, and she follows, only to discover that he has another family. The film ends in near tragedy when she abducts Conor's daughter and the child almost drowns.

The film opens with a shot of Mia; inert and head bent forwards, she faces a window in an empty and derelict high-rise apartment. Initially, the establishment of any specific location is unclear, and Mia's motionless figure is unexplained. Raising her head, the girl is pictured centre frame, and the film then cuts to a shot from a rear position, thus spatially situating her for the spectator. Here, Arnold creates a romantic aesthetic at the outset, with Mia shown in silhouette set against the view from the flats. Far from introducing the area as the rundown housing estate that it is, Arnold cinematographically manipulates the *mise-en-scène* to create a scene of beauty, the camera bypassing the buildings in the foreground to prosaically observe the rural distance.

The director intersperses lengthy takes of scenes like this throughout the film, and in one such sequence we observe Mia first encountering a traveller's horse that is tethered on a rough piece of ground. She gazes through the bars of an iron gate which fences in the site, and this structure fills the frame, forcing the spectator to negotiate the various obstructions to enable a glimpse of what lies beyond, in the same way that Mia must. Mia unsuccessfully attempts to free the horse from his chains, but is chased by one of the inhabitants of the travelling community. A short time later, the girl returns to the site and tries once again to release the animal, and here Arnold creates a sumptuous visual aesthetic similar to its earlier counterpart, and in keeping with Forrest's notion of poeticism. Deploying an extreme close-up of the girl stroking the animal, Arnold suggests a detachment from the reality of Mia's chaotic world, the director enabling a sense of tactility through this act. Arnold contrasts these close-up shots with subsequent images of violence as, when trying to free the horse, she is attacked by the animal's owners and a fierce struggle ensues. When Mia escapes, she runs to the gate and again the images regain their pictorial quality. In this instance, the *mise-en-scène* returns to the housing estate which, through a series of extended shots is seen from a distance with a canal separating the spectator from the high-rise apartments. Fronted by grassland, these edifices appear picturesque and ethereal as the sun sets behind them.

Later in the film, Conor takes Mia's mother, Joanne (Kierston Wareing), Mia and Mia's younger sister Tyler (Rebecca Griffiths) out for the day and, once more, Arnold fuses the aural and visual for aesthetic affect. Conor inserts the music of Bobby Womack's cover of the Mamas and the Papas, 'California Dreamin'' (1969) into the car's CD player and, from this, the film cuts from a profile image of Joanne to Mia. The music is prioritised as Mia's silhouette becomes blurred, merging with the background scenery while the car speeds along. Rather than permitting the camera to remain on her profile though, Arnold cuts to an exterior shot of the landscape now in sharp focus. Pastoral imagery fills the frame, and the words to the song allow Mia a psychological escape, the music and image together creating symbiosis through the aural and visual aesthetic. A cut to Mia as she turns her back to the vehicle's interior and gazes outside structures her as a liminal figure, poised on the brink of a new future and imminent change.

The place that Conor has brought them to is a deserted stretch of river surrounded by fields, and Mia remains at a distance while Joanne, Conor and Tyler stand by the water swatting mosquitoes. Viewed in long shot, and owing to a lack of proximity to the camera, their voices are diminished and they appear distanced in the frame. As Mia approaches the group, Tyler points to a dragonfly, which is filmed in extreme close-up, briefly shifting focus to such striking images of nature. Subsequently, Conor enters the water to catch a fish and invites Mia to follow. Removing her trainers, she wades into the river, and the camera frames her feet as she parts the reeds, the shots becoming lengthy and languorous. At this point, the cinematographer seems more interested in capturing the sunlit dappled foliage than following the characters, and only eventually does the camera tilt upwards to frame Mia and Conor in the water, withdrawing slightly to reveal the two in middle distance and, in part silhouette, knee-deep in the river. Sunlight illuminates the water, providing texture and movement to the *mise-en-scène*, as Conor attempts to and then succeeds in catching a fish. This aesthetic affect offers a prelude to the couple's later sexual act.

Towards the end of the film, Mia abducts Conor's daughter, Keira (Sydney Mary Nash), having tracked him down to the estate near Tilbury docks where he lives with his family. Again, Arnold introduces pictorial imagery to an otherwise traumatic situation. The sequence commences as Mia leads Keira through an area of wasteland, and the camera cuts from the pair to a shot of the landscape, as clouds scud across an otherwise blue sky, the two figures barely visible in the frame. In this scene, what is really waste scrubland appears picturesque in the bright sunlight, and the image remains onscreen for some seconds, enabling an aesthetic which seems divorced from Mia's criminal actions. The camera remains at a distance, and Mia and Keira's voices are barely discernible, before a further edit reveals a cornfield which occupies the foreground of the frame, with two farm machines on the horizon: again this links with Forrest's notion of expressive art cinema, the image prioritised over narrative concerns. At this juncture, the cinematographer lowers the camera to frame the grasses on the edge of the field. Viewed in close-up, and remaining on screen for some seconds, they oscillate in the wind before an edit reveals Mia and Keira walking along a path, the child now fighting against her abductor. Again, poetic imagery is interwoven into the narrative: pausing from shots of the fearful child, the camera rises upwards to frame the sunlight streaming through a network of branches that appear interlaced and overhang the track. In a series of hand-held shots, Mia is shown chasing Keira towards the water's edge whereupon she falls in. For a few seconds, images of muddy water fill the screen, before the child emerges, screaming. Eventually rescued by Mia, Keira shivers on the shore and the two exit the frame, which now carries elements of pathetic fallacy[14] as images of industry form a backdrop to the foregrounded turbulent water.

Arnold's use of lavish scenery in this and other sequences has not remained unnoticed by critics at the time of the release of the film. As Kristin Jones observes:

> At first glance, the modest council estate apartment where much of Andrea Arnold's *Fish Tank* unfolds seems lovely – filled with sunshine, soft colors, and decorative flourishes like seashell wind chimes and a photo mural of a tropical beach … The story unfolds amid lush color and glowing summer light. (2010: 77)

Indeed, the film offers: 'a move away from a traditionally close engagement with real issues and towards a wider concern for the way images and sounds can render reality [defined as] an art-cinema-inclined impulse in realist cinema at the expense of an inward-looking thematic emphasis' (Forrest 2010: 41).

Arnold uses a non-traditional aesthetic in a similar way in her 2011 adaptation of Brontë's, *Wuthering Heights*. For this, she received UKFC funding of £300,000 from the New Cinema Fund, as well as Film4 sponsorship and, as noted, she is the first director to cast Heathcliff[15] as black, and the first female to direct *Wuthering Heights* as a feature film (albeit Coky Giedroyć directed the television version in 2009). Opening with an image of an agitated Heathcliff (older Heathcliff/James Howson) standing dejectedly in a dark, dilapidated and unkempt room, the film has all the ingredients of realist cinema rather than, as one might expect, a costume drama. The young man subsequently throws himself to the floor, and bangs his head repeatedly on the ground in apparent frustration and suffering. At this point, a dissolve leads the spectator into flashback, and the camera, hand-held and set at a low angle, seems to navigate its own pathway through coarse upland grasses to reveal a gloomy and bleak moorland setting. Two dimly lit figures, one hooded, and both with faces in shadow, appear in silhouette against a darkening sky. At this moment the camera reveals a flock of birds circling menacingly above, but the only sound is from the howling wind as the figures head towards the distant murky outline of a stone building. The structure is barely visible through the swirling mist and, as they near the property, their faces remain obscured, torrential rain and dejected barking dogs obstructing their passage.[16]

This sequence, and indeed the entire film, relies very little on dialogue, Arnold's emphasis depending much more on *mise-en-scène*. In line with Forrest's arguments, Arnold acknowledges attempting a visceral style (Fuller 2012b: 78), presenting the spectator with the harsh realities of rural life in the nineteenth century, with the countryside relating to what Andrew Higson (2011) terms 'dirty realism': an expression describing films which usually tell of medieval England and possess:

> a fuller sense of *mise-en-scène*, lighting and cinematography … it is not simply that the landscape becomes bleaker, the dwellings more austere, and the streets, lanes and villages filthier. England/Britain generally becomes a far more dangerous place to inhabit; it is closer to nature, more primitive, less civilised. (Higson 2011: 214–15)

Arnold's interest in nature in *Wuthering Heights* extends beyond this though, and, as Amy Raphael argues:

> Ryan's cinematography is so poetic it almost steals the film. His imagery captures perfectly the heightened physicality of Cathy's longing for a boy as alienated and isolated as herself … Arnold also uses Ryan's lyrical camerawork to reflect Brontë's love of pathetic fallacy. (2011: 36; see Fig. 4.1)

In *Wuthering Heights*, Arnold again introduces the view of an outsider looking in. Arnold's Heathcliff (young Heathcliff/Solomon Glave) is a black homeless boy found on the streets of Liverpool and taken home by Cathy's (young Cathy—Shannon Beer/older Cathy—Kaye Scodelario) soon-to-be-deceased father to be raised with his family. Furthermore, Cathy, though not an outsider looking in, is destined to

Fig. 4.1 Poetic imagery in Arnold's films, *Wuthering Heights*, 2011

a life of unhappiness and she becomes socially distanced from her own background, and reluctant to accept her new surroundings through her marriage to Edgar Linton (James Northcote). From the outset, the story is told from Heathcliff's perspective, a 'shift ... suited to Arnold's more impressionistic style, which is also indicative of the more "art-house" target audience of the film and, one suspects, the production's budget' (Galpin 2014: 96). Cathy's brother, Hindley (Lee Shaw), and eventually Linton, exclude him from their homes and existence and when Arnold revisited the book it was this that made her decide to relate the story from his point of view. Describing her impressions of Heathcliff, she states, 'When I re-read it after many years I found myself fretting about Heathcliff. The ultimate outsider. A vertical invader. I wanted to make it for him. The way he was treated as a boy. The brutality. The way he then turns out. A product of his experience, or of his true nature?' (Arnold 2011: 3). As the bond between Heathcliff and Cathy develops, so Arnold makes greater use of hand-held camera and intimate close-ups to chart their relationship in the isolated moorlands.[17] *Wuthering Heights* was not overly successful at the box office, perhaps chiming with Claire Monk's notion that audiences prefer 'respectful adaptations of important literary works' (2011b: 155).

Clio Barnard

As with *Fish Tank*, the UKFC seemed predisposed to funding projects about childhood and problem families, and the work of film director Clio Barnard is no exception. Barnard hails from a fine art background, with a specialism in conceptual art, and her films are deeply rooted in this artistic milieu. Working in experimental film at art school, she then attended the NFTS, and acknowledges that her training as an artist contributes to her visual style. Barnard has a fascination with the landscape, particularly the Yorkshire moors, greatly admiring the bleakness and beauty of this area (Donald Clarke 2013: 9), an aspect that she brings into play in her work.

Barnard's early films include *Dark Glass* (2006), a story about the instability of memory and the subjectivity of recollection. It is a one-shot story that merges the images of a girl and a woman under hypnosis. Differently, *Plotlands* (2008) is an installation about a community of people, now disappeared, and set on the Seasalter Levels, while *Road Race* (2007) is a forerunner of her later feature film, *The Selfish Giant*, and focuses on the illegal gypsy practice of horse-trap racing on motorways. Barnard then moved into feature-length films, because she believes that 'there are few opportunities for artists to make long-film work. So the fact that this is what Artangel want is very refreshing, because it is so difficult to make work that asks the kinds of questions that art practice asks, but to do that within cinema or television' (in Cocker 2007: 74). She is also interested in the ways in which real experiences can be turned into fantasy through film (Cocker 2007: 73).

Her earlier *Random Acts of Intimacy* (2002) is a short film where she used actors on screen to lip-synchronise to recordings of people recalling incidents of sex with strangers; this technique provided the basis for her later film, *The Arbor*, which focuses on the tragic true story of the circumstances surrounding deceased playwright, Andrea Dunbar, and her illegitimate, half Asian daughter Lorraine (Manjinder Virk). Monitoring Lorraine's life after the sudden death of her mother, who died of a brain haemorrhage at the age of 29, the film centres on her involvement with drugs, prostitution, domestic and sexual abuse, and the manslaughter of her child. Andrea Dunbar, whose first play was also named *The Arbor* (begun in 1977 and staged at the Royal Court in 1980),[18] considered herself an outsider. Barnard recorded audio interviews with members of the Dunbar family and residents from Brafferton Arbor on the Buttershaw Estate in Bradford, where she resided over a period of two years.

For *The Arbor*, Barnard was the recipient of financial support from the Jerwood/Artangel Open, a fund set up by the Jerwood Charitable Trust aimed at tapping into undiscovered British talent in the UK, and £1 million was put together in collaboration with the Arts Council England and Channel 4. Clio Barnard was one of four chosen to benefit with 'plans to work with residents from an English council estate to make a feature-length film using two dramatically contrasting locations' (Brown 2007b: 14). Produced by Michael Morris and Tracy O'Riordan, *The Arbor* was screened at the 2010 LFF, along with Gillian Wearing's *Self Made* (2010) and Joanna Hogg's *Archipelago* (2010).

The film eventually received support from the UKFC at its development stage, and includes archive footage of Andrea Dunbar and her family from the 1960s, with their voices on the soundtrack, as well as recorded interviews from real people to create the script. Actors then play the parts of Dunbar and her family, and address the camera in a semi-documentary style, but the real voices, where possible, are lip-synchronised to create an almost exact match, thus any disjunction between the two is marginally discernible. Barnard suggests that she did this 'to create a deliberate gap between reality and representation, or at least make you aware of the gap' (in James 2010b: 250). For Lib Taylor, 'The film represents its real people with differing levels of corporeal performativity and also through the different genres of documentary, re-enactment and filmed theatrical performance, whereby slippages between a character and actor can be clearly detected' (2013: 375). Certainly, although Barnard's film is instilled with an immediacy associated with documentary, it has been cited, along with others, as an example of innovative filmmaking, blurring the boundaries of fact and fiction.[19]

As noted above, films featuring 'real' existences in everyday life frequently focus on children and youth, and Barnard's later *The Selfish Giant* is no exception. The film depicts social deprivation from the point of view of a child, and the story centres upon two boys, Arbor (Conner Chapman) and Swifty (Shaun Thomas), who come from disadvantaged families and are suspended from school. The boys purloin scrap metal to sell to dealer, Chris Kane, otherwise known as Kitten (Sean Gilder), and eventually they become involved in trap racing. Swifty loves the horses and shows an aptitude for the sport. He meets an untimely death at the end of the film when Kitten coerces the two boys into stealing railway cables and Swifty is electrocuted.

The Selfish Giant was backed by the BFI Film Fund and Film4, and Barnard's decision to 'never go to Cannes unless I had a film there' (2013: 25) was vindicated when she won the prize for the best film at Directors' Fortnight. She attended the film's premiere and confesses to nerves throughout the screening: 'No film is easy to make and there are many struggles and lots of doubts – so to arrive at this point is powerful … Afterwards my friend Kate Ogborn embraces me. "Promise me you will always follow your instincts"' (Barnard 2013: 25). As a result of Barnard's success, and that of Sam Taylor-Wood's bio-pic about Beatles pop star John Lennon's early years, entitled *Nowhere Boy* (discussed in the next chapter), the UKFC announced its intention to promote more work from people who are established figures in the arts, yet first-time feature film directors.

Barnard acknowledges that *The Selfish Giant* is about grief, attachment, separation, loss, mothers and sons. Her mantra is 'don't believe in fairy-tales' (Barnard 2013: 25), albeit the film is loosely based on Oscar Wilde's children's story, also entitled 'The Selfish Giant' (1888). She locates the film within the contemporary economic climate, suggesting that 'This economy is declining and there are not many opportunities for these boys and I guess I find that upsetting. The "selfish giant" of my film is a "selfish ideology"' (in Higgins 2013b: 3), and its poetic qualities are foregrounded through pictorial imagery at the outset. Opening shots show a herd of horses grazing on the skyline; filmed in silhouette the animals are set against a dark sky, and the typography of the title is revealed letter by letter, mobilising an ethereal effect for the spectator. Neither the title nor the picturesque opening betrays the gruelling narrative events that ensue, since the image appears indeterminate and monochrome, and is unaccompanied by any sound. An edit to an extreme close-up of the young boy, Arbor, banging his fists on the underside of a bed and crying out creates a shock effect and a strong juxtaposition with the preceding sequence. The next shot returns the spectator to the darkened landscape, but this time features a boy running alongside a cantering horse. A further edit reveals the two boys astride the animal as they approach a railway bridge, and here a specific aesthetic is created through Barnard's juxtaposition of the mounted riders set against some distant lights, which, it transpires, are those of signal cable thieves on the railway line. Filmed from a distance, and now situated directly on the bridge, which forms a semi-circular archway over the thieves, the boys' faces are dimly lit, and therefore barely discernible. Indeed, although the film is described as 'gritty', 'bleak' and 'realist' (Macnab 2013a: 44), it is also poetic and lyrical, and prioritising *mise-en-scène* over the socio-political issues at stake here appears as a means of dealing with child deprivation sympathetically.

Such qualities are further demonstrated when Arbor and Swifty steal the cable for themselves and successfully sell it to Kitten, the scrap merchant. On securing the deal, the scrap man closes the gate and its bars form a barrier across the screen, until an edit returns the spectator to an image of the horses grazing on the skyline, similar to the one opening the film: this time, though still picturesque, it is daytime. Dominating the frame, the sky and its correspondence with the landscape now creates a tranquil ambience, and the director chooses to focus on the horses for some time, presenting lengthy sequences of the animals devoid of human intervention. Indeed, Barnard introduces a romantic aspect to the *mise-en-scène* through various industrial structures. As Macnab argues:

> cinematographer Mike Eley, who also worked on Ken Loach's *The Navigators*, shoots the film as if it's a kid's adventure story, not just a grim parable about excluded children. He has an eye for landscape and for poetic and jarring positions ... There are spectacular skies that make even huge pylons and factory chimneys seem poetic. (2013a: 44)

An example of this occurs when, at one point, and for no apparent reason, the camera focuses on a pair of cooling towers which loom ghostlike in the mist, before a further edit discloses a flock of grazing sheep at their foot, which the director claims as her favourite shot: 'They [the towers] seem benign and beautiful to me. We could have made that sinister. But we chose to go the other way' (in Donald Clarke 2013: 9) she states.

Following the boys' expulsion from school they spend more time at Kitten's yard, and become involved in his horse-racing enterprise. On the morning of an important race, they arise at dawn, and Barnard chooses to display a set of electricity pylons set in the distance against the morning sky. This image, which remains on screen for some seconds, is then reframed to a further medium shot of the same pylons, before a close-up situates the spectator close to the boys, the only sound an almost imperceptible hum. Barnard thus accords these images considerable screen time, providing a lyrical interlude. Filmed from a relatively low angle, the towers loom large and menacing, and, ironically, it is these structures which will eventually be the cause of Swifty's death at the end of the film (Fig. 4.2).

Barnard's combination of social realism injected with an artistic quality confirms her aesthetic training, and *The Selfish Giant* was praised by critics,

Fig. 4.2 Lyrical and elegiac interludes on urban wastelands, *The Selfish Giant*, 2013

who noted its effect on the spectator through its spiritual qualities: Robbie Collin in his review describes the film as:

> hauntingly perfect … and so skinpricklingly alive does it make you feel to watch it, that at first you can hardly believe the sum of what you have seen: the astonishingly strong performances from her two young, untutored leads; Barnard's layered script; Mike Eley's snow-crisp cinematography that makes the streets of Bradford shine. Unlike her first film … Barnard is working in a more straightforward social-realist style, but like Ken Loach's Kes, the film knells with myth: we get a keen sense of an older, purer England buried somewhere underneath all this junk, from the early wide shots of horses in meadows, idling belly-deep in morning mist, to the extraordinary, almost wordless final sequence that hints at redemption and reincarnation. The Selfish Giant is cinema that tells a nation who we are. (Collin 2013b: 32)[20]

Barnard used her experience in *The Arbor*[21] on the Brafferton estate to make the film, where she encountered two young boys whose lives she mirrored with those of Arbor and Swifty. She explains that her inspiration was the children who were excluded from school and living on the margins (Lamont 2013: 8) but, as she suggests, 'I thought if I am going to make narrative film, then I had better learn the language. I could think about framing, but I needed to learn how to work with actors' (in Donald Clarke 2013: 9).[22]

Lynne Ramsay

From the above analyses, it appears that women film directors attempt to display realism through rich visual imagery rather than symbolic socio-political concerns. Indeed, these issues are raised through 'artistic reflections of reality, using the everyday as a cinematic canvas that houses rich poetic potentials' (Forrest 2010: 38). Correspondingly, Lynne Ramsay's *Ratcatcher* (1999) seems to be one of the first of a number of films to feature such imagery.[23] This film also focuses on children as key protagonists, but, in a similar mode to *The Selfish Giant* and *Fish Tank*, *Ratcatcher* is not a story for children; instead it represents the brutality and beauty of children's worlds from a child's perspective. Ramsay's work fits into a genre of Scottish films about young people, including the work of Ken Loach in *Sweet Sixteen* (2002) and earlier, Bill Forsyth's *That Sinking Feeling* (1979) and *Gregory's Girl* (1984), conforming to a tradition that has a distinctive relationship with the landscape. Indeed, the pastoral is 'tied to film realism as a style of British filmmaking … with the filmic creation of an aesthetic, a poetics if you will, and a politics that involves children and landscapes' (Aitken 2007: 72).

Ratcatcher is not the first of Ramsay's films to feature children. Her earlier *The Gasman* (1996) was a Film School project where she filmed a children's Christmas party and spliced this with imagery of estranged brothers and sisters meeting for the first time. Ramsay, a photographer and later a graduate cinematographer from the NFTS, also directed *Small Deaths* (1996) in her final year there, a film which won the Critic's Prize at Cannes in 1996. As a result, the BFI and Channel 4 sponsored her to direct *Kill the Day* (1997), and it was these productions which initiated the later critically acclaimed *Ratcatcher*, the latter providing the launch for her feature film career.

Ratcatcher is set in the tough urban outskirts of Glasgow, and the film's central character, James Gillespie (William Eadie), is a casualty of his environment where unemployment is endemic and children play on the street unattended. James's parents are marginalised by society owing to his father's unemployment and heavy drinking, and he is abusive to his son. James, through childhood naivety, has a vision beyond his current existence, but this will remain unfulfilled. Having accidentally drowned his friend, he yearns to move out of the slums into the countryside. Though the narrative centres on deprivation, Ramsay injects a poetic quality into the images, particularly in terms of her use of landscape. Early on in the story, James ventures into the countryside; travelling by bus he discovers a new and uncompleted housing estate in a rural area not far from Glasgow where he finds freedom from the poverty of city life. This is visually presented to the spectator when he explores the uninhabited buildings on the site, moving from room to room investigating. At one point, the boy climbs through an empty house window into a beautiful golden cornfield. He runs ecstatically through the crop, before eventually falling to the ground and rolling onto his back, his face upturned towards the blue sky, the camera placed overhead to frame his joyous expression.[24] Ramsay describes her approach to the cornfield sequence, suggesting that she deliberately sought a pictorial quality:

> The shot where he sees a cornfield through the window. I wanted it to look like a painting. I want it to be a frame within a frame … I am particularly interested in photography, stills photography, because basically you are capturing a detail in a person that says something about the whole world at times. So, within a still there can be a lot of narratives. (Ramsay 2002)

James is not the only adolescent sufferer in the film; Margaret Anne (Leanne Mullen) is an awkward pubescent 14-year-old who is mercilessly teased by the local youths, yet offers them casual sex in order to make friends. She is an outsider in relation to the remainder of the Glaswegian group of children, graceless in appearance and ungainly in attitude. Not only does Margaret Anne occupy a fringe position between adulthood and childhood in the narrative, but her social and economic station, as well as the environment in which she grows up, all place her on the edge of society. Left alone most of the day by her single-parent mother, she seeks friendship and affection and, although Ramsay does not make an obvious comment about the absence of a father, we understand that Margaret Anne's situation seems to come out of the combination of financial insecurity and parental neglect. Both James and Margaret Anne are representative of contemporary filmic British social realist youth: figures who are not innocent, yet are themselves victims, excluded from society via poverty and circumstance. Ramsay's film succeeds, however, in marrying brutality with beauty and she also raises questions about children's morality. As

Aitken argues, 'There is a poetic aesthetic at work here – sometimes tragic, sometime hilarious, always poetic' (2007: 84).

This poetic aesthetic is never more present than in Ramsay's later film, *Morvern Callar* (2002), where she tells the story of Morvern (Samantha Morton) from this central character's perspective. Morvern is a young woman whose partner has committed suicide, leaving the manuscript of his book on his computer for her to deliver to a publisher. The girl appropriates this as her own work and accepts a large sum of money in exchange, although the publisher insists they must meet up to finalise details. Morvern is a troubled soul and departs on the trip with her friend, Lanna (Kathleen McDermott), but the two argue and part company. The girl's character complies with Leggott's observations on the rise in representation of 'damaged young women', in particular in films directed by women. As he notes:

> some of the most fascinating statements about the complexity of sexual politics have been made by a group of female directors. Engaging with the interior lives of damaged young women, Carine Adler's *Under the Skin*, Lynne Ramsay's *Morvern Callar* and Andrea Arnold's *Red Road* draw provocative connections between emotional trauma – the death of loved ones – and sexual desire. All three filmmakers find cinematic ways (particularly editing) to express the intensity of their central character's grief, but to render unclear their motivation and extent of their passivity. (Leggott 2008: 103)

Morvern Callar opens with Morvern lying next to her dead partner's body, before a cut reveals his completed manuscript on the computer screen along with a suicide note. She chooses not to inform Lanna of the tragedy from the outset, and they both attend a night club together, Morvern refusing to confront her problems. The next day, however, she puts on her coat and stands, back to the camera, looking out across an expanse of water. Seen in medium shot and in silhouette, she remains immobile, her dark shape mirrored by the colours in the rocks which flank the shore. Ramsay leaves the image onscreen for some seconds, during which Morvern points to one of the islands in the distance, informing her friend that it is 'the island where my foster mum is buried'; this provides some detail about her sorry but otherwise vague background. From here the story unfolds; Morvern sends the manuscript away and dismembers her boyfriend's body. To undertake this deed, she is seen from a low angle trekking through woodland, the bare trees forming upright barriers in the barren area where she intends to bury him. At one point, she twirls around with arms outstretched, her red hat strongly contrasting with the deep blue, cloudless sky, and then proceeds to bury the body, Ramsay injecting a strange but strong visual quality to this process. Seen from a low angle, and barely visible behind clumps of grass, Morvern digs steadily with a small trowel before the camera withdraws, and the girl appears smaller in the frame, with the sun setting over the snow-covered mountains. A further shot reveals Morvern, the deed now done, stamping the ground around where the body is buried. The vivid hues of the bracken in the foreground, the snow-covered peaks and the clear blue sky form a contrast with each other, creating an expressive and artistic image.

Ramsay's later film, *We Need to Talk About Kevin* (2011)[25] is an adaptation of Lionel Shriver's novel of the same name. The film was supported by UKFC money. It premiered at the Cannes Film Festival in 2011 and Ramsay was nominated for Best Director at the BAFTAs.[26] Initially the director was promised funding for the project from the American company Summit Entertainment, but they pulled out after a year leaving only BBC Films and the UKFC as backers. Thus, Ramsay was forced to work on a substantially reduced budget of $7 million and within a limited time frame.

We Need to Talk About Kevin explores the difficult relationship between Eva Khatchadourian (Tilda Swinton) and her son Kevin (Ezra Miller), and Ramsay represents this woman as cold and domineering. Her husband Franklin (John C. Reilly) is the one who really bonds with his son, playing with him and getting up in the night to attend to his needs. Eva, on the other hand, is represented as a career-driven woman who makes her own choices. Told in flashback, the horrific events are revealed as the film progresses. The spectator learns that Eva is a travel writer, but her career is curtailed with the birth of her son, and ultimately her choices become increasingly limited as his transgressive behaviour restricts her independence. Like many of the films discussed in this chapter, *We Need to Talk About Kevin* falls within Mayer's canon of feminist films about family relationships (2016: 157). This is a point looked at by Sue Thornham, who discusses the film within the context of 'new momism' (Thornham 2015), analysing female identity embodied in the maternal melodrama as post-feminist. She suggests that this concept posits the notion of choice: women can have a career, but it is also acceptable to stay at home. Indeed, the mother–son relationship is centrally placed in Ramsay's film, and Eva's constant desire to control is, as Thornham argues, mainstream cinema's response which now features 'mothers as cold and powerful figures who must re-learn maternal softness if they are to be redeemed' (2015: 46).

The problematic mother/child relationship in *We Need to Talk About Kevin* is demonstrated through the institutional spaces that she occupies, such as the hospital and the prison, and the private spaces of her new home when she is forced to move from the buzz of New York to the sedate suburbs for the sake of her child's well-being. These clinical places result from her unwanted pregnancy (the hospital), her son's behaviour (the prison) and her children's upbringing in the house her husband has purchased (the suburbs), described by McGill as 'the stuff of smug suburban nightmares for bohemian Eva' (2011: 18). The lack of freedom that these spaces embody is juxtaposed with Eva's colourful life beforehand, an aspect that is exemplified from the opening sequences of the film, when we see that Eva's work has taken her to the Tomatina, a Spanish tomato festival. Seen from an overhead shot, she appears amid a large group of people throwing tomatoes at each other and bathed in the scarlet juice. The red hues which arise from the fruit celebration not only prefigure her son's terrible massacre at the school, but also Eva's loss of self following motherhood. For Thornham, female empowerment arrives through the free choice of being mother and not mother, yet this situation is not permitted for Eva. Instead, she must conform to the mundane orderliness and ordinariness of suburban life in order to be a good mother, and failure to do so results in catastrophe. Ramsay's juxtaposition of shots here is dramatic and, as the director maintains, in terms of film narratives, women tell a story in a different way to men, who, she suggests, impose a rigid narrative theatrical structure, with an inflexible style of editing (Elsey 2003: 14–15). The film was shot in widescreen with a 2.35:1 ratio, which enhanced the type of *mise-en-scène* that Ramsay wanted, producing 'an epic feel in a film that might easily have felt too interior and claustrophobic' (in McGill 2011: 18). Later scenes of Eva in her first uncluttered place of work as a travel writer are covered with travel posters offering escapism to exotic places. These images, however, are contrasted with her later employment, subsequent to the massacre, in the low end Travel R Us, where she is now forced to work typing and filing. Here, a tasteless drab mural of the mountains sits behind the manager's desk, which is littered with cheap and vulgar souvenirs from foreign countries.

By the end of the film Eva has been punished for her lack of mothering, and, indirectly, for Kevin's crimes. She is assaulted in the street by the locals, her house and car are smeared with red paint, and she is either badly treated or ignored in her place of work by her colleagues. In the final sequences, she appears to accept that she is partly to blame for her son's atrocious crimes (not only does he murder many of his classmates and teachers, he also blinds his sister in one eye, subsequently murders her and then his father), and prepares a room at her new house for his prison discharge. This scene is accompanied appropriately by the non-diegetic music of *Nobody's Child* by Lonnie Donegan. Following a prison visit, the two embrace and appear reconciled and, as Thornham suggests, this act 'seems at once to insist on the maternal relation and a shared responsibility and to recognize Kevin's otherness, the separation of his body *and* actions from her own [original italics]' (2015: 58). Although Ramsay eschews poetic realism here, she focuses on damaged women, dispossessed youth and childhood outsiders.

Samantha Morton

Many of the low-budget films mentioned focus on the child's downward spiral into difficulty and detachment, and Samantha Morton's directing debut, *The Unloved* (2009), is no exception. Funded by Film4 and EM Media, this film was also part financed by a European Regional Development Fund. In terms of its release patterns, it premiered on Channel 4 in 2009, and received theatrical release the following year, Morton choosing television for a first screening because of the wider, domestic audience it would attract (Brunsdon 2012: 464).

The Unloved tells the story of Lucy (Molly Windsor), a child growing up in and out of care in Nottingham where Morton also lived, and draws on Morton's own childhood experiences of care homes in the 1980s. As the director explains, she wanted to achieve those same feelings: 'There have been some brilliant films about children in care ... But I've never watched one and gone, "That's right, that's how it felt." I wanted to make a film that shared with people what it felt like to be in care, to be abandoned' (in Bell 2009: 8). As with *Ratcatcher* and *Fish Tank*, the narrative is told from Lucy's perspective and the cinematography is testament to this, with cameras positioned at child-height level and point-of-view shots to articulate her standpoint.

The film opens with a black screen and the voice of a child praying. This remains on screen for a number of seconds before an overhead view from the top of a staircase reveals a young girl lying sideways to the camera at the foot of the stairs, leading us to presume that she has been involved in an accident. The camera cuts to a number of perspectives, both from the foot of the staircase from the child's point of view, and from above, while the sound of wind chimes adds a whimsical detached quality to the image. An edit to an equally lengthy sequence discloses the girl standing in the living room while being verbally abused as she is interrogated by a man, presumably her father (Robert Carlyle), about the whereabouts of his cigarettes, which she was sent to purchase two hours before. This is told in flashback and, it transpires, is a memory of an event that resulted in a severe beating. In flashback, Lucy stands framed by the window of a sparsely furnished living room, and the camera remains static throughout the painful and violent experience. Seen from a low angle, further demonstrating the child's vulnerability, the man is visible towering above her before he beats her. Returning to the present when Lucy is regaining consciousness, the camera slowly zooms in to an extreme close-up of the injured girl's face. Then a further flashback edits to the child's father facing the camera, followed by the girl's upturned hands appearing in the frame beseeching him. A further cut reveals an out-of-focus shot of a small statue of the Virgin Mary and Child in a sunlit window, and a point-of-view shot of the statue ensues, illuminated by the sun. This imagery intimates a numinous presence in the girl's life, as small gold particles of dust float in the air to offer solace and healing.

In all, the sequence lasts nearly six minutes, Morton taking care to present this in a lyrical, poetic manner to indicate the fantasies that the young girl experiences to escape her impossible circumstances. Described as a film possessing 'its own stringent beauty [using a] muted palette of wintry greys to denote Lucy's private world' (Mayer 2010c: 81), this visual splendour is used to counteract Lucy's miserable existence. This is exemplified when, later, the child goes for a walk alone, and in a series of ruptured and non-sequential shots, she climbs the embankment which borders her house. The camera is now positioned at a distance to observe the young girl emerging from the lower ground, her figure set against a beautiful pastel winter sunset. She stands facing away from the spectator against the pink sky which is illuminated by the setting sun, before walking along the embankment; similar to Arnold's imagery in *Fish Tank*, the backdrop of high-rise accommodation appears majestic and lyrical rather than depressing, and this setting offers Lucy escape yet presents her to the spectator as a liminal figure and an outsider. Indeed, frequently, Morton uses sound to mobilise Lucy's feelings of alienation. In one school sequence in the dinner hall she eats her food and the voices of the other children fade out, as shots of lengthy duration ensue focusing on Lucy's face intercut with images of her recounting various tales to the authorities about her abusive situation. The violence she experiences is never fully explored in the narrative, but the child is taken into care, and scenes follow from outside a hospital waiting room with her social worker interwoven with shots of a car journey: this sequence is filmed from the exterior of the vehicle, the outlines of bare tree branches reflected onto the glass windows and, in turn, the child's face, further informing the spectator of her misery. Subsequently, the voice of the social worker is heard explaining to the child that she must be placed in a children's home, whereupon complete silence reigns.

Throughout the film Morton places great attention on the minutiae of Lucy's life via aspects of the *mise-en-scène*. Extreme close-ups of bowls of cereal, Lucy's washing products, and a dew-covered spider's web fill the frame, and these details are interspersed with flashbacks of time spent with her mother. At one juncture, Lucy goes in search of her and, seen from an overhead shot, she stands in a walled road looking upwards, the brick structure visually overpowering her, thus further reinforcing her loneliness and vulnerability. She is unsuccessful in her quest and, as she walks out of shot, Morton introduces a surreal aspect to the film. Retaining focus on the autumn leaves which swirl in the wind, the girl wanders around a churchyard with a deer grazing nearby and Morton manipulates sound to interject the film with an atmospheric effect, as well as to contrast the periods when she is in and out of the care home. Through this aesthetic approach, Morton attempts to recreate her own memories, as well as the experiences of other children growing up in care and, as Forrest concurs, 'Morton's film treads a familiar thematic path but is enlivened by persistent forays into subjectivity. Stylistic features such as a propensity for long takes, static camera positions and long shots of urban locations transcend the socio-political dimensions of the film by proliferating varied levels of engagement and interpretation' (2010: 32). In fact, the director's attempt to address the issue of care homes through an aesthetically pleasing optic is significant, and Morton argues that this was her favoured approach, rather than create a political statement. As she notes, 'I didn't make the film for that. If I'd wanted to do that, I would have made a documentary. I didn't go for the jugular. I hope I've made a poetic statement if anything' (in Bell 2009: 8).

The Unloved formed part of Channel 4's Forgotten Children season[27] and concludes with statistics concerning the number of children at risk and currently in care. Belonging to a 'rich tradition' of Channel 4 dramas (Cooke 2009: 44), the film was shown at a number of film festivals, including Melbourne and Stockholm. Kate Ogborn, the film's producer, maintains that '*The Unloved* was made for Channel 4 in the hope that it would reach a wide audience and also reach the young audience that it was about. When it was broadcast in 2009 it had the highest viewing figures (over 2m) for a single drama that Channel 4 had had to date' (2016). The film went on to win the BAFTA for Best Single Drama, Lauren Socha was BAFTA nominated for her performance, Robert Carlyle won a Scottish BAFTA and Samantha Morton was nominated for the Douglas Hickox Award at the British Independent Film Awards. Following on from the Channel 4 broadcast it had its international premiere at the Toronto Film Festival, and as the theatrical release in the UK followed the broadcast inevitably it was a smaller platform for the film. As Ogborn comments, 'This was always part of our strategy' (2016).[28]

Joanna Hogg

According to Brunsdon, both *Red Road* and *The Unloved* distinguish themselves from their funding sources with cinematic rather than televisual aesthetics, termed 'film-ness' (2012: 472). Indeed, the above directors offer a lyrical dimension to their work wrought from a social commitment, so to include the work of Joanna Hogg here might seem surprising, yet Forrest incorporates her as part of this categorisation. Hogg's films, particularly *Unrelated* (2007) and *Archipelago* deal mainly with middle-class characters and locations, yet Forrest makes some inroads into situating her work as new British realism as well as part of 'a new moment in British cinema, in which a stylistic concern with everyday life transcends the need for an explicit focus on the "social" in realism' (Forrest 2014). He argues that, in line with social realism, Hogg's films are contemporary, use either non-professionals or unknowns, are characterised by episodic narrative structures and are thematically based on the concept of alienation. However, her use of space, in particular landscape, adds another dimension evincing an aesthetic to explore emotion and isolation.

Hogg, who began her career as a stills photographer making 8 mm films before gaining a place at the NFTS in the 1980s, was inspired by the experimental and avant-garde filmmaker, Derek Jarman. Her early work,

Unrelated, which premiered at the 2007 LFF, centres on a family holiday with all its associated tensions. The narrative follows the character, Anna (Kathryn Worth), who has left her husband at home in order to join her old friend Verena (Mary Roscoe) and family in a rented villa in Tuscany. Also present is George (David Rintoul) and his son, Oakley (Tom Hiddleston). Anna, who spends endless periods of time on the phone to her husband in Britain, is clearly experiencing marital difficulties, and initially befriends the younger group members rather than remain with what the offspring refer to derogatorily as 'the olds'. At one juncture, however, she betrays their confidence, informing their parents that they have behaved irresponsibly when driving home one evening. Consequently, she is ostracised by the youths and this exclusion is demonstrated when the holidaymakers visit a wealthy Italian neighbour for dinner, and Anna is deliberately segregated and ignored. This is exemplified when, at one point, she is asked by Verena to go and locate the youths so that they can all return home together. Reluctantly, she climbs to the tower of the luxurious villa to find them all situated at different windows, looking out onto the landscape. None are aware of her presence, and the camera cuts back to focus on her, centre frame, where she remains unnoticed for some time before exiting unobserved. An edit reveals a later scene when they are walking home, and Verena, her husband Charlie (Michael Hadley) and George are chatting as they approach the camera; again Anna appears at the back, alone and barely visible in the frame; here she is both visually and socially ignored. This motif is repeated throughout, whereby Hogg establishes social relations through her use of space in a process described by Forrest as a 'rhythmic, everyday verisimilitude' (2014). Indeed, in both *Unrelated* and the later *Archipelago*, Hogg deploys long takes of the landscape in a visually aesthetic way to demonstrate isolation, and she retains a minimal use of dialogue to reinforce this aspect.

Hogg uses actors unknown at the time, such as Tom Hiddleston, in *Unrelated*, and the locals in the Italian setting all play themselves. This is a recurring approach in her later *Archipelago*, where she once more mixes actors and non-actors (a classic Italian neo-realist strategy and subsequently a French New Wave and New German cinematic approach). Yet again, the narrative centres on a group of holiday makers, although this time all from the same family. Kate Fahy, a professional actor, plays the mother, Patricia, while Amy Lloyd who plays Rose, the cook, was chosen following the auditions of cooks rather than actors. This was her first screen role and her first professional work. In a similar vein to Arnold,

Morton and Ramsay, Hogg encourages improvisation and features landscapes as symbolic of internal crises. She injects her work with an immobile and strained quality as an autobiographical exploration and, as the director herself suggests, and comparing *Archipelago* to her earlier *Unrelated*, 'I work with a static camera – even stiller here, if anything. But in terms of themes, I'm exploring different territory. In this film I decided to dissect myself. I am a little piece of each of those family members' (in Romney 2010: 37).

Archipelago commences with a black screen as the credits roll, with only the sound of birdsong audible. An edit reveals a large impressionist painting of a landscape which fills the frame, before the camera withdraws a short distance to disclose an artist working within an idyllic and picturesque coastal environment. Some seconds later the man departs astride a bicycle and disappears from view, but the camera does not pursue him. Instead it remains static, revealing the subtle hues of the vegetation which forms gentle horizontals across the film frame in order to create a peaceful scene of the countryside. Suddenly, a helicopter appears, its noise interrupting the tranquillity and this, in turn, implies an impending tension as well as giving an indication of the ways in which Hogg uses space, place and landscape to suggest isolation. This becomes evident in the way that interior scenes in *Archipelago* are used as spaces to display the characters undertaking their routine daily activities, and to expose the family tensions. In contrast, the exterior spaces are filmed in long takes, the characters appearing diminished and distant in the frame to convey their detachment.

Forrest aligns Hogg's style to that of film director Mike Leigh, an aspect that is particularly obvious in the use of crisis points in the narrative when, 'moments of rupture … punctuate the aforementioned replications of narrative episodes [thus creating] a de-socialised realist address' (Forrest 2014). Further, Hogg frequently juxtaposes domestic tensions and associated confined spaces with the broad open seascapes of the Scillies to produce a visually sumptuous aesthetic. Early in the film, for example, the central character, Edward (Tom Hiddleston), has arrived at the family holiday home to spend time with his family before departing to Africa as an aid worker. The tensions are apparent at the outset, but made particularly obvious at meal times when his sister, Cynthia (Lydia Leonard), reproaches him for not getting a proper job and settling down as would be appropriate for his age. His mother, Patricia defends him, and Hogg observes the scene from a distance, not only to include all the characters in the foreground but also to accommodate the kitchen to the rear where the cook, Rose, is clearly listening.

Hogg's style of filming therefore creates a sense of alienation, and although shot on the beautiful Scilly Isles, *Archipelago* is also very much focused on the interiority and claustrophobia of the house (where, incidentally, Hogg sometimes spent her childhood holidays). Edward sleeps in a small attic room and his confinement is emphasised through his height, as shown when he hits his head on the low doorways. This is contrasted with images of him cycling through the landscape where, seen at a distance, he negotiates the lanes, gradually disappearing from sight. A repeated motif is the island's terrain which remains in frame for some seconds, Hogg making no attempt to edit away from the scenery or to retain focus on the characters, instead enjoying the panoramic views. In this respect, Forrest suggests that it is the function of space that is crucial in identifying realist texts, more recently with their poeticising of the post-industrial terrain and landscape as a space for reflection, as seen in the films of Barnard and Arnold. For him, Hogg's films do not use space with a prescriptive working-class emphasis, or what he refers to as a 'revelatory' (Forrest 2014) approach to realism engaging in socio-political debate. Instead, her films, in particular, shift emphasis from realism as a socio-political tool to 'realism as an aesthetic practice' and as a tool for 'social reportage' (Forrest 2014). Hogg's films, according to Forrest, have more in common with 1960s social realism because they 'adopt narrationally loose and ambiguous formal and aesthetic strategies to utilise space, place and landscape as signifiers of contemporary isolation; more in common with the art-cinema influenced British New Wave than with the paradigmatic (didactic) social realist characteristics of Ken Loach' (2014). This, for Forrest, leads to a great understanding of realisms within an international context and Hogg's films can be situated 'within a British realist tradition and as examples of a new moment in British cinema, in which a stylistic concern with everyday life transcends the need for an *explicit* focus on the "social" in realism' (2014, original italics). Indeed, it is the combination of the autobiographical and personal elements of Hogg's work that help to create the realism. Both *Archipelago* and *Unrelated* are films centred on family problems in holiday venues, so, as Forrest notes, hardly fit the Loach pattern of social realism, yet both use non-professional actors (in part), understated dialogue and lack non-diegetic sound, which are all aligned with the genre's more conventional aspects. In addition, sumptuous sunsets, seascapes and cloud-filled skies are liberally interspersed in *Archipelago*, placing emphasis on the poetic potential of the imagery, and these scenes are often elucidated by the resident artist, Christopher (Christopher Baker), who we encountered at the outset of the film, and who has a sensitivity to the land, explaining the colours, the shapes and the contours of the landscape and sea to Patricia.

Despite later receiving much acclaim and recognition,[29] with a recommendation for Best Film at the LFF 2010, *Archipelago* had no support whatsoever from the UKFC;[30] instead it was funded by Wild Horses Films, a small production company run by NFTS graduate, Gayle Griffiths. Similar to *Unrelated*, *Archipelago* was also screened in 2010 at the LFF.

Hogg's later film, *Exhibition* (2013) was also produced by Wild Horses Films, but this time was sponsored by the BFI Film Fund and the BBC. The film's present-day focus is on two artists, a married couple who enjoy a bourgeois lifestyle in London, and is yet another example of outsiders, and people unable to communicate their emotions. The action takes place predominantly in the modernist urban dwelling of professional artists, D (Viv Albertine) and H (Liam Gillick), and Hogg again uses space to reveal personality, permeating the house with a sense of oppression and threat. Once more, Albertine[31] and Gillick are non-actors, a factor which Hogg comments on in interview:

> I wanted to find two strong personalities who could embody the rational versus instinctive dynamic I had conceived. I had planned for my couple to live in the house and get to know each other before filming, but I found Viv and Liam at the last possible moment. They had to get to know each other as the film was being shot. It added a tension and a reality to the film. It's risky but very exciting. (in Sumpter 2014)

In line with many of her contemporary female directors, Hogg scripted the film, but the actors did not learn dialogue beforehand; they were provided with an indication of what they might say as they went along and asked to interpret the narrative themselves. Filming took place over a period of six weeks, and *Exhibition* premiered at the Locarno Film Festival.

Amma Asante

Similar to a number of other women directors discussed here, Amma Asante operates in a poetic realist mode to mobilise spectator emotion through representation of space. Asante sees women in the industry as side-lined, and in particular black women who, she argues, experience too many difficulties in the directing world: as she affirms, 'As a teenage actress[32] ... everybody bar one who directed me was white, male and in their forties' (in Clark 2014b: 31). Born of Ghanaian parents, Asante trained at stage school and went on to become a child actor appearing in *Grange Hill* and *Desmonds*. Her directorial debut,[33] *A Way of Life*, is described as '[o]ne of the most warmly received UK titles in the London Film Festival in the autumn [and] a harrowing drama in social realist mode' (Macnab 2005b: 10), and is set in a Welsh mining village. The narrative centres upon the female concerns of a single-parent mother, Leigh-Anne Williams (Stephanie James), who is also the central protagonist of the film. Leigh-Anne, the spectator learns, is the product of a broken home; her mother committed suicide, her father set up home with her aunt, and her brother, Gavin (Nathan Jones), was taken into care. Seventeen-year-old Leigh-Anne struggles to make ends meet and experiences numerous obstacles in her daily life. Her daughter, Rebecca (Eli Williams, Darcy Williams) has eczema and breathing problems, not aided by the poor state of their living conditions; unable to afford electricity, the girl is forced to use candles and, as a result, the baby is badly burned in an accident. The Turkish neighbour, Hassan Osman (Oliver Haden), is the object of racist attacks by Leigh-Anne, her brother, and their two friends, Stephen (Dean Wong) and Robbie (Gary Sheppeard), and ultimately believing that Osman has reported Leigh-Anne to social services for child neglect, the gang beat him to death. While the content is violent, focusing on racism, physical abuse and underage sex, Asante, in line with a number of her contemporaries, intersperses these savage images with aesthetic pictorialism.

The film opens with Osman's beating, an event which is seen from the perspective of a small boy who is playing football nearby, and the reasons behind this vicious attack unfold as the film progresses. Immediately following this scene, the camera edits to a sequence of dramatic images consisting of a spectacular sunrise over the Welsh hills. Lurid colours fill the frame as the credits roll, and the mining village of Brynteg, near Cardiff, where the film is set, appears nestled in the valley. At one point, a series of industrial cranes are visible on the skyline but, rather than create a sense of menace, shown in silhouette they initiate a dramatic and pleasing affect. A similar juxtaposition occurs when Gavin begins an association with Osman's daughter, Julie (Sara Gregory). He meets her from school and the two leave together, so commencing a romantic relationship. Asante intercuts this liaison with colourful scenes of the industrial landscape: the setting sun again silhouettes the tall industrial chimneys and giant cranes of the locality, and a further dissolve introduces a panning shot surveying the estuary, now bathed in a golden light with the sun centre frame, and the sky now a vivid orange. These shots are accompanied by a soft melodic music to enhance the mood, before the narrative returns to the grim reality of Leigh-Anne's existence.

In the final sequences, a number of serious issues are addressed. Leigh-Anne's child is removed from her home, presumably to be taken into care or to live with her paternal grandmother. Underage and pregnant, Julie confesses her plight to the police, therefore it is unavoidable that Gavin will be in trouble. Finally, it is inevitable that the boys will be arrested for the murder of their neighbour. Throughout, while addressing socio-political concerns such as racism, underage sex, prostitution, single parenthood and abuse, Asante too includes aesthetically audacious images in line with a poetic and art cinema style.

A Way of Life was nominated for a BAFTA, specifically for the Carl Foreman Award—a prize presented to first-time screenwriters, producers and directors as an acknowledgement of exciting new talent.[34] As Asante herself confirms, '[o]ne of the reasons I wanted to make *A Way of Life* was to break some boundaries in terms of what black women like myself are expected to put out there' (in Macnab 2005b: 10).[35] Asante is the daughter of West African immigrants who came to the UK 40 years ago, and she speaks of wanting to address the issues of, and connection between racism and poverty. The film generated positive interest at the Toronto Film Festival, San Sebastian and London, and the director received a £15,000 UK Film Talent Award sponsored by Alfred Dunhill in association with the UKFC.[36]

Asante's directing career continues to flourish and, in 2013, she directed *Belle*, another film dealing with problems of racism in a historical context and with a strong central female protagonist, though entirely different from *A Way of Life*. Set in the late eighteenth century, it is a fictionalised account of Dido Elizabeth Belle (Gugu Mbatha-Raw), the mixed-race daughter of British naval officer, Sir John Lindsay (Matthew Goode). Inspired by a 1779 painting of Dido Belle seated alongside her white cousin, Lady Elizabeth Murray, the film follows the story of Dido brought up in her great uncle's home as part of his family.

The film commences when Lindsay returns home from his journey with the child, and entrusts her care to his uncle, Lord Mansfield and his wife (Tom Wilkinson and Emily Watson). Asante successfully creates Dido as a true heroine and a strong female character; a woman of independent means (she inherits her father's estate), she defies her aunt and uncle's attempts at discouraging her from seeking a suitor, and becomes an activist in the fight against slavery. As Asante acknowledges, 'I didn't want to present a weak woman of colour on screen ... As women we are strong, and we all have our different challenges depending on our history and background and where we come from. Black women sometimes have to have different strengths' (in Clark 2014b: 32; see Fig. 4.3).

The director not only deals with feminism, but also with issues of race and class. Indeed, Asante uses *Belle* to deal with diversity issues through a historical optic. For example, despite her inheritance, Dido must eat separately from her family and is denied a 'coming out' debutante's treatment, unlike her cousin Elizabeth (Sarah Gadon) who, as a white woman, experiences all these privileges. In one sequence, her ostracisation is explicitly stated. She is informed by her spinster carer, Aunt Mary (Penelope Wilton), that they have visitors for dinner. They are the Ashford family, including Lady Ashford (Miranda Richardson) and her two sons, James (Tom Felton) and Oliver (James Norton). Excitedly, she and her cousin discuss their evening attire and how they will have their hair done, only

Fig. 4.3 Amma Asante on set, *Belle*, 2013

to be later informed that Dido will not dine with them. Shown in close-up, she appears distressed but later is forthright enough to question her uncle's decision on why she is considered too low to eat with the guests, to which he cannot or is unwilling to respond. Eventually, she is invited to join the group after dinner; she is asked to play the piano and her accomplishments are outstanding, a point remarked upon by the Ashford family. Asante uses the Zong case, a true story of a slave trader's ship whose captain had the slaves thrown overboard as a result of an insurance scam, as central focus to the narrative—Asante addressing race through past societal misdemeanours. If *Belle* is a costume drama, then it differs in many ways—specifically because, as Mayer points out, 'costume dramas remain prestige film and television productions, and they tend to favour all-white casts' (2016: 98). *Belle* premiered at the Toronto Film Festival, was supported by the BFI Film Fund and distributed by 20th Century Fox International, with Asante only the second black British woman to have directed a feature for a UK cinema release.[37]

Summary

The examples discussed in this chapter are distinctive for a number of reasons. They all have affiliations with the British tradition of social realism, sharing its codes and conventions. However, they also comply with Leggott's arguments, demonstrating that a large number of female-directed films deal with socio-political issues and, more often than not, present them in idiosyncratic ways and through a sumptuous visual style in order to emphasise an argument. These films raise serious concerns relating to troubled childhoods and frequently either reinforce or counteract this through their lyrical representation of the landscape. Often 'desperate women' are central to the narratives and they are presented as outsiders. Furthermore, even when filmmakers such as Asante and Arnold create costume dramas, they seem to transform them into realist films, adopting those conventions associated with the style. *Wuthering Heights*, in particular, offers the spectator poetic images of the landscape imbued with ulterior meaning as evocative of a sense of loss experienced by the characters. In *A Way of Life* Asante's style tallies with Barnard's imagery in *The Selfish Giant* to create an aesthetic affect which is image rather than dialogue led, yet conveys information about the characters and their impossible situations. Samantha Morton's *The Unloved* is perhaps the most personal story of the chapter, and this is evident in the dreamlike sequences she mobilises through her individual account. Apart from Hogg's early work, most of the films discussed here, unlike their documentary counterparts, received lottery funding. Indeed, Arnold has been particularly successful in gaining sponsorship in her career, as has Lynne Ramsay, perhaps suggesting that public funding bodies are predisposed to stories that address the particular issues that these filmmakers raise.[38]

Notes

1. This is not to suggest that social realism exists as a consistent, unified genre. It is more a loose term used to discuss a specific visual style and common themes, often of a socio-political nature. However, it is not the aim of this chapter to offer debate on this. For further reading see Hallam and Marshment (2000) and Lay (2002).
2. See Hockenhull (2016b) for an extended analysis.
3. See Townsend (2008). Statistically, in 2008/9, 22% of children were living in poverty in the UK, and in 2007 the UK had the fifth highest child poverty rate in the EU, with the largest proportion of poor children living in workless families (Bradshaw 2011c).
4. Exceptions to this include Gurinder Chadha whose comedies, such as *Bhaji on the Beach* (1993), contain a social message, dealing with race and immigration in a humorous way. Ostensibly, though, costume dramas dominated British female output during the last ten years of the twentieth century. Examples include: *Orlando* (Potter 1992), Jane Campion's Henry James adaptation, *Portrait of a Lady* (1996), *The Governess* (Goldbacher 1997), *Amy Foster* (Kidron 1997), and *Onegin* (Fiennes 1998).
5. Although this is referred to by Andrew Higson in relation to 1960s New Wave cinema, and discussed in Lay (2002).
6. Prior to this she completed a number of shorts including *Milk* (1998) and *Dog* (2001).
7. Ryan is now Arnold's cinematographer for all her films.
8. The Advance Party production company is aligned with Dogme rules, and more notably the work of Lars von Trier.
9. The other key actor in the film is Martin Compston, who played Liam in Ken Loach's *Sweet Sixteen* (2002). Compston comments on Arnold's experimental style (Verve Pictures *Red Road*: 22), with 'British independent cinema [having] so few truly brave directors' (Verve Pictures *Red Road*: 24).

10. The desperate girls' films such as *Red Road* and *The Unloved* (2009) were made with the participation of television. BBC Films sponsored *Red Road* and Channel 4 sponsored *The Unloved.*
11. John Orr claims that *Red Road* is Neo-Bazinian cinema, as defined by Julia Kristeva. For him the traductive realism suspends identity and, as Stewart argues, in this film Jackie exists in a void, is stranded in a liminal space, and is frequently perceived as 'an image of joyless abjection' (2012: 551). See Stewart (2012).
12. As Nick Roddick points out:

> Just because they are set in tower blocks doesn't make them socially realist ... There is in both films a sense of an individual floating free of (or alienated from, if you prefer) the society in which she nominally lives that harks back ... to the literary tradition that gave us *The Outsider* and *The Catcher in the Rye* – books which, like Arnold's films, are dominated entirely by a single point of view. (2009: 20)

13. *Fish Tank* was shot originally on 4:3 ratio film stock, but because cinemas no longer project in this format it went through a digital process to reduce its size, at the same time giving a more polished effect to the finished product.
14. This is a term used by John Ruskin. Writing in *Modern Painters*, Ruskin argues that many poets attribute human emotions to natural objects, and this could be stretched to include painting and, by extension, film. As art historian Robert Rosenblum points out,

> 'Ruskin was referring in literary examples, to the curious attribution of human feelings to non-human subjects, especially landscape elements; but he might well have been characterizing the new attitude of so many Romantic, and especially Northern Romantic, artists to nature in general and to trees in particular' (1994: 36).

15. In line with the realist school of filmmaking, Arnold's choice of cast is significant in her films, and she uses known and unknown actors. For *Fish Tank*, Katie Jarvis was picked out of a crowd at Tilbury station and James Howson accompanied a friend for the audition, and makes his debut in *Wuthering Heights.*
16. An extended version of this analysis is published in Hockenhull (2016).
17. As Ryan states, 'Andrea forbids tripods on the set. She just loves handheld. She doesn't do it any other way' (in Thomson 2012: 46).

18. Dunbar also wrote a play entitled *Rita, Sue and Bob Too* which was made into a film by Alan Clarke in 1986.
19. For example, Richard Porton (2011) cites three films as examples of innovative documentary film making, (coincidentally, three out of the four he mentions have female directors: Clio Barnard, Marie Losier and Gillian Wearing). He notes that their three films, *Self Made* (2010), *The Arbor* and *The Ballad of Genesis and Lady Jane* (2011), all blur the boundaries between documentary and fiction, which he terms 'modernist realism'. For Porton, these films are imbued with a documentary immediacy with cast members addressing the camera/spectator in a self-revelatory vein, particularly in Wearing's film.
20. This is a factor noted by a number of commentators, including Kate Muir who also acknowledges the film as an 'elegiac and exquisitely photographed package. In *The Selfish Giant*, the moors beyond Bradford's Buttershaw Estate are populated by wild horses and dark, satanic pylons looming in the dusk' (2013b: 32).
21. Both *The Arbor* and *The Selfish Giant* were produced by Tracy O'Riordan.
22. At the time of writing, Barnard is working on her latest film, an adaptation of Rose Tremain's novel, *Trespass.* Funded by the Wellcome Trust and the BFI Screenwriting Fellowship in association with Film4, the narrative focuses on trauma and sexual abuse.
23. This film is discussed in relation to its use of landscape in some depth in my earlier book entitled *Aesthetics and Neo-Romanticism in Film: Landscapes in Contemporary British Cinema.* See Hockenhull (2013b).
24. This film is discussed in Hockenhull (2012).
25. While Ramsay's earlier work focuses on childhood and youth in crisis, her later *We Need to Talk About Kevin* (2011), while using a child protagonist, operates more within the mainstream. However, its themes tie in with this chapter and it therefore makes sense to discuss it in more depth here, with Ramsay's other films.
26. The winner was Michel Hazanavicius for *The Artist.*
27. Morton acknowledges mixing realism and poeticism. The release of her film coincided with a Select Committee report into Britain's care and foster homes which detailed appalling failures in the system, including sexual abuse.

28. To date this remains Morton's only film release.
29. One reviewer, Jonathan Romney, described it thus:

> what we see in Archipelago is an auteur consistency that's familiar in French directors, but rare among Brits, Mike Leigh being an obvious exception. Even so, Hogg brings a new fine-tuning to Archipelago, not least in the visual control: in Ed Rutherford's photography of moody, static, claustrophobic interiors and in the windblown, weirdly tropical Tresco landscapes. In its almost militantly undemonstrative way, Archipelago is a major achievement – a very adult film about people who can't quite grow up. (2011)

30. Although it is unclear whether Hogg applied for a grant, Catherine Shoard (2011) notes: 'not that the UK Film Council was especially forthcoming when it came to Archipelago, whose £500,000 budget was partly stumped up by an aesthetically sympathetic Japanese businessman'.
31. Albertine is a singer and songwriter and former member of the punk band, The Slits.
32. Asante had a regular role in BBC's *Grange Hill* in the 1980s.
33. Prior to this, Asante was mentored by Channel 4 and went on to write and produce a TV show entitled *Brothers and Sisters* in 1998.
34. In 2003, Emily Young won the award with *Kiss of Life*. In 2004 other possible contenders included Shona Auerbach's debut film, *Dear Frankie*, and Juliet McKoen's *Frozen*. In 2004, Tracey Emin also made her debut film, *Top Spot*. Shot on DV and Super-8, the hour long film was aimed at teenagers, but the BBFC rated it 18 and Emin and her UK distributors, Tartan, refused to show it in UK theatres.
35. As Leggott notes, 'Written and directed by a black Londoner, the film offered some hope for a "colour-neutral" film culture, as well as a looser definition of black British cinema' (2008: 109).
36. Asante initially refused UKFC funding because she wanted to retain authorial control. Eventually, she agreed to accept backing to attend Film School for one month.
37. Ngozi Onwurah directed *Welcome II the Terrordome* in 1995.

38. Other filmmakers to consider include Shona Auerbach, who received financial support for her social issue-based drama entitled *Dear Frankie* (2003) in the early years of the UKFC. The film succeeded in obtaining a distribution deal with Miramax in advance of its screening in Un Certain Regard (original and different works which require international recognition) at Cannes. The film toured the festival circuits including Tribeca, Cannes, Edinburgh and Toronto, and was considered for the Carl Foreman Award at the BAFTAs.

CHAPTER 5

Popular Cinema from a Female Perspective

> [There is a] correlation between the underrepresentation of women in the top 200 films and the fact they [the films] are in the action, thriller and fantasy genres. There's significant gender stereotyping and misconceptions about who's allowed to direct in which genre. Women just don't get access to those areas of film. (Richards 2013).

Writing in *The Telegraph*, Beryl Richards's comments suggest that the lack of women directors applies to specific genres and, by default, this refers to mainstream cinema. Indeed, while British cinema is generally renowned for its low-budget films, and women are prolific in this area, they do make popular and mainstream films, although not necessarily, as Richards notes, action, thriller or fantasy films. Phyllida Lloyd, the British film director responsible for the blockbuster *Mamma Mia!* and the bio-pic *The Iron Lady*, observes that most female directors operate on low budgets and a few work more independently rather than within prescribed parameters. As she comments:

> [not many women are] given the reins of a big studio movie. I don't think it's necessarily lack of faith in the vision of a woman, it's just not trusting them with a big pot of cash … On the other hand, it could be – and I feel this myself – that women are drawn to the kind of stories that don't fit into an automatic prepackaged genre. (in McClintock 2011: 50)

S. Hockenhull, *British Women Film Directors in the New Millennium*, DOI 10.1057/978-1-137-48992-0_5

This chapter examines those women directors who make films which are either mainstream in terms of the industry, or films which offer a popular mode of narration. At the outset it is probably worth aiming for some classification of what constitutes mainstream cinema. Paul McDonald goes some way towards a definition suggesting that it is a nebulous term:

> often becoming simply a stand-in for equally ill defined labels such as 'Hollywood' or 'popular'. From the perspective of film-making, attempts to define the mainstream may look towards a certain category or categories of film text. From an exhibition perspective, it is equally and possibly more appropriate to see the mainstream as a product of programming practice. (2010b: 272)

Within this industrial context, mainstream cinema generally consists of established and recognisable stars, the application of a well-known genre, and cinematic spectacle with considerable commercial potential. Beyond the mainstream are blockbusters, which have a number of key characteristics; they rely on the soundtrack as a selling device and also as a merchandisable product; they are well advertised in advance using teaser trailers, television, social media and radio advertising, and have therefore gathered momentum by the time of their release. Blockbusters and some mainstream films rely on product placement, merchandise and tie-ins to supplement box office receipts. Often they have relatively simple and easily relatable storylines which can be summarised in a single sentence, are internationally transferrable and they ensure as wide an audience as possible. There is generally some brand awareness for blockbusters, for example, in the case of *Mamma Mia!* the music of Abba was used extensively for cross-promotional deals and merchandise, and the Bridget Jones films drew on audience familiarity with the Helen Fielding books. Both examples are discussed here and, in addition, while some of the films examined in this chapter might not fit the blockbuster model, for the most part they have been selected because they offer a conventional mode of narration and correspond to a specific genre.

In truth, few women directors are responsible for high-grossing films, but many make popular and accessible cinema. This chapter is divided into sections because the films discussed are diverse, yet fall loosely into groupings. The first part concentrates on high-budget productions which have been financially successful on an international scale, although this—unfortunately—is not a very large component of British cinema, or indeed the output of women directors either. These are known as the 'new women's blockbuster' (York 2010: 4). Referring mainly to Hollywood cinema, Ashley Elaine York has noted the emergence of this new phenomenon post millennium. She argues that films for women prior to this period have supplied mainly a specialist and domestic market whereas the new women's blockbusters have become 'global powerhouses' (2010: 4). Not only do these films offer a change in subject matter, they also rely on ancillary marketing and international box office. York maintains that these are high-concept productions and that:

> This new-found women's genre represented by such films as *The Devil Wears Prada* (2006), *Sex and the City* (2008), and *Mamma Mia!* (2008) are no longer promoted as standalone texts solely marketed to women consumers. Rather, they are advertised in a manner similar to *Jaws* (1975), *Independence Day* (1996), and *Titanic* (1997) and often compete with and eclipse male-driven, big budget vehicles in their total earnings. (York 2010: 4)

The notion of women's blockbusters relies on genre and plot devices that have a broad influence and, in a related way, to those films with a strong male lead. Women's blockbuster franchises offer their protagonists:

> a millennial theme of validation, which was missing in many films of yesteryear. No longer relegated to messages of self-sacrifice or affliction, or held hostage to love (and a male star) or action adventures that altogether deprive them of romantic possibilities, heroines of women's blockbusters live out their fantasies in all respects and come out on top in each and every case. (York 2010: 11)

Furthermore, as Thomas Austin states, these provide a 'dispersible package ... a package designed to achieve commercial, cultural and social reach ... [through] its multiple address to a coalition of audience fractions' (2002: 20). In terms of British cinema, filmmakers such as Lloyd and Kidron have gained substantial sponsorship, enabling them to release films that have had international success, and which have multiple spectator appeal. The first section of this chapter analyses the work of Lloyd and Kidron within this remit.

Another style of filmmaking prevalent with women directors is the bio-pic, and this is the focus of the second section. Not really a genre in its own right,[1] nonetheless, the inspiration for bio-pic narratives is based on real people although often a fictional tale is woven around the facts. The final section centres on humour and comedy, sometimes combined with other issues such as race, class or gender, although another feature of the films mentioned here is the centrality of a female protagonist or a preoccupation and familiarity with the female experience.

The New Women's Blockbuster

While women directors have sought ways of introducing new perspectives to female representations, at times resulting in the disruption of stylistic and narrative conventions, romance has long been a central theme of popular cinema, sometimes with a comedy edge. Sharon Maguire's adaptation of the Helen Fielding novel, *Bridget Jones's Diary* (1996) is a romantic comedy and conforms to York's description of the new women's blockbuster. The film hit number one in both the UK and US, taking $280 million worldwide following its theatrical release—an unsurprising fact given that it was distributed by the large, successful companies, Universal, StudioCanal and Miramax. Sharon Maguire, the film's director, is a friend of the novel's author, and Colin Firth was chosen as Mark Darcy to bring in a star persona, along with Hugh Grant as Daniel Cleaver. Similarly, the charismatic US star, Renée Zellwegger, played Bridget and, for continuity, these stars were used again in the sequel.

Not only do the Bridget films fit into the mainstream category, they also tie in with Angela McRobbie's (2007) notion of post-feminism. McRobbie argues that there is a contemporary focus in popular culture on female characters who are post-feminists. This concept maintains that equality has been achieved and that feminism is no longer a necessary goal for the protagonists. For McRobbie, the post-feminist condition permits the characters to lead independent lives without abiding by the rules of feminism or acknowledging its founding principles. She argues that many films, such as *Bridget Jones's Diary*, feature a strong female who is the product of a good education, relocating to the city to live a 'disembedded' (2007: 36) life, yet these women are gentle repudiations of the movement. For her, the narratives of these films involve fresh female concerns and anxieties which do not comply with traditional notions of feminism. As she proposes, 'there is the fear of loneliness for example, the stigma of remaining single, and the risks and uncertainties of not finding the right partner to be a father to children as well as a husband' (2007: 36). In both *Bridget Jones's Diary* and its sequel, *Bridget Jones: The Edge of Reason*, the spectator is constantly privy to Bridget's thoughts through her diary, many of which express such disquiet and angst. Throughout the film she is witnessed running through various calorie calculations and relationships, and frequent mention is made from the outset of her single status, her ticking biological clock and the choice of career over marriage—all anxieties which do not conform to established feminist principles.

The narrative of *Bridget Jones's Diary* follows a simple structure, and is a comedy based on misconceptions and misunderstandings. Bridget is in love with her boss, Daniel Cleaver, but he is not a serious contender for her affections. In the meantime, she meets Mark Darcy, the son of an old friend of the family, and begins a relationship with him, but not before it is revealed that he and Cleaver are arch-enemies. The film follows a traditional romantic plot of equilibrium and disequilibrium before order is restored at the end. Initially, Bridget is charmed by Cleaver, and she accepts his flirtatious behaviour and innuendo while fantasising about 'very traditional forms of happiness and fulfilment' (McRobbie 2007: 37). This is illustrated when at one point, and told in flashback, she imagines her wedding to Cleaver. The flashback begins with a cut from a close-up of her wistful face to reveal the couple, centre frame, dressed in traditional wedding attire, surrounded by confetti and matrimonial paraphernalia. McRobbie believes that this and other films are:

> hardly rabid antifeminist tracts ... these popular texts normalize postfeminist gender anxieties so as to re-regulate young women by means of the language of personal choice. But even 'well-regulated liberty' can backfire ... and this gives rise to demarcated pathologies ... that carefully define the parameters of what constitute liveable lives for young women without the occasion of reinvented feminism. (2007: 38)

For McRobbie, feminism has been cast into the shadows by certain films (and books) such as this, a condition which represents a shift in direction whereby the progress that the movement has made has all but disappeared or been transformed.

Bridget Jones: The Edge of Reason is loosely modelled on Jane Austen's *Persuasion* (1816) and made by Working Title, a production company renowned for its romantic comedies (including *Notting Hill* [Michell 1999], *Bridget Jones's Diary* [Maguire 2001], *Four Weddings and a Funeral* [Newell 1994], *About a Boy* [Weitz, Weitz 2002] and *Love Actually* [Curtis 2003]). The production of this film and its predecessor tie in with the notion of blockbusters because they exemplify '"the female event film," in which … its release … independent of its qualities as cinema, garners significant media attention because it is an adaptation of an already popular novel, part of a series, based on a historically successful television series, the vehicle for a charismatic star, the re-enactment of a controversial political event, etc.' (Radner 2011: 120).

In terms of narrative, Bridget's character in both films is unambitious, and her main aims in life are to be slim and to marry. She is what Radner describes as a 'stumbler … [a] comic figure whose mishaps elicit the reader's and viewer's sympathy rather than admiration' (2011: 121). In both films, she is to be pitied because of her incompetence and inability to deal with life, but eventually, in each case, she is rescued in fairytale mode by the dependable, desirable, wealthy and successful Mark Darcy.

Produced by Universal Pictures, StudioCanal and Miramax, *Bridget Jones: The Edge of Reason* is a high-budget production, costing an estimated $40 million to make. Kidron spoke of her intention with the sequel 'not to disappoint people's love of the first *Bridget* movie. It had been very much taken to heart, so there was an emotional responsibility to deliver another good experience for the audience' (in Hunter 2005: 17), and, in blockbuster mode, Kidron's film opened in the USA and UK on over a thousand screens on the same day. Despite poor reviews from the critics (Kermode 2004: 45; Quinn 2004: 6; Winter 2004: 41), in particular with reference to Kidron's direction, the film achieved box office success, eventually covering its budget on cinema screenings alone before DVD sales, tie-ins and additional merchandise revenue. *Bridget Jones: The Edge of Reason* was partly filmed in Thailand, and the Thai government began to uphold the country as a film-friendly location, using the Bangkok Film Festival as a self-promotion venue, and with the further aim of encouraging tourism. The film was awarded the Nielsen EDI International Gold Reel Award for taking more than $100 million in non-US box office revenue during the year following its release.

In a similar mode to Kidron, prominent film director Phyllida Lloyd also achieved phenomenal success with her 'women's blockbuster', *Mamma Mia!*. Lloyd, who studied drama and English at Birmingham University, began her career in theatre, training originally as a theatre director and working at the Bristol Old Vic, the Royal Exchange, Manchester and the National Theatre. In 1999 she directed the stage musical *Mamma Mia!* in the West End, based at London's Prince Edward Theatre, and this production became an international phenomenon both in Britain and on Broadway, earning an estimated $2 billion. Even so, Lloyd is probably best known for her screen debut adaptation of the Abba musical of the same name and, in order to make the play into a film, she surrounded herself with an all-female crew comprised of production designer Maria Djurkovic, editor Lesley Walker and cinematographer Haris Zambarloukos.[2] The same female team responsible for the stage show were also retained, including producer Judy Craymer, who claimed that the songs were the true protagonists of the film (in Delgado 2008: 68), and writer Catherine Johnson. Lloyd was so familiar with the musical and had such in-depth knowledge of its nuances that she was able to use it to effect and, as Zambarloukos points out, 'Phyllida's unique vision of the project comes from the fact that she was there at the inception and has lived with the play for nine years. She knew every line, every note and every nuance of emotion, and was determined to achieve something magical' (in Anon. 2008b: 24). Filmed in Greece and at Pinewood Studios, Lloyd retained the same camera crew in both locations because of the specificity of equipment (heavy grip equipment and cranes), rather than employing Greek staff. She also decided to use 2.40:1 widescreen aspect ratio because of the horizontality of the dance sequences, and much careful preparation went into the production, which lasted 20 weeks longer than anticipated.

The story for *Mamma Mia!*, along with other films which fit into the women's blockbusters category, was high concept with a simple plotline. Competing in the same year with films such as *The Dark Knight* (Nolan 2008) and *The X-Files 2* (Carter 2008), and, unlike films that contained troubled and altruistic women who had the possibility of a better life, *Mamma Mia!* 'offers a theme not of affliction or of sadness or even primarily of romance, but rather of affirmation that viewers too can "have it all"' (York 2010: 8). The women in this film are not relegated to traditional representations such as wife and mother, and the suggestion here is that gender difference is in flux. *Mamma Mia!*'s narrative follows Donna Sheridan (Meryl Streep), a free-living and emancipated ex-hippie who is popular and carefree, and has refused marriage to raise her daughter, Sophie (Amanda Seyfried) alone on a Greek island. Donna is not answerable to men or a victim of male abuse; rather, men are accountable to her, a point exemplified when her three ex-boyfriends turn up to attend Sophie's wedding, and to claim paternity. In this and other similar films, the modern female is not marginalised but represented in a way that is relevant to contemporary women's lives, a factor meant to mobilise spectator identification. True to form, ultimately Sophie makes the same choices as her mother, thus demonstrating a similar independence of spirit by refusing to marry at the end of the film, although she remains with her partner. Radner argues that the film is about conventional heterosexual relationships and female friendship, both between Donna and her friends and Donna and her daughter. For her:

> the film presents independent, energetic and resourceful heroines, in this case two – one who has raised a daughter on her own, and manages to triumph against all odds to achieve her happy ending, and another capable of engineering a suitable wedding for both herself and her mother, and in so doing provides herself with a husband and a father. (Radner 2011: 129)

Mamma Mia! concerns human emotions and relationships, and the script was constructed around the music, with sophisticated aesthetics, a rapid editing pace and sumptuous imagery—all indicating an idyllic and harmonious way of life. In line with the blockbuster, films such as this have taken a leaf out of *Titanic*'s (Cameron 1997) book, which garnered a strong female following by mixing spectacle, simple narrative structure, and high-concept global marketing, with 'image, narrative, and advertising … conceived, pitched, and marketed in one fell swoop: in a single-sentence catchphrase that easily translates among cultures and across borders' (York 2010: 8). As one poster's teaser statement suggested, 'Take a Trip Down the Aisle You'll Never Forget'. The women are represented as exotic and colourful and to be envied and 'The entire cast to that end lives in a laidback tropical oasis that, at once, promises freedom and extravagance to every sutured viewer' (York 2010: 13) (Fig. 5.1).

Because she was so familiar with the story, Lloyd was specific about the visuals of the film, adopting an idiosyncratic style and, as Zambarloukos states, Lloyd 'knew the story well and knew how to deal with actors … She wanted the camera to be a real participant, and we went for a quirky style; we really wanted it to be a rollercoaster of a visual experience' (in Hope-Jones 2008: 39–40). The planning process concerning location went on for six months, and crane shots were used throughout to capture the exotic setting. For the sequences that take place in Donna's café, for example, real location and built sets at Pinewood were juxtaposed, and in both cases, wide sweeping shots combined with hand-held camera were deployed to investigate the characters' emotions. Songs were not deemed just musical numbers, but had a narrative seam running through each of them. With the song 'Voulez-Vous', for example, a number of facts emerge about Sophie's relationships, and Lloyd uses crane shots to

Fig. 5.1 The new womens's blockbuster, *Mamma Mia!*, 2008

give a general impression of the scene followed by investigative cinematography to select emotional interludes and expressions. Although the words of the songs are often meaningful, they do not always enhance the narrative, and characters break off from conversations to engage in song and dance routines. Indeed, as with the classic musical, this film integrates narrative and spectacle and 'music and song [act] as a formal thematic and ideological "bridge" which helps reconcile the dichotomies' (Mundy 1999: 57).

The women's blockbuster often crosses genres to create appeal and *Mamma Mia!*'s style is evocative of early Hollywood musicals which incorporate song and dance routines into the structure of the film, while women's lives are explored 'in the form of female bonding, mischief, and mayhem as reminiscent of the screwball comedies of the 1930s and 1940s' (York 2010: 12). Another aspect of the women's blockbuster is that it provides attractive characters leading exciting and exotic lives. In this respect, Meryl Streep was named as one of the most popular American stars (York 2010: 10), and the Greek setting of the film adds the key ingredients of escapism, luxury and possibility.

If, as York claims, films such as *Mamma Mia!* offer a departure from chick flicks, by representing 'lifestyles that foreign and domestic audiences both appreciate and aspire to' (2010: 4) then this and other similar films have broad appeal in terms of age, gender, and international markets. Backed by Universal, the film presented a built-in awareness of the stage musical, and its stated aim was 'to crack £20 million here [UK], and thereby beat *Moulin Rouge* to become the UK's biggest ever musical box-office hit' (Gant 2008: 9), which it succeeded in doing within less than two weeks of its release.

Overall, *Mamma Mia!*, produced by Pathé and BBC films, was a phenomenal box office success, costing $15 million to make, and grossing $609 million worldwide, making its director the most successful female director in history until *Kung Fu Panda 2* (Yuh 2011). Further, in 2008 it was rated number six among the top 100 worldwide grossing films, along with 14 other women-led films, with its contemporary subject matter and plot lines offering a package equally suitable for image and advertising. The film, though a British production, was also produced by Tom Hanks among others,[3] and marketed towards a more mature population who were not necessarily regular cinema goers. This was a 'typically BBC audience, so you can't advertise to them … and there's a real need for publicity to reach them. This audience tends to react to films that are very relevant to them, or ones that become such a cultural event that they feel the need to participate' (Gant 2008: 9).

A significant part of the budget was spent on marketing the film after its release, particularly in terms of the participatory element which enabled audiences to sing along with the words, probably remembered from or associated with their youth. *Mamma Mia!* maximised subsidiary markets, and in this case the soundtrack was an exceptional added marketing bonus, with potential appeal on an international level. Released three weeks after the film's debut it became the number one selling iTunes album and the top internet album of the year and ultimately sold over 3 million copies. New Line publicised the soundtrack alongside the DVD release of the film, which further benefited the franchise. The film was promoted on the internet, and Biolage, the film's official beauty sponsor, ran an essay competition, the winner receiving a professional wedding day stylist to create a hairstyle of their dreams.

The film opened in the UK on 3 July 2008 and extended elsewhere in Europe before its North American release on 18 July 2008; although an international winner, *Mamma Mia!* was not a runaway hit at the US box office but has now become the biggest UK film ever in its home market and the highest grossing musical ever (Walsh 2011: 34). Indeed, day one sales of its DVD made it the fastest selling of all time in the UK, reaching 1.7

million units following its launch in November 2008, and beating *Titanic*. It was the top film in other markets too, from Iceland and Germany to South Africa and, as Universal Pictures International president, David Kosse, claims, 'In markets that were less musical-focused, we pushed it as a romantic comedy with music, and where they do like musicals, we pushed it as a musical with romantic comedy elements' (in Mitchell 2008: 7). The film's distributors offered a second experience with 'singalong' screenings launched in late August, thus rejuvenating it. *Mamma Mia!* was a US/UK co-production, and the overseas markets for such films are of prime importance. Furthermore, it did not glamorise its characters or take itself too seriously. As Maria Delgado points out:

> This is a film that isn't afraid to scratch beneath the veneer with which Hollywood too often adorns its products. Heels are shown to be treacherous to walk in, looks are preserved through lotions, potions and surgery, and bodies sing and dance in a range of idiosyncratic ways. There's a real pleasure in watching a narrative that can laugh at its own evident artifice and delight in sending itself up. (2008: 68)

Mamma Mia!'s success propelled its distributor, Universal, to the top of the charts in home entertainment taking 18.1% of the market share.

Danish-born Lone Scherfig also makes romantic films, and *One Day* fits the category of mainstream cinema although not in the same way as *Mamma Mia!* More recently Scherfig moved into making British films. To provide some background to her career, she began directing commercials and television dramas. She graduated from the Danish film school in 1984, and worked in Dogme[4] films, initially releasing *Italian for Beginners* in 2000. This film, which follows the life of a recently widowed young clergyman in Copenhagen, was a success, showing at the Toronto International Film Festival, and around the world. It gained distribution rights with Miramax for North America and Mexico taking over $20 million in global box office revenues within its first three months of release. The film attempts to show real people with serious problems, but in a light-hearted comedy mode, establishing Scherfig as a significant foreign-language director. In terms of her filmmaking, and in line with Dogme productions, Scherfig aims to 'get very close to the truth. It [Dogme] adds authenticity and intensity to a film by showing what is going on right here in this very moment' (in Bernbom 2001: 38).[5]

Scherfig moved to work in the UK, leading to her later film, *Wilbur Wants to Kill Himself* (2002), which is a dark romantic comedy, and a Danish, UK, Norwegian, French co-production supported by Scottish Screen and set in Glasgow. It was co-written by Scherfig with Anders Thomas Jensen, and the producers were Sisse Graum Olsen and Gillian Berrie from Scotland's Sigma Films, the latter making an application for UK lottery money through Scottish Screen. This was a positive move as Scottish Screen wanted to forge stronger links between the Nordic countries and Scotland, and subsequently committed over £400,000[6] to the film, with the Glasgow Film Office providing £40,000 to be used on production facilities in the region. The Danish Film Institute provided over £250,000 development money for the screenplay, although it saw its responsibility as mainly supporting Danish-language films so could not commit to the same level of funding as Scottish Screen. Scherfig also managed to secure £150,000 from the Nordic Film and TV Fund, £260,000 from the Nordisk Film Biografdistribution, and television sales to TV 2 Denmark and SVT Sverige, and a pre-sale to Les Films du Losange in France. Zentropa Entertainments also made a 30% equity investment in the production. In sum, the final budget was £2.5 million, with Scottish funders providing 30% of the money and Nordic funders the remaining 70%. As a result, *Wilbur Wants to Kill Himself* was shot on location in Glasgow and at Zentropa studios in Denmark, and Scherfig established a proven track record in securing funding. She was also successful in aiding with the marketing of the film. A promotion reel was sent to Cannes film festival, where Scherfig introduced the film, and subsequently Trust Film Sales, the marketing branch of Zentropa, secured a number of international pre-sales. During post-production, the film was test screened in both Glasgow and Copenhagen but throughout the process Scherfig retained control. First screened in Copenhagen, *Wilbur Wants to Kill Himself* opened on 40 screens on 8 November 2002, topping the box office takings in its first five weeks. Eventually it secured international theatrical distribution.

Scherfig moved on to direct the romantic drama, *One Day*, which is an adaptation of a David Nicholls's novel, in 2011. Described by film critic, Philip French, as a 'disappointing film … thin, superficial and sentimental' (2011: 26), *One Day* is a romantic conceit and ends in tragedy with the death of the central female love interest, Emma Morley (Anne Hathaway). Scherfig follows Nicholls's structure of focusing on a couple, Emma and Dexter (Jim Sturgess), on their agreed reunion one day per year subsequent to their initial meeting in the late 1980s at university. It is only in the latter part of the film, however, that they strike up a romance, marry and have a child. The film ends following Emma's death, and Dexter takes their daughter to Arthur's Seat in Edinburgh where he and Emma spent their first morning together.

One Day offers mainstream potential because it falls loosely into, what Robert Murphy (2001) might describe as, a 'City Life and Fairytales' category. As he suggests, romantic comedies in late 1990s British cinema 'show life in Britain as exciting, glamorous and full of romantic possibilities, and are constructed like fairytales' (Murphy 2001: 292). While referring mainly to films such as *Notting Hill* and *Four Weddings and a Funeral*, he argues that the criteria include that they centre on romance, 'mythologise their setting and social relationships, allow coincidence and magic to determine events and structure their narratives in such a way that the protagonist of the story undergoes a series of tests or ordeals before achieving his or her goal' (Murphy 2001: 293). The films, according to him, begin with a deficiency which must be resolved 'a curse which has to be removed … or a harmonious situation which is disrupted and has to be restored' (Murphy 2001: 293).

To align the film with Murphy's arguments, *One Day* begins in the present but quickly reverts to the past and the graduation of the young Emma and Dexter. They meet on Saint Swithin's Day in 1988, and, despite their relationship not initially burgeoning into romance, they strike up a friendship. The lack which must be remedied is that they remain as friends and do not consummate their love, and they pretend to prefer to continue as companions rather than lovers. Happiness is their magical quest, and the curse is that they are unable to state their true feelings. On a trip to France, Emma informs Dexter that she was once attracted to him, and they swim naked together and nearly fulfil her desire, but he destroys the moment by snubbing her. This is a recurring event throughout the film, whereby their relationship reaches equilibrium but is disrupted after each meeting.

Emma also conforms to, what Murphy defines as a 'fairytale archetype[s]' (2001: 294). She is the Cinderella who becomes a Princess, albeit Dexter cannot see that, and her sad life is only enhanced when Dexter (Prince Charming) is around. For his part, he is young and handsome and doesn't comprehend what he is missing until it is too late. Initially she is unglamorous and ungainly, seen wearing heavy boots and glasses, a ruse to make her appear plain and unfeminine. However, by the end of the film, in fairytale style, she has undergone a transformation. When Dexter meets her in France she is elegant, sports a chic haircut, and has a successful jazz musician boyfriend. It is now that Dexter realises his mistake. Emma leaves him to go to the bathroom and, seen from an overhead shot, he viciously stabs her boyfriend's photograph with his finger, this image shown parallel with Emma closeted in the bathroom as she agonises over her relationships. When the realisation hits Dexter that he is in love with Emma, disequilibrium occurs yet again. However, the situation is quickly resolved when Emma too recognises that Dexter is the right match for her and the two embrace on the banks of the River Seine in Paris. At this point, the camera is poised at a high angle to frame the romantic *mise-en-scène* demonstrating that their situation is consolidated.

Part of the film's appeal occurs through the use of archetypal figures, and Dexter falls into Murphy's notion of 'Sleeping Princes and Frogs Waiting to be Kissed' (2001: 295). As Murphy points out, 'Although they are handsome and attractive to women, the male protagonists have none of the...characteristics of conventional heroes' (2001: 295). Indeed, Dexter, apart from being good looking, is initially an unlikeable character. He is a womaniser, takes drugs, has little time for his dying mother and, as a TV personality, is described in the film as 'the most annoying man on television'. Even his mother abhors his behaviour, informing Emma at one point that she loves her son but doesn't like him very much. Dexter must be rediscovered as a decent person to redeem himself, and this he does only when he marries Emma.

'Villains and adversaries are much less formidable in these films than in traditional fairytales' (Murphy 2001: 295), even if the rivals in this film tend to be underplayed. Callum (Tom Mison), Dexter's university friend has an affair with Dexter's first wife, Sylvie (Romola Garai), but this is subtly expressed, and no exchange is witnessed between the two opponents, Scherfig dealing with the situation in a few short scenes. Furthermore, and again in true fairytale pattern, London remains the 'city of delights'. At one point the couple both attend a mutual friend's wedding and Dexter and Emma move outside of the venue to chat in private and sit intimately outside on a rooftop, the London Eye visible and illuminated in pinkish hues in the background: in all, a fairly obvious romantic backdrop. As Murphy suggests, the fairytale films use London as a setting, 'but not one which found favour with critics ... these films deliberately recreate London as an enchanted setting where unlikely romances can blossom' (2001: 296). This also occurs later when Dexter has set up his own café business, and he appears at home in a rustic London bistro, the café represented as organic, cosy and family oriented.

When Dexter and Emma later marry, the spectator is led to believe that they will live happily ever after but, again, a state of imbalance occurs when Emma is knocked off her bicycle and dies. The situation is only redeemed when he returns to their meeting place with their child and, despite being bereaved, sees a future for himself and his daughter.

In line with mainstream features, Scherfig uses known stars, worked on a relatively high budget of $15 million, and the plot is straightforward and uncomplicated. The film was a success for Scherfig, gaining US backers. It was sponsored by Film4 and distributed by Universal and opened on nearly 1,800 screens in America. It made more than $5 million at the box office in its opening weekend in August and by the end of September had grossed nearly $14 million in box office receipts in USA alone.[7]

The Female-Directed Bio-pic

The above fall largely into the romantic comedy genre but, in terms of popular cinema, the bio-pic is also favoured by a number of female directors. Difficult to define, the bio-pic is loosely inspired by real people, and the filmmakers have woven fictional tales around facts. The ones included here use real names and tell the story of that person. In this section I discuss three films: Scherfig's *An Education* is loosely based on the memoirs of Lyn Barber growing up in the 1960s, and this is what Ellen Cheshire would describe as a 'thinly-veiled bio-pic where character names have changed but are considered to be based on a known person' (2015: 5) and a fairly anonymous person becomes a celebrity. As Cheshire notes, 'the little-known lives of protagonists … have been translated into box office and award-winning hits without a great deal of public foreknowledge of their subject' (2015: 7). With *The Iron Lady*, Lloyd chooses to focus on the latter part of Margaret Thatcher's life while looking back over her career. In a different vein, *Nowhere Boy* is based on known Beatles' pop star, John Lennon, focusing on his early life and, in particular, his relationship with his aunt and mother.[8]

An Education is Scherfig's second English-language film.[9] The screenplay was written by Nick Hornby,[10] who encountered an article in the British literary magazine *Granta*, written in 2003 by Lynn Barber about her experiences growing up in 1960s Britain before the swinging '60s took off. He eventually adapted the screenplay from these brief personal memoirs and, at this stage, the BBC supported the project with the sum of $10 million. The company Endgame came up with the remainder of the budget, and the film featured in the 2009 Sundance Film Festival. CAA was selling *An Education* and they received multiple bids, with American rights going to Sony Pictures Classics for $3–4 million. The release date was crucial and, according to independent production company distributor, Entertainment 1, the film needed to stake an early claim in the film awards and was set to premiere at the LFF. Entertainment 1 purchased the film at the American Film Market based on a script and a short promotion reel and, as the company director, Alex Hamilton, suggests, 'In theory it was a relatively, in inverted commas, "small" British movie that needed careful handling ... It wasn't a big Cannes splash from an established international director' (in Gant 2010: 11). Hence the poster design emphasised the romanticism of the tale, avoiding any of the seedier sides to the story. The film was launched on 9 October 2009 in the USA to a $40,000 per screen average during its opening weekend on four screens in New York and Los Angeles.

In line with her Dogme training, Scherfig shot *An Education* on location in London, Oxford and the Isle of Man, with some hand-held filming in Paris. The film created a star out of Carey Mulligan, who takes the lead role, playing Jenny. Indeed, Mulligan was specially selected by Scherfig because of her specific characteristics such as 'fragility and strength' (in Haun 2009: 15). Despite her Danish background, and the fact that she was only an infant in the 1960s, Scherfig obsessively researched the period, observing that, 'England is such a strong culture. The way that people live and behave and the class system – the seeds of that postwar period – that is not something that you could do without first of all being interested in it and also being interested in doing it correctly' (in Haun 2009: 16). The result was that the film was described as 'naturally cinematic and yet completely English' (James 2009: 8).

In terms of its visual style, *An Education* avoids experimental aesthetics in favour of a focus on social and societal nuances, and the fact that the film is set in the early 1960s meant that Scherfig could explore postwar English austerity. This enabled her to introduce Jenny's parents Jack (Alfred Molina) and Marjorie (Cara Seymour) as a product of their time; accordingly, they are unworldly and avaricious, seeing in Jenny's relationship with property developer David (Peter Sarsgaard) a wealthy married future for their daughter who was otherwise bound for Oxford. David, it is later revealed, is married and a crook, and eventually she leaves him. Although she is barred from school, Jenny goes on to study privately and wins a place at Oxford and, in the final sequences she visits her ex-teacher, Miss Stubbs (Olivia Williams), to ask for help. Here, Scherfig juxtaposes the *mise-en-scène* to present contrasts: Miss Stubbs's house is sparsely furnished in comparison to the opulence of David's abode, but she is surrounded by books and paintings, exemplifying an academic home and thus a shared affinity between the two women. The seasons change and Jenny's letter arrives to inform her of her acceptance at Oxford. In the final montage sequence, various famous Oxford landmarks are shown with Jenny's voice-over stating her return to a life envisioned before she had met David:

> So, I went to read English books, and did my best to avoid the speccy, spotty fate that Helen had predicted for me. I probably looked as wide-eyed, fresh, and artless as any other student ... But I wasn't. One of the boys I went out with, and they really were boys, once asked me to go to Paris with him. And I told him I'd love to, I was dying to see Paris ... as if I'd never been.

Although *An Education* hinges on a female as central character, Scherfig tries to distance herself from the type of project she considers stereotypical for women. As she suggests, 'Everyone sends me scripts with these sweet stories ... I've done that already. I want to make a movie with chases and explosions. I want to blow things up' (in Zeitchik 2009b: 21). Even so, the director revisits the 1960s from a feminist perspective, with Jenny as a free spirit who eventually chooses a university life, made possible for her through increased access to education for women.

According to Hornby, Scherfig had quite an input into the film's ending, which she interpreted in a manner that he had not himself visualised: 'She really wrung out everything in that scene I hadn't been able to see' (in Lisotta 2010: 8). The film took seven weeks to shoot and Scherfig aimed for a style consonant with the British Free Cinema movement and the Nouvelle Vague to chime with the period. She used the renowned and experienced cinematographer John Boorman, who deployed Cinemascope to make the film 'look real so the audience feels that the film recognises its audience. I always work with the audience in mind. I'm their representative to a certain extent' (in Forde 2008: 12).

An Education received three Oscar nominations, including one for Carey Mulligan as leading actress, Hornby for Best Adapted Screenplay, and Best Picture categories for producers Finola Dwyer and Amanda Posey. It also received eight BAFTA nominations, with Mulligan recommended in the Orange Rising Star category.

Despite the universality of the story, *An Education* is told in a straightforward way. It is not a high-concept film, nor does it use known stars yet it was successful at the box office. Lloyd's bio-pic on Margaret Thatcher, *The Iron Lady* (2011), on the other hand, uses a known established star with Meryl Streep playing Thatcher, but the film follows a different track to her earlier musical. Its narrative charts the late prime minister as the key protagonist. Funded by Pathé, Film4, Goldcrest Film Production and the UKFC Development Fund and Film Fund, *The Iron Lady* was predicted to divide audiences (Anon. 2012: 78) because of its deferential and sympathetic, yet misguided portrayal of the British Conservative prime minister. Costing $13 million to make, the film received a US release before going worldwide. Again, Lloyd employed a female-only team, believing that this was essential and, rather than centring on politics as one might expect given the focal character, the narrative centres on memory loss: as she states, 'Abi Morgan, the screenwriter, and Meryl and I are all interested in the details, the miscellaneous fragments. It's a film about memory and strays into territory you wouldn't expect a big political film to stray' (in McClintock 2011: 50).

Selecting key moments in Thatcher's life, and told in flashback, rather than chronicling her entire career, *The Iron Lady* received mixed reviews. Described as a 'humanizing, at times touchingly sentimental drama' (Rooney 2011: 76), the film opens with Margaret Thatcher in her 80s, as a widow and with dementia: a subject used because it was briefly alluded to in her daughter, Carol Thatcher's autobiography, *A Swim-on Part in the Goldfish Bowl* (2008). Indeed, Carol commented that her mother sometimes did not realise that her husband, Denis Thatcher, was dead, and this is developed as a repeated motif, if not the main theme in the film, Lloyd using a subjective camera throughout to show Thatcher's point of view, and, in turn, what it might feel like to have dementia.[11]

All through *The Iron Lady*, Lloyd isolates Thatcher both literally and metaphorically. At the opening of the film an aged hand is seen in close-up reaching for a bottle of milk from a corner shop shelf. It belongs to an elderly and demented Lady Thatcher who is subsequently pushed to one side by a young man in a suit, a yuppie of the type promoted by her in the 1980s. She is clearly confused, making her solitary status in the shop all the more concerning and implausible within the narrative. In the flashbacks to her Cabinet days, she is also separated and shown as an outsider through her female status. This is exemplified when she arrives at the House of Commons for the first time and is sent to the Ladies Members' Room: predictably deserted, its interior contains a single chair and, ironically, an ironing board suggesting traditional female chores. At a state banquet she is the only female present among her Cabinet colleagues, and, at one point she sarcastically cries out, 'Gentlemen, shall we join the ladies?'

Thatcher's clothes also reinforce her enforced detachment. Filmed from a low angle shot, her cream-coloured court shoes are highlighted and conspicuous among the highly polished black brogues worn by the men. Later, in a Commons' debate, she is again isolated through her costume. Clad in a pale blue outfit, she is prominent among the otherwise male attendees who are entirely dressed in black. This imagery recurs when she becomes prime minister and has her photograph taken with her Cabinet. Placed centrally within the frame, and dressed in a strong blue outfit as opposed to the dark male attire, she is evidently the only female present.

Denis's ghost becomes a key motif in *The Iron Lady*. He is present in Thatcher's imagination until near the end when, in an emotional farewell, he departs her life. To aid his passage, she carefully packs his bag, and he kisses her on the cheek, and, appearing spectre-like in silhouette, walks down the corridor to the front door. Filmed in slow motion and accompanied by rousing non-diegetic music, the sequence commands emotion and mobilises spectator identification with the ex-prime minister. To reinforce this aspect, the film cuts to Thatcher's saddened face as she attempts to persuade him not to leave. Nonetheless, the imaginary Denis advances towards the door, the use of a slow-motion montage further signalling that he is a figment of her demented imagination. 'I don't want to be on my own' she states, and the camera focuses on her face in close-up to encourage spectator compassion. 'You will be fine on your own', states Denis, 'you always have been', and the camera zooms out as he disappears in a halo of light, further enhancing his numinous presence.

The constant reappearance of Denis in Thatcher's imagination imbues the ex-prime minister with a likeable disposition which otherwise might not be the case. She mildly chides her husband when he puts his feet on the bed with his shoes on, and later laughs when he dons a chiffon scarf and pretends to be an Indian subordinate. The pair operate as a comedy duo, engaging the viewer in their banter, and the film alternates throughout between the present and flashbacks of her private and political life, including documentary inserts of real events such as the Brighton bombings at the Conservative Party conference in 1984. Following Thatcher's reminiscences, Lloyd includes close-up images of her face in the present day, where she appears confused and vulnerable, Streep's countenance tearful as though to affirm such emotions. Thatcher is also represented as a feminist, informing Denis early in their courtship that she will never be a stay-at-home wife on the arm of her husband, Lloyd thus rendering the prime minister as strong yet exposed.

If, in *The Iron Lady*, Lloyd favours the subjective camera to evoke sympathy by placing the spectator in Thatcher's position, then arguably she simultaneously alters history in the process. For this reason, critics were not always positive in their reviews, suggesting that the film created Thatcher as a vulnerable character and 'produces an alibi for the film's view of history and politics which positions Thatcher … as a "victim", … [that] is achieved through recurrent scenes of angry men shouting at her or looming menacingly into view and repeated shots of her framed alone as an isolated figure' (Wearing 2013: 321). What is doubly shocking about the film is that it shows Thatcher as infirm while she is still alive. In this respect, the film has been described by Fuller as 'Thatcher without Thatcherism' (2012a: 67), and he points out, in a critical way that, 'as thrilling as it is to watch Streep imitate Thatcher, *The Iron Lady* feels like a missed opportunity, not to blame and cast aspersions, but to weigh and assess' (2012a: 68). However, not all critics were dismissive. For instance, John Walsh highlights similarities between Lloyd and Thatcher, and argues that this is why the film should be sympathetically received. He claims that:

> It's tempting to draw parallels between the film's director and her subject – the tough indomitable woman who storms the barricades of a men's club (film direction, Parliament) and triumphs by force of individual will. Tempting but hardly the real story. Phyllida Lloyd is undoubtedly a major figure in British theatre and filmland, a freelance who has directed rapturously received plays in all Britain's major theatres and who confidently helmed the most successful British-made film of all time. But she seems to have succeeded by her unique powers of empathy with collaborators, especially with women. (2011: 34)

The collaborators that Walsh alludes to are the women in key positions, including the scriptwriter Abi Morgan, the editor Justine Wright and the star Meryl Streep.

Not all the filmmakers mentioned here offer massive marketing potential. Indeed, a number included in this chapter came to prominence from art backgrounds in the 1990s, but went on to make feature film productions often in the form of a bio-pic. Some of Taylor-Wood's later work, for example, also falls into the bio-pic category and her films display a different style of filmmaking. To provide some details of her early career, Taylor-Wood was originally identified as part of the phenomenon of Young British Artists which included Tracey Emin and Damien Hirst, and studied at Beaconsfield Community College. She started out as an artist creating installations and in 1998 she was nominated for the Turner Prize, thereafter being commissioned to create a video portrait of a sleeping David Beckham for the National Portrait Gallery. In 2000 she was commissioned by Selfridges to wrap its entire Oxford Street store while renovations were carried out, and to achieve this feat, she created one long 900 feet photograph based on three panoramic shots taken with a revolving camera and spliced together. The work was entitled *XV Seconds* and various celebrities were invited to take part in the shoot including musician and singer Elton John, and actor Ray Winstone.

Her later series, *Five Revolutionary Seconds*, comprises panoramic 360-degree photographs taken over a number of years in the homes of friends and family and these formed the basis of a Sam Taylor-Wood one-woman retrospective exhibition at the Hayward Gallery in 2002. Described by its contributors as 'a platform for all forms of uncensored artistic expression' (McKie 2006: 49), Taylor-Wood's two-hour collaboration *Destricted* (Matthew Barney, Richard Prince, Larry Clark, Marco Brambilla, Sam Taylor-Wood, Marina Abramović, Gaspar Noé 2006), consists of a film divided into seven shorts, all drawn from the contemporary art world. Taylor-Wood's contribution, *Death Valley*, is set in the American desert landscape and is intertextual, drawing on John Schlesinger's *Midnight Cowboy* (1969) and Wim Wenders's *Paris, Texas* (1984) for inspiration.

Her debut feature, *Nowhere Boy* (2009), rather than focusing on the height of the Beatles' fame, follows the early life of the young John Lennon (Aaron Johnson) who was reared by his Aunt Mimi (Kristin Scott Thomas) in the absence of his natural mother, Julia (Anne-Marie Duff). Taylor-Wood is, in some respects, experimental in her approach to this work, using appropriate sound tracks to enhance the narrative, and creating visually striking imagery through innovative use of flashback. The film opens with a shot of Lennon walking through Liverpool as a young boy. In this sequence, and throughout the film, the director uses music, not only to add realism but also to make specific statements about Lennon's life. For example, during the opening credits, Taylor-Wood uses Jerry Lee Lewis's *Wild One* (1958) to explain Lennon's personality as a cheeky, uncontrollable boy. This plays over various sequences, including one where Lennon is in the headmaster's office, another in which he drops his trousers and exposes himself to his fellow female pupils, and one where he is travelling dangerously fast and precariously in a vehicle. Through music and cinematography, the spectator is left in no doubt that Lennon is indeed a wild boy. Additionally, rather than focus on the music of the Beatles, Taylor-Wood uses soundtracks contemporary to Lennon's childhood and, by concentrating on the star's youth, *Nowhere Boy* avoids the dramatic tension between his onstage and private life.

Further use of emotive soundtrack occurs when Lennon meets his mother Julia after some years apart, and they visit Blackpool together. Again, music is used to enhance the narrative, the tempo and words of Dickie Valentine's *Mr Sandman* (1954) aligning the spectator with the fun time mother and son are having. They try on and purchase cowboy hats, pose in the Hall of Mirrors, where, in a fast-motion sequence, the distorted images of the pair create a surreal effect. A little later, and set against the sunlight shining on the sea, the two walk along Blackpool pier and the words 'Mr Sandman bring me a dream, make him the cutest that I've ever seen' are heard, enhancing the magic of the moment for Lennon concerning his renewed relationship with his mother. Taylor-Wood continues in this vein when, later in the film, Lennon recalls the time with his mother in Blackpool, and, as he sits in his bedroom holding the cowboy hat, a cut reveals the remembered images of the sea before he slips into a dream sequence. Subsequently, a series of flashbacks of his traumatic childhood occur,[12] which becomes a recurring motif in the film.

Afterwards, when Lennon forms his first band, The Quarrymen, he performs at a local fête, and this first recital narratively marks off the start of his career as a pop singer. The group sing the traditional Liverpool folk song about a prostitute, 'Maggie May', and as he says the words 'You dirty robbin' no good Maggie May'; the camera frames Julia's distressed and bewildered face to demonstrate that she realises that the comments are clearly directed at her. Taylor-Wood continues throughout the film to use music to explain the mother/son relationship. On his birthday, David Whitfield's 'My Son John' (1956) is played as Julia brings a cake into the room alight with candles. Lennon however asks for the music to be turned off 'before I start crying in pain', and the camera cuts to frame Julia, whose happy demeanour changes to one of dejection, the music used here to clarify the characters' emotional states. After Julia is killed in a road accident, John and his Aunt Mimi patch up their differences and, in an emotional exchange, she is awarded the status of parent before he leaves for Hamburg. As he departs and walks away, the music to Lennon's 1970 song, 'Mother', is played, specifically using the words 'Goodbye' over the closing credits. Although the director introduces Lennon's music as biographical backdrop, she therefore also focuses on the singer's personal suffering through the use of sound.

While Taylor-Wood incorporates source music to effect in *Nowhere Boy*, one of the problems she experienced was being able to afford the rights to the soundtracks given the relatively low budget of the film. As Kevin Loader, one of the producers suggests, 'The key is to get a music supervisor who is extremely well connected with the record companies and knows how to get quick results that fit with the budget of the film' (in Macnab 2009b: 10). For *Nowhere Boy*, about 6% of the £6 million budget was set aside for music, the soundtrack for which was overseen by Ian Neil, who was also responsible for that of Whitecross's 2010 film, *Sex & Drugs & Rock & Roll*, the Ian Dury bio-pic. A soundtrack album from the film was produced, adding to its after sales and helping to recoup costs. As Loader suggests, 'If you can get a record company to partner with you on the release of the soundtrack album, you can often get them to discount some of the prices on music used in the film' (in Macnab 2009b: 11). Featuring a number of cover versions performed by The Quarrymen, the film utilises few original Lennon/McCartney songs. Additionally, it avoids the conventions of the musical genre, and the diegetic and non-diegetic songs only serve to enhance the narrative.

This film, as with other music bio-pics, employs visual and aural experience to drive the narrative, yet critics seemed disappointed that Taylor-Wood's portrayal of this national British emblem was not more avant-garde. Trevor Johnston admired its quality, but felt that the flashbacks were little more than plot devices and, 'given the auteurist expectations created by Taylor-Wood's track record in the art world, it's hard to discern a distinctively personal take on the material, or indeed the medium' (2010: 49). The film did not set out to, or achieve, blockbuster status, but made Taylor-Wood a significant name in feature filmmaking. She not only offered the young Lennon a voice, but also created space for the female figures in his life: his mother and aunt. *Nowhere Boy* opened on 172 screens in the UK and was financed by the UKFC's Development Fund and the Premiere Fund along with Film4, and the Canadian financier, Aver Media. The UK post-production company, LipSync Productions also aided the project.[13]

I conclude the bio-pic section with a film about the beginnings of feminism which primarily uses female protagonists (albeit fictitious) to further the narrative. Sarah Gavron's 2015 release, *Suffragette* opened the LFF in 2015, a year which was dubbed 'the year of the strong woman' (Ritman 2015: 112). To provide some background, the director graduated in English from York University, later gaining an MA in Film Studies from Edinburgh College of Art before studying film directing at the NFTS. Attending a directing class with Stephen Frears, she was not only influenced by his work, but also that of Mike Leigh and Ken Loach, as well as Jane Campion's film, *Angel at My Table*. In 2003 she directed, as noted, *This Little Life* for the BBC, which earned her a BAFTA for Best New Director, and in 2007 she went on to direct the Film4/UKFC sponsored *Brick Lane*, an adaptation of Monica Ali's 2003 novel of the same name. Gavron was subsequently nominated for a BAFTA and British Independent Film Award for Best New Director.

Brick Lane centres on the story of Nazneen (Tannishtha Chatterjee), who is sent to London from Bangladesh for an arranged marriage. The film won a Silver Hitchcock and Best Screenplay at the Dinard Festival of British Cinema and, from this, Gavron went on to receive sponsorship from Film4 for *Village at the End of the World* (2012)—a documentary about the 59 inhabitants of the remote Inuit settlement of Niaqornat in north-west Greenland.[14] Sponsored also by the Danish Film Institute, and distributed by documentary distributor Dogwoof, *Village at the End of the World* was criticised for its lack of female focus. As Isabel Stevens notes, 'Given the director's previous female-centred dramas, it's also surprising that women's voices are in the minority here, and it's a shame that the position the women occupy in what appears to be a very patriarchal society is never investigated' (2013: 109).

A lack of female focus is clearly an issue that Gavron addresses in her more recent film, *Suffragette*. The film was sponsored by Film4, Focus Features and Pathé, and not only opened the LFF[15] but also paved the way for discussions between actors and directors about the current situation regarding women in the industry.[16] The LFF's director, Clare Stewart, promoted the film as an important feminist intervention in mainstream filmmaking, and of the LFF's 2015 line-up, roughly 20% were female directors. Moreover, at the same event, a symposium was held with Geena

Davis's Institute on Gender in Media. The scriptwriter for the film, Abi Morgan,[17] worked collaboratively with Gavron on the project, and the remainder of the team involved in the film consisted of Alison Owen and Faye Ward (producers). Gavron believed the film to be timely, coinciding with a new wave of feminism (Williams 2015: 66), and between her and Morgan they researched extensively in archives such as the Women's Library at the London School of Economics, the Museum of London and the National Archives, in order to complete an accurate picture. They consulted specialists on various historical events and on force-feeding and its psychological repercussions.

Gavron's decision not to concentrate on the aristocratic names associated with the Suffragette movement, such as Emmeline Pankhurst and Emily Wilding Davison, was innovative; instead, she made the lead character working class. Carey Mulligan played the fictional[18] laundress, Maud Watts, and by doing this, Gavron suggests, she was able to give a voice to those women who had not previously had the opportunity (in Lewis 2015: 41).[19] Gavron's remit was not only to depict women's struggle but also their radicalism and, besides, she especially wanted to show the brutality they experienced at the hands of authority, particularly the law. The police officer in the film, Inspector Arthur Steed (Brendan Gleeson), was Irish and, as Gavron explains, 'There were a number of Irish in the force ... and many of them fought the Fenians. The surveillance methods they used in Ireland were adapted for use with the suffragettes' (in Garcia 2015). Steed's job of surveillance brings him close to the female protagonists, and through this connection, the narrative suggests that he finally recognises that the law is wrong. Gavron achieves this through the use of mobile camera, particularly in the rally sequences, to provide a more realistic effect. She admits that such an approach was undertaken with the goal of moving away from the style of filming associated with period drama: 'I wanted *Suffragette* to be focused on being there, and feeling it, being aware of all the grubbiness and grime' (in Smyth 2015: 9). To further achieve her aim, she created a number of close-ups, staying 'very close to these women, [and] observed very tiny shifts ... We also wanted to be unflinching and not shy away from the pain, anguish, and horror of it' (in Smyth 2015: 20). Before the end credits, Gavron produces a scroll revealing the years when women gained the vote in various countries across the world, and following the film, a number of feminist societies were started in schools and universities.

Comedy and Race in Women's British Cinema

The final section in this chapter uncovers the category that dominates women's popular culture: comedy. One director, Gurinder Chadha, has been prolific in this field for some time, and has made inroads into raising issues concerning Indian women living in the UK. Born in 1960 in East Africa, Chadha's family moved to London when she was 2 years old, hence her interest in diaspora and immigration. Initially she studied broadcast journalism at the London College of Printing, and started work for television as a reporter and a documentary filmmaker for the BBC. Chadha was working as a researcher when the BFI launched its New Directors scheme, to which she submitted *I'm British But*. In 1990, she set up her own production company and made her first feature, *Bhaji on the Beach*, which was released in 1994. Earning a nomination for the Best British Feature at the BAFTAs, the film also highlighted Chadha as the first British Asian female to direct a feature film in the UK. *What's Cooking?* (2000) followed and was shown on the opening night of the Sundance Film Festival, and voted joint Audience Award winner in the New York Film Critics 2000 season.

Chadha's work deals with social issues and racial tension through a comedic rather than documentary style and, as Alison Butler observes, Chadha has used her own 'experience of hyphenated identity or mobility between cultures as the basis of dramas of cultural difference which insist on its presence *within* communities, families and individuals' (2002: 110, original italics). The director's innovative methods and talent were supported early in her career when she received UKFC funding for the comedy about racial differences and tensions, *Bend It Like Beckham* (2002). Exploring the world of a Sikh family whose daughter, Jesminder Kaur Bhamra (Parminder Nagra), prefers the game of football to the traditions associated with her upbringing, *Bend It Like Beckham* received positive critical reviews and, although made on a budget of just over £3.5 million, went on to become a box office success in both the UK and USA.[20]

Bend it Like Beckham (2002) is not just a comedy, but is also about the class system in Britain,[21] and Chadha herself comments on the way the film:

> works on so many different levels. So if you're an American kid who likes football it works for you; if you're Punjabi and you've grown up in Southall or Hounslow it works on a completely different level. There are so many

> references to our existence and the complex way we handle things … [we] make people who are not Indian understand our world from our perspective … the idea that people can enjoy it on different levels is quite subversive, because what you're doing is actually lulling people into your world, then telling them about racism, about our culture, about all kinds of things they're not really expecting. They just think it's a comedy. (in Nagra 2014: 26)

The film opens with a football match on-screen and a voice-over commentary as the central character, Jesminder (Jess) Bhamra scores a goal. The televised live match then cuts to a commentary hosted by Gary Lineker, with John Barnes, Alan Hansen and Jess's mother (Shaheen Khan), albeit the latter is not initially visible on-screen. When she is eventually introduced by Lineker, the camera withdraws to reveal Mrs Bhamra, Jess's traditionally dressed Indian mother, complaining about her daughter 'showing her bare legs to 70,000 people' thus demonstrating, in a humorous way, clashes in culture. In this, and Chadha's later films, she interrogates contemporary British and Asian cultural stereotypes in terms of race and gender. Irene Gedalof (2011) argues that *Bend It Like Beckham* has generally been read in the context of other British Asian films of its period, such as *My Beautiful Laundrette* (Frears 1985) and *East is East* (Din 1999), whereby the diasporic family is brought into mainstream cinema. Indeed, the marketing of the film promoted the notion of the problems that a Sikh Punjabi family experience living in London and adjusting to Western ways, and this is also demonstrated narratively because Mrs Bhamra insists on continuing with her Indian traditions, and as a result presents obstacles for her daughter.

To provide contrast with Jess's need to escape her cultural strictures, much of the narrative centres on Jess's sister, Pinky (Archie Panjabi), who is to be married. In her analysis, Gedalof argues that the wedding and the football pitch share visual commonalities in that 'Both are sites of sexism, homophobia, and unequal gender dynamics, but both are also sites of the embodied pleasures of the different rituals of dance and sport and of investment in and the pleasures of connectedness' (2011: 138), thus enabling Jess to operate in both spaces. Jess's home life and her sister's wedding preparations are colourful and brightly lit, and these scenes use frequent close-ups to suggest confinement, juxtaposed with the exposed, yet less colourful, area of the football pitch. The underlying representation of home and family is conservative and restrictive, and in line with this,

Jess's strict parents only want her to settle down according to Indian traditions. This is shown in the early sequences of the film when Pinky takes the unwilling Jess shopping; here the streets are packed, and the camera focuses on the crowds of people intercut with shots of the girls' faces. On Jess's return home, she is coerced into a game of football in the park, and she, and the other players are shown in medium shot enabling the spectator a less cluttered vision.

Gedalof argues that the film has possibilities for a more negotiated reading by female viewers. Rather than necessarily signalling domestic constraint, Chadha focuses on the film's portrayal of 'complexities of homemaking in the context of migration' (Gedalof 2011: 135). In fact, the outside spaces 'are not problem free … Rather than one space being represented as absolutely other, both inside and outside are represented as spaces that demand the negotiation of a multiplicity of differences … Cinematically, both spaces offer openness and closure, darkness and light' (Gedalof 2011: 137).

Bend It Like Beckham is a film that attempts to evoke stereotypical representations of the diasporic experience for white Western spectators through comedy. To this effect, Chadha produces a 'palatable foreigness' (Marciniak 2007: 187) by injecting humour into the film. At one point during the engagement scene, which is set in the Bhamra house, the sound of mobile phones ringing is accompanied by the incongruous image of a row of elderly Indian women all searching their bags. The fact that they are traditionally attired in saris, yet fully embrace modern equipment and technology, is not lost on the spectator.

Bend It Like Beckham involves the two sports of football and cricket to suggest the marriage of the two cultures. Chadha emphasises this by using traditional Indian music during the final football game of the film, when Jess leaves her sister's wedding early, changing her clothes in the car to prepare herself for the match. This is intercut with the wedding dancing and, when her friend, Juliette Paxton (Keira Knightley) scores a goal, the cheering crowd are juxtaposed with the raised arms of the wedding dancers. Adorned in a bright pink hat, Paula Paxton (Juliet Stevenson), Juliette's mother, cheers along with her husband, her attire aligning her with the bright clothing of the Indian wedding guests. When Jess scores a goal, the camera edits between the applauding team players raising Jess in the air, and the groom raising his bride above the guests accompanied by the music from *Nessun Dorma* (Tito Beltrán). Chadha thus mixes Asian and Western music and, further, she introduces both mothers of the girls as stereotypical, hysterical comedy characters, whereas the fathers are sensible and level headed and are ultimately the ones who permit their offspring to follow their dreams. For example, Mrs Bhamra is situated outside of British culture, signified by her traditional dress and language, and Mrs Paxton is typically English in her attire, peculiarities and colloquialisms, even wearing an elaborate hat to watch her daughter play football. At the end of the film, the two families reconcile any differences, Mrs Bhamra offering Mrs Paxton a handkerchief as they wave their daughters off to compete in America.

Owing to the subject matter, Chadha experienced problems raising the appropriate funds, with absurd suggestions that Indian girls don't play football. As Chadha herself recalls, the UKFC were not responding to equal opportunities issues: 'I was furious ... Eventually I went to see John Woodward at the UK Film Council. I said that whenever there are panels to talk about diversity I'm wheeled on as a British film-maker of colour, but here I am struggling to make a fucking film about a person of colour and getting nowhere' (2004: 37). Woodward looked at the script and made the appropriate minor changes, and these were incorporated and funding granted.

In a similar vein to *Bend It Like Beckham*, Chadha's 2004 film *Bride and Prejudice* is also a site of connection between two different cultures. It offers a Bollywood twist on Jane Austen's novel and was heavily promoted by Pathé before its UK theatrical release, and distribution by Miramax. The film follows Mr and Mrs Bakshi (Ampam Kher and Nadira Babbar) who are seeking husbands for their four daughters, Lalita (Aishwarya Rai), Jaya (Namrata Shirodkar), Maya (Meghnaa) and Lakhi (Peeya Rai Choudhuri). Described by the director herself as 'a multi-national, multicultural crowdpleaser that touches on American imperialism, the way the west looks at India and what people regard as backward or progressive' (Chadha 2004: 37), *Bride and Prejudice* involves an Indianisation of a very British novel as a way of appealing to a mass audience. As Chadha observes, 'We're all brought up with this obsession to get us married. The film was supposed to be like an Ealing comedy but with a different perspective, one that was a discourse on the Asian community – but perhaps it was too Asian' (in Nagra 2014: 27).

Bride and Prejudice is a referential pun, not only on the novel, but also on two conflicting cultures, and a pair of differing film industries: Hollywood and Bollywood. As Cheryl Wilson suggests, 'within the context of Austen studies and Bollywood film history, *Bride and*

Prejudice can be viewed as a film that integrates two well-suited partners – the Bollywood form and Austen's comedy of manners – to both preserve and update the cultural critique of the original' (2006: 323). Co-written with Paul Mayeda Burges, slightly different versions of the film were released to Western and non-Western viewers. Nevertheless, it is aimed at a multinational audience and, just as the novel *Pride and Prejudice* questions the influences which affect cultural identities, so *Bride and Prejudice* is a postmodern interrogation of cultural stereotypes. In line with her previous films, Chadha uses a female central protagonist, and this time, for the Director of Photography she chose a Bollywood cameraman whose credits include *Taal* (Ghai 1999) and *Devdas* (Bhansali 2002).

Bride and Prejudice is a comedy which disavows the conventions of Bollywood cinema, yet relies on it to explain its approach to issues of class and gender. The film provides viewers with the familiar and the strange and pokes fun at the importance of a good marriage, both for Indian and British culture, drawing on the original Austen novel by implication. Frequent allusions to other Bollywood films also occur: Lalita falls into Darcy's arms, a sequence which pays tribute to *Barsaat* (Darshan 1949), and the family, in pursuit of Wickham (Daniel Gillies) and Lakhi, follow the couple into a screening of *Purab Aur Pachhim* (Kumar 1970) at the National Film Theatre. Likewise, the film breaks off, Bollywood-style, to incorporate song and dance routines, and to move into dream sequences at regular intervals. Throughout, Chadha references the correlations between Western and Indian music; for example, when Balraj gets up to dance, Miss Bingley (Indira Varma) informs Mr Darcy (Martin Henderson) that he is about to perform the Indian version of MC Hammer. Thus Chadha incorporates Indian dancing into representations of community, but in subversive mode, aiming through music 'to tell Asian stories in marketable ways' (in Nagra 2014: 29).

Bride and Prejudice is accused of reinforcing generalised global perceptions of India regarding subjects such as arranged marriages and spicy food (Ramachandran 2004: 44), and it pokes fun at cultural nuances and differences. Early on in the film Mrs Bakshi sits with her friend, who informs her that the new arrival in town is Mr Balraj (Naveen Andrews), who is from the Uppal family of Delhi, is a barrister and lives in Windsor. Clearly impressed by status, Mrs Bakshi perceives him as akin to royalty. Later, when in England, she sits with her female family members lamenting that no one wants to marry her daughters. The four women sit around a coffee table, an English china rose-covered teapot placed in the foreground seen in extreme close-up, reflecting both nations' relationship with tea.

It is the cultural differences that present the most tensions within the film. At one point, Darcy comments on what he describes as the backward system of arranged marriages, to which Lalita responds that it is no different to a global dating service. These tensions are never fully resolved as, at the end of the film, Darcy appears when Lalita has almost lost hope of ever seeing him again. He bangs an Indian drum festooned with flowers, and the camera cuts between the couple as he advances towards her. Conventional close-ups, intercut with images of the family who nod their approval, ensue, before the film edits to frame the couple as they embrace. A cut reveals a happy Hollywood-style ending, with Balraj and Jaya astride a heavily adorned elephant, followed by Darcy and Lalita also seated on an elephant with a Just Married sign attached to the animal's rear. There is, however, no explanation of the lead up to this situation nor a complete resolution. Darcy's early objections are not settled and none of his family appears at the wedding.

Having gained UKFC funding, filming took place largely in the UK as well as Goa and America. However, *Bride and Prejudice* did not achieve success at the BAFTA ceremony, possibly because, as Allan Hunter observes, 'BAFTA is generally less kindly disposed towards obviously mainstream multiplex fare, erring on the side of artistic achievement rather than commercial success which suggests that *Bride and Prejudice* would be unlikely to secure significant nominations – although it may be a contender for the Alexander Korda Award' (2005: 17). Chadha confesses to being a 'populist' with her films in an attempt 'to change people's minds ... The whole point is about challenging racism' (in Nagra 2014: 26).[22]

Continuing in the comedy genre, filmmaker, Debbie Isitt, relies more on television funding to finance her films: the *Nativity* trilogy. Isitt's work is not only renowned for its humour but also its social commentary, which she typically presents through the comedy family film. Comparable to Lloyd, Isitt also began her career as a theatre director before moving into television films such as *Nasty Neighbours* (1997) and her BAFTA award-winning adaptation of Jacqueline Wilson's *The Illustrated Mum* (2003) for Granada Television. Her film career largely consists of a trilogy including *Nativity!* (2009), *Nativity 2: Danger in the Manger* (2012) and *Nativity 3: Dude, Where's My Donkey?* (2014).[23] All three are popular farces starring well-known figures such as Martin Freeman, David Tennant and Martin Clunes respectively.

Nativity!, the first of the trilogy, is a BBC Films and Screen West Midlands production and is set in present day Coventry. The central character, Paul Maddens (Martin Freeman), is a schoolteacher, and he is placed in charge of a school nativity production. Traumatised by a past poor review of a production he organised, he must garner publicity, so fabricates a story informing the school that his ex-girlfriend, Jennifer (Ashley Jensen), who is now in Hollywood, is bringing her prestigious friends to the play. Paul is in competition with the local prep school teacher, Gordon Shakespeare (Jason Watkins), and ultimately, through a variety of misunderstandings and problems, loses his job. Even so, closure is achieved at the end. The film commences with voice-over which deals with five years of Paul's life in a few moments, and Paul's school is presented, in contrast to that of his contemporary, as full of unruly pupils unable to spell. In comparison, Gordon's pupils are well behaved, competitive and smart. Isitt relies on timing, facial expressions and witty dialogue to create humour, and, as social comment, she constantly parallels the two schools using a fast editing pace to compare the characters. A confident Gordon dresses in the robes of his former university, and has an orderly, gifted class, whereas Paul wears a cardigan, teaches an unruly group and is in constant personal crisis. Comedy is also created through Paul's teaching assistant, Mr Poppy (Marc Wootton), who behaves in a similar manner to the children he works with, running to grab his coat at the end of lessons, constantly flouting the teacher's instructions and generally behaving in a disorderly fashion. The film follows the popular format of centring on the final show. This takes place, with the children performing their song to the public, and the headteacher makes a moving speech in their praise while commenting on the fact that many are from socially deprived backgrounds. As she states, 'Everyone expects them to go down the drain', but by the end of the film, and in true popular musical style, the show goes ahead and Hollywood, in the guise of Paul's ex-girlfriend and her studio boss (Clarke Peters) arrive by helicopter. Paul stages a laudable performance in the evocative ruins of Coventry Cathedral, the children feel valued and equilibrium is restored.

Isitt wrote and directed the sequel, *Nativity 2: Danger in the Manger*, which was sponsored by Creative England and follows a similar trajectory to its predecessor. Again set in St Bernadette's primary school, this time Poppy auditions the children for a Song for a Christmas competition. Rival school Oakmoor once more attempt to sabotage St Bernadette's success and the latter are forced to hike, river raft and climb mountains in order to arrive at their Welsh venue on time. Again, the children are from deprived backgrounds, one boy, the spectator is informed, not having spoken since his father left the household. The last of the trilogy, *Nativity 3: Dude, Where's My Donkey?*, was privately financed and also set in St Bernadette's. Marc Wootton carries on as Poppy, but this time actor Martin Clunes plays the teacher, Mr Shepherd. Poppy is rehearsing a nativity play, but the donkey kicks Shepherd in the head causing him to lose his memory. The film follows a similar pattern to the previous two films, and equilibrium is restored at the end, but not before the previously conservative Shepherd becomes a flamboyant dresser and changes personality. In a happy ending, he marries his fiancée, Sophie (Catherine Tate), and the characters dance on the Empire State Building. For this sequence, Isitt creates a magical feel, with the lights of New York seen initially in the distance as Shepherd takes a walk around accompanied by the music from various Christmas carols. Suddenly his memory returns and, at the last moment, he prevents Sophie from marrying someone else. In a conventional romantic ending, Shepherd appears at the entrance of the church dressed in a white suit with silver shoes and, seen centre frame, he approaches the camera down the aisle towards his fiancée. The film closes with a cut to the top of the Empire State Building, and joined by Poppy and the children of St Bernadette's, and even the offending donkey, all dance and sing as the camera withdraws. In all three films, through comedy, Isitt comments on social inequity.

Summary

This chapter commenced with mainstream or popular cinema as a model for analysis, yet these terms are imprecise, and in some cases difficult to define. Clearly the Harry Potter series and the James Bond movies fall into this remit because they follow the formula laid out by McDonald. Even so, they are US funded and intended and marketed as blockbusters with a wide release and all the accompanying tie-ins and merchandise. Also, they are clearly based on action and fantasy, and, as documented here, these are not genres in which women often work. Nevertheless, as demonstrated, women do make films which are box office successes, although when Sue Harper wrote that 'One thing is certain: a few women directors in the 1990s have moved into the mainstream' (2000: 235), she cannot have anticipated that, apart from Lloyd and Kidron, the 2000s would see women produce so small a number of blockbusters.

An exception is Lloyd's *Mamma Mia!*, which emerged as the 'new women's blockbuster', with a strong female lead, an exciting character who lives out her fantasies through an exotic lifestyle, with romance as its central theme. Nonetheless, even though women make few blockbuster productions, as the title of this chapter indicates, they do make popular, innovative and successful films. Indeed, British women directors have been financially successful on an international scale, whether their output consists of bio-pics or comedies. The bio-pics discussed here either hinge on a female central character (*The Iron Lady*, *An Education*, *Suffragette*), or offer prominence to female characters as in Taylor-Wood's *Nowhere Boy*. However, the category that dominates is comedy, which tends to deal with social issues and racial tension through a humorous style. Frequently, filmmakers use their own experience of hyphenated identity or mobility between classes and cultures as the basis for their dramas. What is apparent is that the variety and content of some of the work discussed here not only suggests skill and expertise in the craft of filmmaking, but also a concern to imbue mainstream cinema with female issues and to offer a voice to women through a variety of genres.

Notes

1. Ellen Cheshire (2015) attempts to define this through a series of guidelines and parameters.
2. Zambarloukos had worked on *Enduring Love* (2004) and *Venus* (2006) with film director Roger Michell, and *Sleuth* (2007) with Kenneth Branagh: both of whom came from theatrical backgrounds.
3. Hilary Radner aligns *Mamma Mia!* with *My Big Fat Greek Wedding* (Zwick 2002), suggesting that this 'highlights … the ways in which Conglomerate Hollywood uses industry figures such as Tom Hanks to provide counterprogramming to studio-produced tentpoles' (2011: 129).
4. Dogme principles were created by four Danish film directors, including Lars von Trier, and these evolved into a trademark for Danish film and television productions. The vows are to shoot on location using natural light and sound in order to seek a new means of expression. Based on a return to auteurism, their manifesto stipulated that the traditional rules of story, acting and theme must be obeyed instead of special effects.

5. The film won the Silver Bear Jury Prize at the Berlin Film Festival. Her previous films, made in Denmark, include *The Birthday Trip* (1991) and *On Our Own* (1998).
6. All figures are approximate and provided here to show the proportion of sponsorship awarded by the different funding bodies.
7. Scherfig's most recent British film released in 2014, *The Riot Club*—funded by Film4 and the BFI, and distributed by Universal Pictures in the UK—is set at Oxford University and is based upon a centuries-old debauched all male dining society, the Bullingdon Club. The film is described as a 'sobering attack on a culture of inherited privilege and power in Britain' (Anon. 2014: 25), and is adapted from the stage play *Posh* (2010) by Laura Wade. Tracking the appalling and debased behaviour of a group of ten Oxford undergraduates, *The Riot Club* makes intentional allusion to figures, then in the Cabinet, such as David Cameron, George Osborne and Boris Johnson, and their membership of the club in their early years at Oxford. The film involves an overview of upper- versus working-class dynamics using Old Etonian, Miles (Max Irons), and his working-class girlfriend, Lauren (Holliday Grainger) as the central characters, and gender and class differences are played out in the film. Wade wrote the script and was present for most of the time on set, and the film was produced by Peter Czernin who was also at Eton with Cameron. *The Riot Club* is a satirical sketch of the English class system, and divisions are further emphasised when Lauren is summoned and offered £27,000 for sex, which, as Dimitri (Ben Schnetzer) reminds her, is worth three years' tuition fees. Scherfig was chosen to direct the film because she isn't English and because 'it would be interesting to have a female director "and also somebody who wasn't from England, to get her view on class"' (Williams 2014: 40). In terms of cinematography, she represents each youth as an individual, and exposes the corruption of this stratum of society. Indeed, the film closes on one of the more obnoxious of the characters, Alistair Ryle (Sam Claflin), as he walks away from a meeting with his wealthy father, Jeremy (Tom Hollander), assured that he will not have to pay for his crime due to their high-level connections. Ultimately, he is offered an internship in a prosperous firm if he shields the club. *The Riot Club* received wide European release, but limited release in USA.

8. The bio-pic based on a musician often offers further opportunities for merchandise and reissues of CDs and films.
9. Scherfig's commitment to raise money comes from her belief that English-language films are the way forward for any commercially minded director, despite also taking pleasure in making films in her home country. Beeban Kidron was initially to direct the project, but dropped out when she received the green light from Working Title for *Hippie Hippie Shake* (unreleased).
10. As Hornby suggests, what drew him to the novel (based on Barber's own experiences) was that the author has a 'strong, sometimes confrontational voice in her profiles' (2009: 49).
11. However, according to Sadie Wearing, the film 'renders dementia a virtually "disembodied" experience, subject to Thatcher's famously indomitable "will" whose main function is, arguably, to merely provide a "narrative" alibi for the partial political perspective of the film' (2013: 318).
12. Lennon went to live with his aunt and his mother was barred from seeing him.
13. Taylor-Wood's latest film, *Fifty Shades of Grey* (2015) was a US/Japanese production and her success with *Nowhere Boy* enabled her to acquire US funding from Universal Pictures and thus move more into the mainstream. The film was distributed by Universal's UK distribution arm, Universal Pictures International, and was aimed at a female audience. It was described as 'a romantic fantasy and a fairytale, a story of sexual awakening' (Giles 2015: 64) and likened to 'the great expressive excesses of Douglas Sirk's Hollywood melodramas, lavish women's pictures such as *Written on the Wind* (1956) with its theme of unrequited love' (Giles 2015: 64). The film was passed uncut, cost $40 million to make, and to date has achieved over $166 million at the box office.
14. *Village at the End of the World* commences with an aerial view of an immense vista of a landscape consisting of mountains and the continuous expanse of an iceberg towering over a tiny cluster of homes. This bleak setting forms the backdrop for the ensuing combination of observation and interviews, but, far from romanticising the existence of the Inuits, Gavron shows the hardship of day-to-day living, including the slaughter of whales and polar bears for survival. The director selects the lives of a number of characters over a year as the Inuit people are threatened with the closure of a halibut fac-

tory, their main source of income. Subsequently, though, they form a collective in order to effect purchase.

15. Although it was actually shown three times that year.
16. This was not the first time a feature film directed by a woman opened the LFF. Other films include *Scrubbers* Mai Zetterling (1982), *Strange Days* by Kathryn Bigelow in 1996 and *In the Cut* by Jane Campion in 2003.
17. Morgan wrote a play entitled *Splendour* in 2000, *Sex Traffic* (2004)—a series for Channel 4, the screenplay for *Brick Lane* (Gavron 2007), *The Hour*, a BBC drama, and co-wrote *Shame* (2011) with Steve McQueen.
18. Although she is fictional, she is based on real people such as Hannah Mitchell, Annie Kenney and Annie Barnes. See Smyth (2015).
19. Gavron laments the lack of representation of women in lead roles in cinema in general, noting that none of the Oscar-nominated films for 2014 featured a female lead protagonist. See Gavron (2015: 288).
20. An estimated £3.5 million in total. See: http://www.imdb.com/title/tt0286499/ (accessed 4 December 2013).
21. At the time of writing Chadha is working on turning this into a musical. See Nagra (2014).
22. Chadha's later, *Angus, Thongs and Perfect Snogging* (2008) is a US/German/UK funded production based on the novels by Louise Rennison. The film, sponsored by Paramount, Goldcrest and attracting some UKFC support was 'aimed at audiences on both sides of the pond' (Mayer 2008: 52). A transnational success, it focused on teenager, Georgia Nicholson (Georgia Groome) and her group of friends. More recently, on 28 March 2014, Chadha began filming on location in Southall, Ealing and at Ealing Studios a British comedy entitled *It's a Wonderful Afterlife*. Bend It Films produced the film, which cost £6.5 million to make and was distributed by Hanway Films. Finance was also raised from the Indian Film Company of India and Coficine, the French bank—Chadha's aims 'to show you can make films with people of colour that make money' (Chadha 2004: 37). In a similar vein to Chadha, Pratibha Parmar's films use comedy to explore racial tensions. Parmar is a Nairobi-born British director of Indian descent. After studying for a degree at Bradford University she attended Birmingham

University's Centre for Contemporary Cultural Studies, co-authoring a book with Paul Gilroy and Valerie Amos about race relations in 1970s Britain. Her early work consists of documentaries and shorts and she later directed the documentary *Alice Walker: Beauty in Truth* (2013). This film did not gain theatrical distribution, although, as Sophie Mayer argues, 'Parmar was able to reshape the bio-doc subtly, interweaving a portrayal of artist-activist with a portrait of Walker as gardener, living the truth and beauty of her writing through her interconnected nurturing of the land and community' (2016: 196). *Nina's Heavenly Delights* (2006) is Parmar's first feature film and introduces a number of themes to the narrative, including lesbian relationships within a Scottish-Asian society. Funded by Scottish Screen, the film adopts a Bollywood approach, introducing singing and dancing at appropriate moments to underscore the comedy. In January 2015, Parmar continued with her documentary work with *Intercourse: The Life and Work of Andrea Dworkin*. The film was a US release costing $1 million to make and focuses on the controversial feminist writer, Andrea Dworkin, through various actors at different stages of her life.

23. Prior to this, Isitt directed *Confetti* (2006), which was sponsored by the BBC and Screen West Midlands. The film is a mockumentary and gained widespread theatrical release making over £635,000 in its opening weekend.

CHAPTER 6

Alternatives to Mainstream and Classic Modes of Narration

There are a number of alternatives to mainstream fiction and classic modes of narration, and this chapter examines the work of women directors in this arena. It commences with an attempt at a broad definition of these 'alternatives', which are frequently described as counter-cinema, experimental cinema and avant-garde, although, in many respects, the work and techniques defy labelling. Counter-cinema is founded on the premise that ideology is embedded in mainstream cinema through its formal language, and it is this that filmmakers challenge and subvert by breaking with conventional codes of narration. This occurs through the disruption of linear cause-and-effect relationships, lack of narrative closure, and the rupturing of spatial and temporal relations. Furthermore, a process of distanciation is also a feature of counter-cinema and all these ingredients dislocate the traditional organisation of mainstream cinema. Feminist counter-cinema theory and practice materialised through the work of Laura Mulvey and Claire Johnston who argued that mainstream cinema is dominated by patriarchal ideology, and the only means of breaking with this authority is to produce a style of filmmaking dictated by a feminist aesthetic. Such an approach subverts patriarchal control, introducing non-linear structures, lack of continuity editing and non-psychologically rounded figures that we don't know and cannot comprehend. Avant-garde cinema also creates dissociation by challenging the codes and conventions of classical-style cinema. Originating in art history, the term dates back to some early

S. Hockenhull, *British Women Film Directors in the New Millennium*, DOI 10.1057/978-1-137-48992-0_6

nineteenth-century French painting which was seen as an attack on the establishment and its traditions. Avant-garde is a military term meaning an advance military group attacking the enemy ahead of the main army and, as Michael O'Pray asks, 'With film in mind, we may ask who represents the main army and who the enemy?' (2003: 3). For him, mainstream cinema is the army whereas the avant-garde is 'the advanced group foraging for new techniques, forms of expression and subject-matter' (2003: 3). Avant-garde cinema is located within a short period of history, although it can be used to describe aesthetic practice in general. Experimental cinema is also relevant to mainstream film and can denote changes in technique and 'simply provides traditional cinema with more variety of expression ... experiment does not imply radical social or political ideas often associated with the avant-gardes' (O'Pray 2003: 5). Counter-cinema and avant-garde cinema often, but not always, tend to be independently financed and are thus relatively free from aesthetic constraints, and the final product is frequently the result of a collaborative work. Whether it be counter, avant-garde or experimental, as Alison Butler contends, 'Under the influence of the women's movement, an agenda emerged ... which prioritised the body, the personal and the intersubjective power relations ... with a distinct set of concerns of its own' (2002: 59).

The body, the personal and intersubjective power relations are characteristic of non-mainstream cinema translated as an autobiographical stance. Even though, as Judith Mayne (1990) argues, women have difficulty saying 'I', because historically their relationship with cinema has been, in Mulvey's terms, passive, and also because the film industry has a different relationship with men than it does with women (1990: 97), much counter-cinema, and avant-garde and experimental films have an authorial self-inscription. The filmmakers offer an autobiographical or personal aspect which encourages self-reflexivity and a revelation of the process of filmmaking. However, as Mayne concedes, 'The notion of authorship is not simply a useful political strategy; it is crucial to the reinvention of cinema that has been undertaken by women filmmakers and feminist spectators' (1990: 97).

The 'I' impediment that Mayne refers to is sometimes addressed in non-mainstream cinema by women appearing in their own films, as actor or voice-over, or working with autobiographical content, although there are a number of other ways to perform authorship, including the self-inscribed mode of documentary and fiction films. This may involve the filmic self-portrait and essay where authors are associated in the exploration so that

'The frame becomes the metaphor demarcating both the authors' place in the world they film and the impossibility of containing themselves within a rigid narrative or image' (Sayad 2013: xxiv). Sarah Turner's film, *Perestroika* (2009), fits into this category, her work using fine art practices to create an intensely visual aesthetic as metaphor for her feelings. However, in addition to creating a dialogue about herself, she also becomes fictionalised in the process, blurring the boundaries between fact and fabrication. Not only is *Perestroika* semi-autobiographical, it also traverses the borders beyond the personal to more extensive subjects such as global warming, documenting the landscape and the environmental damage inflicted through climate change, as well as the director's anguish and sorrow at this and other events that have occurred in her life.

Filmmakers such as Sally Potter, who is 'undoubtedly the most imaginative of the new directors' (Harper 2000: 201), produce varied work and, to date, her output has been discussed in some detail by various scholars (Fowler 2003; Mayer 2008, 2009a). Through the formal language that she deploys in films such as *Yes* (2004) and *Rage* (2009), she challenges conventional codes of narration, distancing the spectator and denying equilibrium at the close of the film. While her later *Ginger & Rosa* (2012) fits more into the tradition of mainstream cinema, using known actors as psychologically rounded characters, and linearity through cause and effect, there is no narrative closure. Moreover, Potter includes biographical details from her own youth to self-inscribe the film, hence its inclusion in this chapter. In addition to Potter's films, documentary cinema, mainly in terms of women using a direct mode of address, is included here for consideration separately from the films discussed in Chap. 3. This is because it emerges in the work of filmmakers such as Gillian Wearing and Sophie Fiennes as a creative artefact rather than a message, the filmmakers adopting various forms in their work, particularly in the components and features of construction they deploy. As Sayad suggests, 'The documentary may also be a vehicle for self-investigation' (2013: xxiv), and in Wearing's films her authorial presence functions as a vehicle to prompt the subjects involved to express their own feelings.

Sally Potter

Potter studied dance and choreography at the London School of Contemporary Dance before becoming an apprentice at the London Film-makers' Co-op. She made a number of shorts between 1969 and

1971 prior to her launch of *Thriller* (1979), a protest about female death in classical tragedy, and financed by the Arts Council of Great Britain. The film's success led to more funding opportunities and, in 1983, Channel 4 and the BFI awarded a grant of £250,000 for her first feature release, *The Gold Diggers*. Potter's early work developed alongside feminist film theory for a time, although it is also relevant to consider her oeuvre in relation to authorship in that she deliberately makes herself the authoring presence. *The Gold Diggers* was shot in Iceland, and involves an all-female crew and cast;[1] it adopts a Marxist stance telling the story of two women trapped by capitalism and patriarchy. Exploring women as economic and cultural symbols, this production, and indeed much of Potter's early work, rejects film as purely a representational medium by avoiding the appropriation of women for the male gaze, as identified by Mulvey;[2] instead she deploys an alternative film form to counter narrative's 'visual pleasure', thus also dispensing with the suspension of disbelief. Potter continued to make features such as *Tears, Laughter, Fear and Rage* (1986) and *I Am an Ox, I Am a Horse, I Am a Man, I Am a Woman* (1990)—both for Channel 4—and *Orlando* (1992), a highly aesthetic and radically feminist film with a contemporary take on Victorian life. Made with European Co-production Funds, *Orlando* was a costume drama of sorts, and a relative success, making over $1 million at the box office.[3]

Her work in the new millennium continues in this vein with *Yes*. The dialogue is totally in verse and here Potter deliberately flouts the mainstream filmic conventions of editing and framing, the camera frequently moving between shots that encourage subjectivity, especially her own subjectivity. Set in London, the narrative focuses on a married couple who barely speak to each other; She (Joan Allen), an Irish/ American scientist, and Anthony (Sam Neill). She meets a former Lebanese doctor, now a chef, referred to throughout as He (Simon Abkarian) and they have an affair. In the meantime Anthony makes advances to She's teenage goddaughter, Grace (Stephanie Leonodis), which results in a breakdown of their marriage. She and He conduct their relationship through stories of their past growing up in troubled countries: She grew up in Belfast and He in Lebanon. The couple part but are reunited, this being shown in a series of passionate embraces through a sequence of dissolves.

Yes opens with the sound of a machine running, although the screen is almost blank apart from what appear to be particles of dust in the air. This is the debris created by the cleaner who speaks first to the camera/spectator. Here Potter defies the suspension of disbelief as the maid

(Shirley Henderson) initiates the story by telling us tales of Anthony's infidelities. Such an approach deliberately presents a female articulation in Anthony's world to construct him as a dislikeable character, and the maid divulges information about his extra-marital affairs as she fishes condoms out of the toilet, while explaining the processes involved in her indiscretion.

Indeed, throughout the film, Potter flouts the rules of classical film-making, inserting black-and-white footage without explanation, as though the characters are visible only through the optic of surveillance. In one sequence, She and Anthony are at a formal dinner where He is working. Through a series of edits, Potter eliminates the other guests focusing on He and She and the creation of their liaison. A cut to an extreme close-up of a washbasin alters the location, and She emerges from the cubicle and gazes into a mirror. Her inner thoughts are heard as an internal diegetic voice-over suggesting possible reminiscences about a conversation held earlier with He, although this is unclear. From an overhead shot She comes into sight in the grand hallway of the building, but Potter changes the hues and appearance of the film, presenting the scene in low resolution to give a CCTV effect in order to suggest surveillance. Subsequently, She hands He a note and the camera reframes him in medium shot, whereby the colour, previously drained to almost a monochrome effect, reappears.

Later in the film, She presents an illustrated talk to a group of people in a room. She introduces a slide of a sperm and the image fills the frame before blurring and then dissolving into an extreme close-up of a drain. This links with the cleaner's earlier exposure of Anthony's infidelity and returns the spectator to the microscopic specks of dust that opened the film. As Mayer suggests, 'What appears to be an intimate love story is presented as a parable about the physics, politics and metaphysics of visibility and invisibility related directly to the audience by the Cleaner' (2016: 194). Throughout, Potter retains a distancing effect, observing conversations between the lovers at a remove, and sometimes obscuring them completely, only retaining their dialogue. Moreover, the director deals with the passage of time through a series of microscopic close-ups of the sperm which She analyses under a microscope, and then cuts to images of He in the kitchen and a series of fast-motion shots to progress the narrative.

All the way through *Yes*, Potter specifically gives voice to the cleaners as they are the only people to directly address camera. We are never given background information about these women but they are prioritised by Potter as key characters. In another example, She collects her god-daughter Grace from school and they go to a swimming pool. They discuss weight and age in the changing rooms, and a cleaner (Barbara Oxley) is seen in the background mopping the cubicles before approaching the camera with a knowing smile. When they have left the space, Potter keeps the camera on the cleaner rather than follow the pair out, prioritising her and permitting her the same knowledge as the spectator as well as direct address.

In line with a classical Hollywood ending, the film offers some resolution, as He and She are reunited; He has returned from Beirut and She from Belfast and they meet in Cuba. Thus, despite all odds, ostensibly the film has a happy ending. However, Potter provides the spectator with no such fairytale or assurance. Indeed, as Mayer points out, 'In mainstream cinema, romantic resolution overshadows and simultaneously underscores the restitution of social order at the end of the film. The suspended time of *Yes*'s conclusion offers no such guarantees. Rather than "happily ever after", the ending offers "happily for now"' (2009a: 201). Mayer attributes this to the final scene in which the place is 'neither geographically located nor tied into the film's narrative space' (2009a: 201), thereby leaving an air of uncertainty. Intended as one of several shorts about love in Paris (although this altered, culminating in a feature), *Yes* was funded by the UKFC's New Cinema Fund.

Her later *Rage* (2009) was also UKFC financed through the same fund, and is set in New York. The film concerns a schoolboy, Michelangelo (Sally Potter), who interviews by phone 13 characters associated with a New York fashion house which is about to launch a new perfume. Never seen, although from the comments made it is assumed that he is a young non-white male, Michelangelo hesitantly types each day of the filmed action which he then blogs. At one point the spectator is informed that he is crying but we don't see this, instead we are reliant only on verbal information. The notion that the spectator is watching a series of interviews, which are then posted online, is innovative and replicated in the multi-platform release pattern of the film which was undertaken through a synchronised satellite premiere at multiple cinemas, DVD release, with the option of free online or mobile phone streaming.

In *Rage*, Potter grants the spectator agency and co-authorship of meaning. Using star names such as Jude Law (Minx), Judi Dench (Mona Carvell), Eddie Izzard (Tiny Diamond) and Steve Buscemi (Frank) to name a few, the film provides a comment on capitalism and ethics with the result that 'a celebrity perfume looms larger in our consciousness than the devastating impact of globalised capitalism' (Mayer 2009b: 69). The film follows a similar format to Potter's earlier *The Tango Lesson*, which is a UK/France/Argentina/Japan/Germany co-production in which Potter plays a film director, and which also concerns voyeurism, excess and surface appearance.[4]

Indeed, in *The Tango Lesson*, and also in *Rage*, Potter is aware of Mulvey's critique of fetishism, and therefore professes to subvert the dominant male gaze, instead assigning the 'to-be-looked-at-ness' to the male lead (see Guano 2004). Each person in *Rage* is a fictional employer or employee of the New York fashion house, and each is interviewed and appears alone in medium shot in the frame against a colour background, Potter thus introducing a type of visual minimalism. Michelangelo is in fact Potter, who injects her own presence as she hand-holds the camera, inviting a voyeuristic gaze from the spectator. Within the narrative, Potter creates a murder, but this occurs within the confines of the on-screen conversation of the protagonists, thereby forcing the spectator to work at constructing the narrative from the dialogue to create a mock documentary. The film is thus difficult to categorise, but is described by Potter as possessing a 'no-waste aesthetic, which is now paradoxically appropriate for recession filmmaking' (in Nick Bradshaw 2009a: 39). In the final sequence, Lettuce (Lily Cole), one of the interviewees, takes the camera from Michelangelo and turns it on him, but there it ends, and Potter is never disclosed as the fictitious character. In making low-budget films the director takes responsibility to keep the costs down and in this case, Potter decided to be progressive with her release strategies. Shot on HD, *Rage*, as noted, was released concurrently to cinemas in its traditional format, and on DVD, the internet and mobile phones in a serialised form. It premiered at the BFI Southbank with simultaneous releases around the country and an interactive satellite broadcast Q&A.

Potter's later *Ginger & Rosa* is unusual in that it is her most intelligible film to date and, for this reason, does not fit well into this section. However, it is included here because its subject matter is rooted in Potter's youth, and also because its political agenda is still current and topical. The narrative is straightforward and centres on the friendship of two 17-year-old best friends, Ginger (Elle Fanning) and Rosa (Alice Englert), as indicated by the title. In this, Potter traverses from oppositional-style cinema to a more mainstream production, yet one that questions gender identity and politics in the 1960s. Set in 1962, Ginger and Rosa were born at the same time on the day of the Hiroshima bombing, and their mothers met in hospital. Rosa is the product of a single-parent family and has enjoyed a liberated upbringing, whereas Ginger's two parents have been present throughout her childhood, but now prepare to separate. Ginger's father (Alessandro Nivola), a left-wing academic and Second World War conscientious objector, leaves the family household, but his political legacy remains with his daughter, who becomes a member of CND, regularly attending meetings. Rosa and Roland, Ginger's father, commence an affair, and Ginger discovers her father's infidelity when all three stay on his boat. Rosa becomes pregnant and Ginger is arrested during a peace march. Natalie (Christina Hendricks), Ginger's mother, is a woman who gave up her career as an artist (as did many of that generation immediately post-war) to raise a family. Made with BFI and BBC funding, and supported by the Danish Film Institute, *Ginger & Rosa* is a film about intensity of emotion and mother/daughter, father/daughter relationships. Potter chose the year 1962 because it was the time of the Cuban missile crisis and CND protests, as well as an innovative period in filmmaking and youth culture. Employing the cinematographer, Robbie Ryan because of his hand-held camera skills and distinctive application of light (in Mayer 2012: 34), Potter tells the story primarily from Ginger's perspective—Ginger representing her own experiences. The backdrop to the narrative is explained by the fact that the director is politically motivated and was active at Greenham Common in the early 1980s, and more recently the Occupy London camps, fighting for a greener environment and campaigning against the causes of climate change.

Ginger & Rosa opens with a shot of a grainy red screen which fills the frame, before a mushroom cloud is seen erupting into the sky. A fade to black reveals a devastated landscape devoid of human inhabitants, the camera panning left to right as a subtitle 'Hiroshima 1945' appears on the screen. This opening of the Hiroshima bombing heralds the turbulent relationships in the film, which commence at the outset as Ginger and Rosa's mothers give birth simultaneously. Seen from an overhead shot, the two mothers scream and pant as the girls are born. At one point they reach out, and their joined hands are shown in close-up, set against the austere blue background of the hospital. Potter moves the narrative swiftly forward, cutting immediately to a shot of the girls' fathers waiting outside, before a further edit displays a back view of two young girls seated on swings holding hands. The camera pans out to reveal Natalie comforting Rosa's mother, Anoushka (Jodhi May), who is in tears. A further edit shows an extreme close-up of Rosa's face watching her father walk from the house carrying a suitcase. Within the space of just over two minutes, Potter has eclipsed time and reached the year 1962, putting the age of the girls at 17.

Not only does *Ginger & Rosa* cover CND and single parenthood in the 1960s, but the director also demonstrates the unfairness of the education system at that time: Rosa fails the 11 plus, the spectator is informed, and this fact is shown through the two different lives that the girls lead. Potter also perceives Natalie as part of a generation of lost women. Initially, she shows her as an anxious parent, and the only person in the relationship to keep a check on her daughter, but throughout the film she pays the price for this, and is excluded from the close tripartite rapport between Ginger and her father, Ginger and Rosa, and Rosa and Roland. Later, Natalie serves up dinner to Roland and Ginger, who are seated opposite one another smiling conspiratorially. They eat without comment, unaware that Natalie has remained standing, awaiting thanks for her efforts. Potter highlights Natalie's frustration in the ensuing conversation, and Roland accuses her of martyrdom, emphasising that he has 'been working all day', thus reinforcing his wife's subordinate and unemployed status. He further advises Natalie to take up her painting again, or get a job, and the camera focuses on her distraught face, her make-up smudged by tears as she retorts rhetorically, 'Anyway, what kind of job could I get?' It is only when Roland leaves and begins an affair with Rosa that Natalie gains true independence and takes up painting again. Ginger returns home following the discovery of her father's infidelity and learns that her mother has started rebuilding her life, *Ginger & Rosa* revisiting the past now from a feminist perspective. Natalie's independence is short-lived, however, when she finds out that Rosa is having an affair with Roland and is pregnant. The camera frames a hysterical Ginger, who reveals this information to her mother, whereby a cut from the girl's point of view frames Natalie's face as she digests this news, Roland seated on the staircase behind. As a result of this betrayal, Natalie then takes an overdose.

The melodramatic narrative unfolds against a politicised milieu through which Potter injects an autobiographical element. She was taken on Ban the Bomb marches, and sees herself in the young teenage girls, particularly Ginger. This is foregrounded in Ginger's relationship with her godfather, Mark (Timothy Spall), and his partner, Mark Two (Oliver Platt). Both participated in the Ban the Bomb marches, the spectator is informed, and Mark Two's sister Bella (Annette Bening) is also a political activist, encouraging Ginger as a militant.

The final sequences show Ginger and Roland seated in the hospital at night time awaiting the outcome of Natalie's attempted suicide. An edit reveals that it is now daylight, and the pair remain at the hospital. Ginger writes poetry based on her friendship with Rosa, and the words are heard through internal diegetic sound:

> We had a dream that we would always be best friends. When we were born, for some it was the end. Now it seems there may not be a tomorrow, but despite the horror and the sorrow, I love our world. I want us all to live. Now Rosa, you've asked me to forgive. One day, if mum survives this bitter night, then we shall meet again and I will say 'I loved you Rosa' don't you see. But we are different. You dream of everlasting love. Not me. Because what really matters is to live, and if we do, there will be nothing to forgive ... but I'll forgive you anyway.

Throughout the monologue Roland, his eyes closed, is visible in the background. He apologises for his behaviour, but Ginger ignores him and turns away. She is prepared to forgive her friend, but not her father. Her face remains in close-up, whereas Roland is now marginalised in the frame and, here, Potter gains some closure, with the final message suggesting that women emerge strong and in control although we are unsure whether Natalie will survive, and whether Rosa and Roland will continue their affair.

Potter believes this to be her most comprehensible film to date. Given that *Orlando* (1992), a reworking of Virginia Woolf's novel, concerned gender ambiguity, and *Yes* was written in rhyme and takes a feminist perspective, *Ginger & Rosa* follows a narrative trajectory of equilibrium, disequilibrium and closure in a more traditional format, leading film critic Lisa Mullen to pan the director for using a biographical approach. As she states, 'By aiming for a light touch, Potter has made her framework so flimsy that it totters under the weight of the tragic upheavals it unfolds. It's odd to find such a bold filmmaker holding back so stiffly, and you come away wondering if the material was just too personal for her to close in on' (2012: 89). However, as Mayer points out, *Ginger & Rosa* forms part of contemporary British feminist cinema which is 'deeply concerned with trauma, not as a spectacle, but a route to representational justice ... A film such as *Ginger and Rosa* negotiates perceptively through the double binds of public/private and visible/invisible, not least through its attention to the secrets of the archive that allow for a thoroughgoing re-vision of historical girlhoods' (2016: 96). The film opened at various film festivals in 2012, including the US Telluride, the Toronto International Film Festival and the LFF, and gained a reasonable box office success, taking nearly $50,000 in its opening weekend on three US screens.

Sarah Turner

The aforementioned Turner studied Fine Art, Film and Video at Central Saint Martins in the late 1980s, followed by an MA at the Slade School of Art. She was mentored by Lis Rhodes and was involved in the female distribution companies, Circles and Cinenova. In her seminal film, *Perestroika*, Turner and her companion travel by train across Siberia to Lake Baikal. The film takes place where a close friend of Turner's died 20 years earlier and, throughout the journey, Turner, who is the producer, writer, editor and cinematographer of the film (along with Matthew Walter), records her thoughts. Although chiming with the British interest in landscape in the work of other avant-garde directors such as Derek Jarman, Chris Welsby and Patrick Keiller, this film looks instead at the Soviet landscape which is documented twice: once when Turner visited the terrain 20 years previously between 1987 and 1988, and the second between 2007 and 2008.

Visually, Turner's work draws on her art background using experimental aesthetics, and based on experience, yet with the emphasis on ecological concerns. This approach is exemplified in her earlier *Ecology* (2007) where the spectator is enlightened via the point of view of a mother and child, Turner juxtaposing sound and image to construct memory. *Ecology* was screened as part of the Derek Jarman series at the Serpentine Gallery, and, for Turner, who experienced a head injury that causes retrograde amnesia and so is unable to recall the initial journey, the film creates rather than records experiences. The replication of the earlier journey parallels the storytelling, as the framing narration moves between past and present, functioning as an 'environmental allegory. Are we all ghosts passing through as the world moves outside the frame of our (overheated) windows?' (in Darke 2010: 47).

In *Perestroika* Turner therefore performs both fact and fiction simultaneously. Early on in the film, in a semi-fictionalised account, she informs the spectator in mournful tone of her imagined death in a cycling accident, and throughout the film she places herself in fictional situations. The death she really refers to is that of her close friend, Sîan Thomas, who died in a cycling accident in Siberia some years after she and Turner had first visited there.

Ostensibly though, the film is about climate change but, rather than focusing on this as a fact-finding procedure, Turner creates a sublime set of images 'full of ominous portents: steam rising from the water is smoke, tourists taking holiday snaps are dancers on a volcano and, in an apocalyptic vision, Baikal becomes a lake of fire awaiting the final sunset' (Darke 2010: 47). The film is dominated by travelling shots, yet opens with a static hand-held image of the lake which fills the frame. Turner's voice-over explains the journey, both emotional and physical, that she is making. She cuts between images of the lake and a completely black screen as her commentary suggests she was 'manic' and 'reckless' when she experienced her fictional cycling accident. Turner recounts her own death and rebirth after the incident with a car, an allegory for her own memory loss, and the film therefore follows a loosely autobiographical vein throughout. She never appears on-screen, and only occasionally does the spectator catch a glimpse of her face in a night train window, which presents her as a disembodied spectral figure, anchored solely by her elegiac voice-over. As Sayad argues, 'what *Perestroika* attempts to frame visually is less the author's body than the landscape that mirrors her subjectivity' (2013: 60). The film is not only autobiographical but is a lament for, and tribute to both her friend Thomas and to the landscape. To achieve this, Turner compares early video material from her previous trip, which shows a landscape covered in deep snow, with the same places filmed in the new millennium in order to make the political statement; in other words, the more recent footage now has little snow due to climate change.

Perestroika mixes stills with video; the diegetic sound sometimes matches the visuals but at other times Turner interjects haunting noises and chanting, and Turner's voice-over description is non-synchronous to image. As Butler argues, in women's experimental cinema there is a prevalence of films that 'play against the conventions of synchronised sound to create separations and disjunctions of body and voice' (2002: 78). This, she suggests, is because to synchronise the two only results in 'impoverishment and entrapment' for women in the Hollywood tradition of filmmaking (2002: 78). Turner certainly moves away from the predictable, and introduces a personal voice although we rarely actually see her. Despite this, she draws on her own lived experience at times, thus inscribing herself into the film. Indeed, Turner suggests that *Perestroika* is a ghost story, because 'it explores how experience is framed through memory – memory as a set of stories we tell ourselves and others' (in Darke 2010: 47).

Later in the film, night time on the train turns to day as Turner continues to film through the window of the Trans-Siberian Express. Using long takes, she focuses on the trees visible through the train windows, their branches forming a pattern against the bleak grey sky. Additionally, she introduces the sounds of the camera shutter to accompany the images thus drawing attention to the filmmaking process itself. To further emphasise this point, the shots subsequently appear as a series of stills rather than as a continuous sequence. As Paul Newland suggests, 'in this film the notion of the journey also becomes a profoundly rich metaphor for life, death, memory and mourning' (2013: 6), and while the film documents Turner's travel, her verbal memories reconstruct the past for the spectator. Described as possessing a 'formalist rigour' (Darke 2010: 46) in line with the traditions of the London Film-makers' Co-op, *Perestroika* maintains a rhythm throughout. Similar to other female documentary-makers concerned with the environment, Turner also notes the changes that have occurred at Lake Baikal since she shot footage there 20 years previously. The film carries multiple meanings and these are never fully explicated by the filmmaker, nor become obvious to the viewer. Instead, spectacular images of the landscape are presented which are open to interpretation; for example, towards the latter part of the film, Turner captures the final rays of a setting sun and the rich orange and red hues fill the frame, this time accompanied by African-style tribal singing, but no explanation is given.

Perestroika continues to maintain a separation between Turner's voice, which fixes her in off-screen space, and the on-screen images that are intensely visual, yet ones she does not fully describe, instead remaining removed, impassive and unemotional in her explanation. Further, we are frequently spoken to by the director as though in a personal address. Ultimately, the film is not only autobiographical, it also explains Turner's experiences and what she is feeling, and is an 'environmental allegory' (Darke 2010: 47); indeed, it gives information about Siberia and climate issues, and provides a larger picture of global concerns. The film was funded by Film London Artists' Moving Image Network, the Arts Council England and Film London, and was also subsidised by the University of Kent's School of Arts.

Gillian Wearing

In 2007, the UKFC issued an invitation for a number of British artists to put forward a proposal for a feature-length film, and Turner Prize-winner Gillian Wearing was one of the artists to do so. The result is a disturbing combination of fact and fiction entitled *Self Made* (2010). Despite only previously directing shorts and videos, Wearing, who left school at 16 with no qualifications, felt comfortable moving into full-length films: as she explains, 'Once you work in moving film it's very hard not to think that you want to engage with the cinema ... I did feel like an artist making my film, though the film is for a cinema not an art gallery' (in de Witt 2011: 12).

The film owes a debt to some of Wearing's earlier films such as *Confess All on Video. Don't Worry. You Will Be in Disguise. Intrigued? Call Gillian* (1994). In this, the faces of the participants are hidden behind masks and they subsequently confess their inner thoughts and transgressive fancies. In both *10–16* (1997), and her three-screen video allegory, *Drunk* (1997–9), which showed at the London Serpentine Gallery and the Musée d'Art Modern de la Ville de Paris in 2001, a number of children's voices overlay the figures of adults, processing a variety of audible thoughts. This and other films by Wearing reveal the significance of the authorial presence by constructing a complex set of relationships between the filmmaker, the spectator and the subjects. The later *Family History* (2006) makes autobiographical reference to reality television, and the viewer is made aware that there is both a re-enactment and a revisitation in the process. Wearing hoped that the audience would benefit from the experience of watching the film by reflecting more on their own lives as a result. Throughout her career she has situated human stories, particularly those of ordinary people, at the nucleus of her films, and she claims that these are akin to portraits.

In order to recruit for the film, Wearing placed adverts online, in newspapers and job centres, as well as in *Time Out*, for people to appear in *Self Made*, with the proviso that they could either play themselves or a fictional character. She received thousands of replies, and seven were eventually chosen because Wearing liked them and they had good stories. These included Asheq Akhtar, Dave Austin, James Baron, Simon Manley, Jerome Prince, Lesley Robinson and Lian Stewart. The respondents were trained by the method actor tutor, Sam Rumbelow, in various styles of acting and modes of exploring their own emotions and memories. Wearing was drawn to method acting because she felt it was close to emotional truth, thus 'allowing yourself and your body to be truthful with your character' (in de Witt 2011: 12). This involved rigorous improvisation workshops before the participants acted out their personal dramas.

The film commences with a definition of the word 'method' before she cuts to a shot of a man approaching the camera. She tracks him for some seconds before cutting to a rear view as he walks down an alleyway accompanied by the non-diegetic sound of a meditative chant. Wearing continues to document his progress, but the spectator is denied any knowledge of this person, as he walks around a residential area before throwing a carrier bag to the floor. The film cuts on the sound of a man coughing and the film's title and Wearing's name appear. A further edit reveals an extreme close-up of a woman's face as she explains that the camera knows whether a person is photogenic or not—her conversation inane and unrelated to the previous sequence. This opening is therefore non-linear and it is only later that the initial sequence makes sense and is linked to subsequent developments. An inter-title reads 'Lesley replied to an advert' and then the advert appears asking 'Would You Like to Be in a Film: You Can Play Yourself or a Fictional Character?' All the respondents then introduce themselves on camera, providing some short autobiographical details. The film continues as Rumbelow introduces them to breathing exercises and meditation, the director filming the procedure and then their reactions to it. However, whereas Wearing proceeds with the aim of documenting what she sees, she undercuts this realism with techniques such as inventive editing. An example of this occurs when the group act out a scenario where Lian must envisage a meeting she has just had with her father, with whom she has a problematic relationship. Throughout, the group are asked to identify their personal problems, neuroses and demons, the purpose of this being that their sketches enable catharsis. In this vignette, the group are all assembled on seats which are meant to represent a carriage on the London Underground. One by one they depart as though passengers, but Wearing does not show their exit, using invisible editing to eventually reveal only Lesley and Lian remaining on the imaginary train, the latter appearing lonely and distressed. Throughout, Rumbelow attempts to make the group improvise and experience different sensations, and these occurrences enable the emergence of their inner feelings and emotions. All of the group members talk to camera to explain their personal circumstances, hurts and disappointments, and they then are placed in situations pertinent to their history. The results are five cameos (two of the group members are not included although this fact is unexplained) based on the participants' fantasies, ranging from explorations of difficult family relationships, to their confrontation of bullying in childhood.

In one scenario, another story is built around Lian and her negligent father: Wearing recreates a Shakespeare *King Lear* sequence, Lian playing Cordelia. The director admits to being influenced by the 1974 observational documentary entitled *The Family* (Watson), which disrupted convention and was exploitative, raising questions of voyeurism. In a similar way, she perceives *Self Made* as a 'convergence of drama, psychotherapy and social experiment' (Fisher 2011: 76). An edit from Lian in medium shot talking to camera reveals a theatre stage which is filmed from a high angle. This cuts to her 'father' asking the family to declare who loves him most. At this juncture we hear Lian/Cordelia's inner diegetic thoughts expressed: 'What shall I do? Love and be silent' she states in character but also in relation to her real feelings. The confusion for the spectator lies in the blurring of fact and fiction given that Lian plays Cordelia, yet re-enacts and expresses her inner thoughts concerning her father. At the end of this sequence Lian leaves the stage, and the camera cuts to a shot of her with her real father explaining that, as a result of the film, she has made contact with him and they are in communication on a weekly basis—thus she achieves emotional release. Wearing continues to film the other group members, but this time reverts to improvisations and method acting in the warehouse rather than, as she does with Lian, on stage. Furthermore, she follows them out into the changing area in order to capture their 'off-screen' reactions to the day's filming.

In a later and shocking sequence, James enacts an event on a train. Seated opposite Simon, he confronts then attacks him. In an invisibly edited scene he is seen vigorously and viciously punching a dummy, although initially it is Simon that he assaults while shouting expletives and obscenities. The spectator learns that James was bullied as a child, and this has made him angry and aggressive. Later, a re-enactment takes place outside his house where he is stabbed by a group of youths. Wearing then edits to James describing his experience before showing her filming the film, thus drawing attention to the filmmaker within the filmmaking process. Later, when Wearing provides Lesley with screen space to undergo her healing processes, she switches to black-and-white images of the bare branches of trees swaying in the wind. A further edit reveals Lesley carrying some heavy bags along the lane and, as the imagined scenario is wartime, one must assume that Wearing is reverting to monochrome either for the purposes of realism (monochrome film stock was more readily available then) or to signify the distant past. However, Lesley remains herself, rather than acting in character. At one juncture, she is accosted by a man who attempts to seduce her but he is rejected because, as we have been led to believe earlier, Lesley was abused by her father as a child.

In another vignette, Wearing shows Dave talking about Mussolini and the image is of him after his death hanging upside down. This is shown in a photograph, and then the film cuts to a close-up of Dave, in the same position, blood streaming from his nose. When Asheq's turn arrives, his personal cameo returns to the opening sequences of the film whereby he is revealed as the mysterious person whom the spectator first encountered, but this time, when he drops the bag, he lives out his fantasy of kicking a pregnant woman whom he encounters on the street. The spectator learns that, as a child, Asheq witnessed his mother's abuse by his stepfather, and Rumbelow encourages him to relive the attack, but this time with a dead pig which he has hung on the wall.

In sum, Wearing's film uses documentary techniques such as talking heads, but she subverts conventions by filming the filming taking place. Throughout *Self Made*, she permits the spectator to see the preparation of the vignettes, with Rumbelow extracting emotional past experiences and memories from the participants. As Lucy Reynolds argues, '"Self Made" draws the viewer into patterns of identification familiar from the television makeover genre, with its narratives of redemption and emotional transformation' (2010: 26). Reynolds was reviewing Wearing's film as a contributor to the BFI LFF in 2010, and she attributes its style to the advent of the camcorder and a lineage of British TV culture. Although she confesses to struggling with funding to finance her work and she argues that the application process can thwart confidence (in Enright 2011), on this occasion she was fortunate. *Self Made* was produced by Kate Ogborn and co-financed by the UKFC Development and New Cinema Funds, Northern Film and Media, the Arts Council, Channel 4, Britdoc Foundation and supported by Abandon Normal Devices Festival.[5]

Sophie Fiennes

In a similar vein to Longinotto's and Ayisi's unassuming style of filming discussed in Chap. 3, documentary filmmaker Sophie Fiennes also allows events to unfold in front of the camera, although her refusal to dominate the film results in a more experimental style. Born in Suffolk, Fiennes briefly attended art school before working with Peter Greenaway from 1987 to 1992. Influenced by the director's experimental techniques and ideas, she began making her own films for the BBC, including short documentaries such as *Lars from 1–10* (1998), and *The Late Michael Clark* (2000) about the iconoclastic Scottish dancer and choreographer. Her later *Because I Sing* (2001) is a documentary about the collaboration of a number of London choirs, and was coordinated by Artangel, an organisation which commissions and produces experimental projects. Consisting of 16 different singing groups installed under one roof in the Roundhouse, a London performing arts venue, for two nights, Fiennes's documentary demonstrates how the event came together. *Because I Sing* illustrates the diversity of London's population, including the London Gay Men's Chorus, South Hampstead School for Girls choir, a Congolese choir, a Maori group, a Jewish choir and a Welsh male voice choir.

Hoover Street Revival (2002) was Fiennes's first feature documentary, and told the story of the preacher, the Reverend Noel Jones, of a Pentecostal church community in Los Angeles. Fiennes was drawn to the subject following a visit some years earlier when she listened to his hypnotic sermon. As she acknowledges, 'I was astonished by it – the charisma of the preacher and the whole event of church. I was amazed by how sophisticated that sermon was ... he had me glued to my seat, even as everyone around me stamped their feet up and down the aisles' (in Macnab 2002: 10). Made for approximately €0.5 million, *Hoover Street Revival* was shot using borrowed money and credit cards. The film not only documents the celebratory church services, but also, what at times transpires to be the very difficult daily existence of the mainly black congregation. It achieved theatrical release and was showcased at the Edinburgh Film Festival, the Locarno Film Festival and the Adelaide International Film Festival.

Throughout *Hoover Street Revival*, Fiennes offers the spectator intimate and sometimes shocking events, such as the moment when a woman discovers the death of her son while recording is taking place. Filming in a rundown black neighbourhood known for its drug problems and gangland shootings, Fiennes retains control of the project, operating the camera and sound system herself. Similar to Longinotto, she avoids a voice-over narration and shuns an obvious auteur approach by not appearing on camera, instead claiming that she tries 'to use the grammar of cinema' (in Macnab 2002: 10) alone as a means of expression. Fiennes also uses a minimal participatory style in her work: as she admits, 'I'm not an investigative, in-your-face newsmaker who is going to find out who you really are, or what terrible crime you really did. I like to sit back and be amazed or moved by what I observe' (in James 2001: 29). Her aim is to interpret: as she states, 'I'm just the translator, the midwife of reality ... I've my own response, but the material speaks for itself' (in Russell 2004: 79) she affirms. *Hoover Street Revival* adopts the standpoint of the congregation to assign the Reverend Jones with a numinous status, and Fiennes partly achieves this effect through slow-motion cinematography, or else she integrates aerial shots into the film to take a deistic position which is more direct and realist. Fiennes encourages the subjects to speak for themselves, and consequently the film constructs a collage of voices. In many respects, Fiennes creates a world akin to fiction by revealing the plot gradually. By using helicopter shots she forces the spectator to work in order to understand what is taking place. Moreover, as situations develop, she makes spontaneous decisions about what might be included. At one point, by chance, she captures a drive-by shooting and incorporates it into the film; in another instance she permits the Bishop's sermons to narrate the story. Ultimately, *Hoover Street Revival* is Fiennes attempt 'to make the veil between the subject and the audience as thin as possible' (in Russell 2004: 79).

More recently Fiennes directed *The Pervert's Guide to Cinema* (2006), which was a collaborative project with the Slovenian Marxist philosopher and cultural critic Slavoj Žižek. Although the potential audience for this film is unclear, it is an introduction to Žižek's thoughts on various films over the past fifty years using reconstructed sets and location photography. In an interview with Marty Fairbairn about this film, Fiennes describes her creative style and her experimental techniques:

> You learn to make choices about how to frame things and what the framing does to the subject and knowing what that framing might do. To me, it's like sculpting in time but it's also sculpting with imagery, concentrating on how to render the three-dimensional world into two-dimensional pictures; what does that do and how much time do you leave a shot on screen. It's an alchemical thing. But there's also a science to it. The thing is to broaden the grammar of that science beyond the grammar of cinema which says,

> conventional filmmaking, which insists on beginnings, middles and ends, three acts, reverse shot A-B, now wide shot. I'd like to approach filmmaking differently. (in Fairbairn 2006: 41)

Recounting the making of *The Pervert's Guide to Cinema* as similar to painting, Fiennes notes her admiration for the 'enduring physicality' of cinema and its potential (in Fairbairn 2006: 42). While the film offers similarities to a Film Studies lecture, Žižek is seen as a Hollywood-style character, this emphasis introduced through Fiennes's deployment of classical shot/reverse shots. Žižek, who built his career out of psychoanalytically interpreting Hollywood characters, acts as himself and Fiennes's style of editing creates the feeling that he is present.

From a thematic perspective, *The Pervert's Guide to Cinema* was followed by Fiennes's more recent film, *The Pervert's Guide to Ideology* (2012), which replicates, to some extent its predecessor, but is a 'bolder project and a riskier gamble' (Mullen 2013: 87). Again a film about Žižek, and funded collaboratively by the BFI and Channel 4, along with the UKFC, this recent observation on the philosopher's work uses classic, well-known and little-known films to explain their ideological impact.

Fiennes had previously received UKFC funding in 2002 via the New Cinema Fund for *Hoover Street Revival*, but did not benefit directly from lottery funding for her later release, the documentary, *Over Your Cities Grass Will Grow* (2010), based on the life of the German painter and sculptor, Anselm Kiefer. Instead, Fiennes was forced to seek alternative sources to finance her ideas.[6] As the director points out, '[t]here is nowhere you can go to in Britain; there are very few pots of money, unlike in France. I did go to the Film Council, to the New Cinema Fund and I was sharply turned away on the basis that they had urgent narrative priorities' (in Higgins 2010b).[7]

Kiefer's work centres on the cultural wreckage of the Third Reich, and Fiennes's film documents his enormous environmental installations based on this subject. This project began in 1993, when Kiefer acquired a large tract of land in Barjac, southern France and proceeded to build installations both below and above ground. Due to leave the area, he requested that Fiennes film the final result, which consists of three distinct areas: the amphitheatre, the tunnels and the towers, the latter containing a series of rooms and chambers which represent a collection of the artist's thoughts and memories. Roughly divided into three parts—an unpeopled scene, scenes of Kiefer at work, and an interview—the film took nine months to edit. As Fiennes suggests in the voice-over commentary, her film was always destined to be 'visually led'. Further, she eschews a typical documentary which shows the work of an artist through interview. Her whole approach is observational and her style is formed by the subject.

The opening shot of *Over Your Cities Grass Will Grow* is presented in a visually dark and menacing manner. It commences as Fiennes's camera centre-frames a single light bulb in what appears to be a gloomy concrete windowless room, a single music note aurally accompanying the image, fostering a sense of the uncanny. The room is lead-lined and is the smallest space in the compound. Fiennes continues to produce an exploration of Kiefer's massive constructions by selecting unusual angles, with the camera frequently pursuing a slow-moving trajectory in what appears, on the surface, to be a subterranean world. A sense of danger and the unknown is mobilised when Fiennes's film investigates a variety of rooms, and the camera has to travel, thus assuming an omniscient viewpoint. Here, the director succeeds in capturing Kiefer's own sense of loss, filming broken pots and walls splattered with what could easily pass as bloodstains. Areas appear as though they have recently been vacated in a hurry, and some are littered with fragments of reinforced concrete, indicative of bomb damage (the director suggests Gaza) and the Blitz. One of the rooms represents Kiefer's past in post-Hitler Germany, and contains racks of shirts, while another displays numerous rows of toothbrushes. A further space discloses piles of dusty bundles of papers bound together in a derelict area that is scattered with what look like extracted human teeth, although they are actually synthetic, taken from impressions of real teeth and scaled up. Repeatedly, and throughout the film, this accumulative wartime detritus might be interpreted as referring to the Holocaust. As Fiennes suggests, 'Being a German after the Holocaust had such a huge impact on his work' (Fiennes 2011), although these images are simply there rather than any explanation being provided. However, the artist chooses to work with specific materials such as ash and straw, articles that he uses derived from a poem about Auschwitz entitled 'Death Fugue' by Paul Celan.

To further distance the spectator, Fiennes avoids establishing shots, thus not providing any spatial reference. For example, at one point during the Barjac filming she presents an extreme close-up of what looks like a map. This is clearly not the case as it is a home-made, textured artefact, but Fiennes never withdraws the camera sufficiently to expose the real object and so this remains a conundrum. Fiennes refers to *Last Year in Marienbad* (Resnais 1961) in her voice-over in the documentary[8] as a work that orientates and disorientates, and this is true of her film about Kiefer. The artist later moves his operation to Paris, where he continues working in a studio and, at one point, Fiennes films him breaking great shards of glass on its floor. Here she intersperses images of the artist throwing the glass to the ground and then withdrawing the camera to reframe an enormous structure made of glass topped by a book containing Kabbalistic reference. At one juncture Kiefer carefully selects various pieces to place in the pocket of a child's dress that he has glued to a massive canvas and daubed with symbols. Shown from an overhead shot, the piece of clothing is a filthy, hooded gown with numerous pockets sewn on its front which Kiefer refers to as Abu Ghraib.[9] The artist then chalks each pocket with a number—the ten attributes of god. Throughout the film, Fiennes roves around the area, juxtaposing outdoor space—the views often obliterated by trees—with claustrophobic interiors.

Using lengthy contemplative shots and avoiding voice-over, Fiennes's visual style echoes that of a number of the filmmakers discussed here: her work is a study which avoids direct interviews with Kiefer, merely observing him and his assistants at work as they operate cranes, bulldozers and forklift trucks on his 35 hectare installation, thus providing the subjects their own autonomy. As she suggests, 'I was very keen to privilege the audience's imaginative response before they heard Kiefer speak, because as soon as words come, they become the total authority' (in Stevens 2010: 11). When Fiennes does include interviews with the artist she uses a third party as a mediator, one of the consultations being conducted by a German journalist with whom Kiefer discusses the root of much of his inspiration—boredom. The closing shots of the film, accompanied by the dense sound features of György Ligeti's orchestral piece *Atmosphères*,[10] focus on the towers Kiefer has erected. This sequence, apart from showing these structures framed against a yellow sky, creates a 'distinct post-apocalyptic feel and features some of the most exquisitely choreographed sequences of visionary art, decayed architecture, and futuristic music – courtesy of Ligeti – in recent memory' (Chang 2011: 16). Ligeti is best known for the soundtracks of Kubrick's films, such as *2001: A Space Odyssey* (1968), *The Shining* (1980) and *Eyes Wide Shut* (1999), and Fiennes uses his work to create suspense and a lack of clarity, and ultimately she achieves a monumentality of sound in support of Kiefer's images.

Achieving inventive ways of dealing with complex imagery, the film centralises the landscape and is largely devoid of people during the first 15 minutes, and the finished product is as much about the artistic process (both of making the installations and the filmmaking) as about the completed work. Fiennes's approach was evolutionary, showing the images she had filmed to Kiefer as she progressed rather than meticulously planning. She describes her technique as:

> quite frontal which he [Kiefer] liked. Even when I'm shooting with a small video camera I'm taking a tripod with me. I'm not doing that type of ersatz documentary in which the camera moves all the time. That seems to me a pastiche of documentary that's been employed by fiction film-making recently to convey some sort of idea of authenticity. (in Stevens 2010: 11)

The pertinence of the visual style of *Over Your Cities Grass Will Grow* is that it was shot on film to achieve a textural quality and thus made with the big screen in mind. Low budget, the film was made using private finance and a variety of grants, including contributions from ARTE France[11] and the Rotterdam Film Fund.

Summary

A characteristic of non-mainstream cinema is its authorial and/or autobiographical stance, and counter-cinematic, avant-garde and, to some extent, experimental filmmaking all encourage a relationship with cinema which is active rather than passive. As part of the process of self-inscription, the filmmakers offer a personal aspect to their films, appearing as actor or voice-over, or working with autobiographical content. Sometimes they traverse borders beyond the personal to explore more extensive and global subjects or to include broader political dimensions in their work. Sally Potter's films present a counter-cinematic approach, where she flouts conventions associated with the mainstream or, in the case of *Ginger & Rosa*, offers an historical optic based on her own lived experiences. Turner's work, on the other hand, uses experimental and avant-garde aesthetics, but informed by events, and with an emphasis on ecological concerns. In *Perestroika* she performs fact and fiction simultaneously, with her voice-over explaining the journey, both emotional and physical, that she is making across Siberia. The film is as much autobiographical as a mark of respect to both her friend, Thomas, and to the landscape, and she draws attention to the filmmaking process in place. Wearing's films use documentary techniques such as talking heads, but she subverts conventions by filming the filming taking place.

Throughout *Self Made*, she permits the spectator to see the preparation of the vignettes unfold as well as the final sketch, and the film explores the tension between the public and private in the respondents, and the distortion of boundaries in performance. Finally, Fiennes likens her film-making to sculpting and *Over Your Cities Grass Will Grow* shuns the typical documentary format to familiarise and destabilise simultaneously, the director achieving resourceful ways of presenting complex imagery.

Notes

1. Women electricians had to be recruited from outside the unions because there were no female members.
2. See Mulvey (1975). The bulk of female-directed films during this period shied away from the mainstream, seeking alternative funding and audiences. Laura Mulvey is a prime example and her films and academic writing are most prominent during the 1970s. She is particularly known for her scholarly feminist ideas which underpinned films such as *Penthesilea, Queen of the Amazons* (1974), co-directed with Peter Wollen, and *Riddles of the Sphinx* (1976), which is a conversion of the Oedipus myth and was funded by a £20,000 grant from the BFI.
3. Costume dramas dominated to a considerable extent during the last ten years of the twentieth century. For example: *Orlando* (Potter 1992), Jane Campion's Henry James adaptation, *Portrait of a Lady* (1996), *The Governess* (Goldbacher 1997), *Amy Foster* (Kidron 1997), *Onegin* (Fiennes 1998).
4. Potter wrote the screenplay— a mix of fact and fiction—which received Arts Council funding. Potter plays herself; she meets an Argentine tango dancer who subsequently gives her lessons. Based on an event from her own life, *The Tango Lesson* is 'about the *imbalance* [original italics] of power between man and woman—a theme for which the tango itself stands as a potent metaphor' (Monk 1997: 54).
5. An organisation which invites works of art that challenge definitions of art and the moving image.
6. This controversy was exposed by *The Guardian* film critic, Charlotte Higgins (2010b), who revealed that Fiennes had unsuccessfully approached the UKFC, Arts Council England and Tate Media as potential funders for her film.

7. However, although Fiennes failed to gain UKFC backing in the production process, she eventually received £8,000 for the film's promotion. This is not to suggest that female film directors were less likely to be funded by the UKFC, or indeed to make applications, particularly in its final years of existence as statistics show. Proportionally they appear to have benefited on an equal level to their male counterparts. An overview of films released during the period suggests that limited funding was available for filmmakers, irrespective of gender. Similarly, those involved in large-budget projects tended to seek external funding, often relying on US studio support.
8. Her voice-over was later added. See Fiennes (2011).
9. An Iraqi prison where the US Army and the CIA tortured detainees during the war in Iraq.
10. The music was originally commissioned in 1961 by the South West German Radio.
11. A Franco-German TV network.

CHAPTER 7

Conclusion

In 2016, the Best Director category in the British Academy Awards was won by the Mexican film director, Alejandro G. Iñárritu, with the other nominees including Todd Haynes, Steven Spielberg, Ridley Scott and Adam McKay. This all-male line-up suggests that, despite the various diversity policies instigated during the early part of the decade, not a lot has changed. Indeed, while in the UK in the same year debbie tucker green's *Second Coming* (2014) (sponsored by Film4 and the BFI Film Fund) was nominated for the Outstanding Debut by a British Writer, Director or Producer BAFTA, this was the sole female-directed film to be put forward in this category, and the director was unsuccessful, despite the film receiving favourable reviews.[1]

This is not to suggest that there is a paucity of female British talent. Indeed, this study has identified a large number of key female film directors and analysed their productions through various dimensions, taking into account funding strategies, production, distribution and exhibition methods, as well as aesthetics and genre. Their innovative methods for fundraising, and their flair for unusual stories told using a rich visual vocabulary has important resonances for future women filmmakers. As documented, some of the films examined offer a feminist stance or present life from a female perspective, and the filmmakers included here can be considered auteurs in a broad sense, although many work collaboratively. What is apparent is that most women filmmakers direct films relevant to women, work as part of a team and also undertake many

S. Hockenhull, *British Women Film Directors in the New Millennium*, DOI 10.1057/978-1-137-48992-0_7

of the above-the-line positions themselves. The films' subject matter is often targeted at a female audience, and this is particularly evident in the work of the documentary filmmakers, who frequently address a significant or empowering agenda in their work. In fact, documentaries form the major part of female film production in Britain and repeatedly centre on issues of concern for women. Women produce films about environmental activism, societal and cultural phenomena, and adopt contentious approaches to inner city life; through various techniques, such films tend to be observational, yet interventional presenting them an important voice. The narratives of these films might be local or international but, whichever they are, women directors embrace happenings that occur on a global scale and relay them in a personal way, often pursuing their convictions as activists and campaigners long after their film is completed, as well as becoming advocates for their cause. For directors such as Longinotto and Ayisi, the women they document are empowered to become their own agents of change, or, in other situations, the films become an instrument for the disclosure of societal injustice and a means of obtaining an answer.

British women directors work across a variety of genres, and funding for low-budget films which express societal concerns has proven available and beneficial. The resultant examples discussed here often focus on the notion of the outsider in the appearance of a troubled central female protagonist, a 'lost girl', or on the theme of deprived childhood and youth. Aesthetically their problems are emphasised by the use of landscape, either rural or industrial, which is deployed through an intensely visual and romanticised approach to create emotional significance rather than deal confrontationally with the social and political issues at stake. In addition, many of these films, as with Morton's *The Unloved* for example, have a personal story to tell.

Financial support for higher budget and more mainstream filmmaking tends to be derived from Hollywood, and, sadly, only a minority of women make blockbusters, particularly in the action and fantasy genres, Lloyd's *Mamma Mia!*, as a 'new women's blockbuster', being an exception. However, women do make a substantial contribution to popular and financially successful mainstream cinema, although, as demonstrated, this is rarely acknowledged at the various award ceremonies. What is apparent is that a number of these films offer strong female characters in lead roles. Furthermore, some directors bring into play their own experience of gender, race, class and cultural mobility as a foundation for their stories. Britain's long-standing tradition of women's independent, avant-garde and experimental cinema continues, and a recurring characteristic of this non-mainstream cinema is its authorial and/or autobiographical stance—the filmmakers discussed here introducing their own stories and experiences through an atypical optic. Additionally, these filmmakers use experimental and avant-garde aesthetics to navigate from the personal to the wider global politics at play while frequently drawing attention to the filmmaking process itself.

In terms of the current state of play, despite the demise of the UKFC, a number of emergent British women film directors in the UK are at the moment in receipt of BFI funding, which is attributable to measures being put into place to address the disproportion between male and female directors. Indeed, with headline accusations that 'sexism is still rife in the drama world' (Brown 2010), the BBC partnered Directors UK to explore ways of increasing the number of women directors working in film and television. In addition, as noted in Chap. 2, the November 2013 BAFTA event chaired by Baroness King on Diversity in the UK Film and Television industries was followed by the 2014 *Screen International* and *Broadcast* cross-industry conference to consider the inequities faced by women in UK film and television. Greater inroads were made in 2015 with the BFI Three Ticks Scheme for all BFI lottery funded projects, and filmmakers to benefit include Tehran-born, but French- and British-based Tina Gharavi, who made her directorial debut in 2012 with *I Am Nasrine*, a film about two Tehran refugee siblings, Nasrine (Micsha Sadeghi) and Ali (Shiraz Haq), who were illegally smuggled into the UK. The film was BAFTA nominated in 2013 for the Outstanding Debut by a British Writer, Director or Producer category and for the Douglas Hickox Award in the British Independent Film Awards (2013). More recently, Rebecca Johnson, who was mentored by Paul Greengrass as part of the Guiding Lights scheme, directed *Honeytrap* (2014). Sponsored in part by the BFI Film Fund, the film was nominated for the BFI's Best British Newcomer Award and for an award at the South by South West Film Festival in Austin, Texas.[2] Destiny Ekaragha is another budding filmmaker, and *Gone Too Far!* (2014) is her feature debut, based on Bola Agbaje's award-winning, if episodic, comedy play about South London teenagers and black British identity also titled *Gone Too Far!* Made with support from the BFI Film Fund, BBC Films and Skillset, the film is part observational social comment on identity and part sitcom slapstick humour. *Gone Too Far!* was not well reviewed,[3] but it is set apart from other films about black characters in inner cities due to its tone and genre.

At this point, Ekaragha is only the third black woman to direct a British feature film and *Gone Too Far!* falls within the change-over period from UKFC funding to the BFI Film Fund, suggesting that the former's diversity policy was instrumental in highlighting the disproportion of women film directors in the UK, and also in encouraging greater cultural diversity. Nonetheless, for Ekaragha, the acquisition of funding was initially difficult because *Gone Too Far!* was not easy to categorise. The reasons for this, as Ashley Clark notes, she puts 'down to potential investors' inability to fit the film into a box' (2013: 20). For her, 'It wasn't the [film's] structure that was holding us back. It was certain companies not getting it and saying: There's no audience for this. Any film with young black boys in it is called "urban"' (in Ashley Clark 2013: 20). Subsequently, the BFI agreed to fund it for the sum of £35,000 for further development and £357,000 for production, the complete budget amounting to nearly £1 million.

Other recent female filmmakers to acquire BFI funding include the documentary makers, Jeanie Finlay and Jane Preston. Finlay's work focuses on telling other people's stories, with her ideas usually grounded in the music scene. *The Great Hip Hop Hoax* (2013), assisted by the BFI Development Fund, recounts the tale of two rappers who claim to be from America, and even sign record deals with UK companies, only to be exposed as originating from Scotland. Her later documentary, *Orion: The Man Who Would Be King* (2015), is about the singer, Jimmy Ellis, a man who adopted Elvis Presley's persona as a masked vocalist named Orion. The film acquired finance through the BFI Production Fund, the Arts Council of Wales and Broadway Nottingham. Jane Preston operates as both producer and director on her films, and her credits include the television documentaries *Graffiti Wars* (2011), *Britain's Biggest Beauty Queens* (2012), *Fatal Flight 447: Chaos in the Cockpit* (2012), *Being Paul Gascoigne* (2013) and the film documentary *Gascoigne* (2015).[4] These are just a few examples of the many women currently making films, and, although I commenced this book with ruminations on the gender of the nominees and winners of the BAFTA Best Director category with worrying findings, with the wealth of British female talent currently in circulation in directorial roles, and with the new faces emerging under the auspices of the Diversity Fund, the future for British women film directors will hopefully turn out to be more promising.

Notes

1. Lisa Mullen notes the director's 'impressive talent for punchy, eloquent dialogue' (2015: 64).
2. Johnson is an ardent advocate of equality and she speaks of the need for diversity in British cinema. See Killian Fox (2015).
3. Lisa Mullen was critical of the film's characters' one-dimensionality, especially as it is written by a woman. However, she praises the way it is handled. As she suggests, 'it's unusual to find a portrayal of mostly non-white urban life that doesn't fall back on the gritty stereotypes of crime and violence' (Mullen 2014: 75).
4. Not all current filmmakers are in receipt of BFI finance. Claire Lewin, for example, raised money from private finance for *I Am Ali* (2013), which is a US/UK co-production and was distributed by United Pictures International. Other directors too numerous to include here, but worthy of mention, include Virginia Gilbert with *Long Way From Home* (2013), M.J. Delaney and *Powder Room* (2013) and Kerry Skinner and Stewart Alexander with their directorial debut *Common People* (2012). Elaine Constantine also made her first appearance in 2014 with the privately funded film *Northern Soul*, about the dance movement that commenced in the north of England in the 1970s, and, in a more mainstream vein, experienced film and television director Mandie Fletcher revisited the television series, *Absolutely Fabulous* (1992–2012) with the film of the same name in 2016. Produced by Fox Searchlight, *Absolutely Fabulous: The Movie*, at the time of writing, has made over $830,000 in its opening weekend and $25.7 million worldwide.

Bibliography

Abeel, Erica (2007) "Red Road" *Film Journal International* Vol. 110 Issue 3 p. 37.
Adler, Tim (2009) "Mamma Mia! Rakes in the Money, Money, Money" *Screen Finance* Vol. 22 Part 7 p. 3.
Aitken, Ian (1993) *Film and Reform: John Grierson and the Documentary Film Movement* London, New York: Routledge.
Aitken, Ian (1994) "Stop the Serbian Juggernaut" *New Statesman and Society* 30 December Vol. 16 p. 15.
Aitken, Stuart (2007) "Poetic Child Realism: Scottish Film and the Construction of Childhood" *Scottish Geographical Journal* Vol. 123 Issue 1 pp. 68–86.
Akbar, Arifa (2008) "Hollywood Embraces Britain's Black Film Talent" *The Independent* 10 May p. 8.
Amber Online http://www.amber-online.com/sections/about-us/pages/the-workshop-agreement (Accessed 23/06/2015).
Ames, Katrine (2008) "The Surprising Career of Penny Woolcock" *Opera News* Vol. 10 pp. 38–39.
Andrews, Nigel (2014) "The Riot Club: Film Review" *FT.com*http://search.proquest.com.ezproxy.wlv.ac.uk/docview/1613632296?pq-origsite=summon (Accessed 07/07/2015).
Annesley, Claire, Gains, Francesca, and Rummery, Kirstein (eds) (2007) *Women and New Labour: Engendering Politics and Policy?* Bristol: Policy Press.
Annesley, Claire, and Gains, Francesca (2007) "Feminising Politics and Policy: The Impact of New Labour" in Claire Annesley, Francesca Gains, and Kirstein Rummery (eds) *Women and New Labour: Engendering Politics and Policy?* Bristol: Policy Press, pp. 3–24.

S. Hockenhull, *British Women Film Directors in the New Millennium*, DOI 10.1057/978-1-137-48992-0

Annual Report Creative Skillset creativeskillset.org/assets/0000/0256/Annual_Report_2009-10.pdf (Accessed 08/09/2015).

Anon. (1922) "Peggy Hyland's Plans" *Kinematograph Weekly* 4 May p. 54.

Anon. (1943) "Review: The Flemish Farm" *Kinematograph Weekly* 12 August Vol. 1895 p. 18.

Anon. (1944) *Picture Post* 9 September p. 16.

Anon. (1946) "Review: The Way We Live" *Monthly Film Bulletin* Vol. 13 Issue 152 p. 108.

Anon. (History and Civic Viewing Committee) (1949) "Review: Children of the Ruins" *Monthly Film Bulletin* Vol. 16 Issue 185 p. 91.

Anon. (1951a) "Review: To Be a Woman" *To-Day's Cinema* Wednesday 30 May n.p.

Anon. (1951b) "Review: To Be a Woman" *Monthly Film Bulletin* Vol. 18 Issue 210 p. 302.

Anon. (1954) "Review: The Million Pound Note" in Josh Billings (ed) "Reviews for Showmen" *Kinematograph Weekly* 7 January p. 14.

Anon. (1957) "Review: Windom's Way" *Kinematograph Weekly* 26 December p. 15.

Anon. (2000) "Women in Film" *Filmwaves* Vol. 10 pp. 26–31.

Anon. (2005a) "Bridget Jones: Golden Reel Record" *Screen International* 8 July p. 3.

Anon. (2005b) "Films: The Five Best Revivals" *The Independent* 12 November p. 25.

Anon. (2005c) "Ones to Watch" *New Statesman* 4 April Vol. 134 Issue 4734 p. 43.

Anon. (2006) "Margaret Thomson: Obituary" *Daily Telegraph* 10 January http://www.telegraph.co.uk/news/obituaries/1507401/Margaret-Thomson.html (Accessed 11/08/2014).

Anon. (2007a) "Documentary Maker Bidding for Major Film Award" *South Wales Echo* 31 January p. 19.

Anon. (2007b) "Up On the Roof with Angel Art Genius" *Evening Standard* 11 May p. 1.

Anon. (2007c) "Football Is Bridging Gap Between Women" *South Wales Echo* 22 September p. 15.

Anon. (2008a) "Mamma Mia! Hot Steps Past $400m" *Screen International* 31 October p. 4.

Anon. (2008b) "Mamma Mia! Makes the Leap to the Big Screen" *British Cinematographer* Issue 28 pp. 24–25.

Anon. (2008c) "Film Festival Set to Be a Big Hit" *South Wales Evening Post* 10 November p. 7.

Anon. (2008d) "A Whole Other Story Behind the Scenes: Action and Cut!" *The Western Morning News* 21 October p. 13.

Anon. (2009a) "1 DAY Gang Culture Film Dropped from Cinemas in Birmingham" *The Telegraph* 30 October http://www.telegraph.co.uk/culture/film/film-news/6462775/1-DAY-gang-culture-film-dropped-from-cinemas-in-Birmingham.html (Accessed 25/05/2015).

Anon. (2009b) "The Age of Stupid" *Evening Post* 26 March p. 64.

Anon. (2010a) "Lynne Ramsay's Ratcatcher" *Critical Quarterly* May Supplement Vol. 52 pp. 156–170.

Anon. (2010b) "Actor Hurt Narrates Story of Irish Racing Stable" *Belfast Telegraph* 16 March p. 22.

Anon. (2010c) "Film Investing – Fast Becoming a Risky Business" 9 August http://search.proquest.com.ezproxy.wlv.ac.uk/docview/741432986?accountid=14685 (Accessed 28/05/2015).

Anon. (2010d) "Stars Who Have Backed the Campaign" *Derby Evening Telegraph* 27 May p. 14.

Anon. (2011a) "Ask Lucy Walker What Was the Most Difficult Challenge She Faced in Making the Startling (and Terrifying) Documentary Countdown to Zero and She Pauses and Gives It Some Thought" *Sunday Independent* 19 June p. 4.

Anon. (2011b) "Kim Longinotto" *New Internationalist* Issue 445 p. 61.

Anon. (2012) "Cheekbones and Chidings: New Film: The Iron Lady" *The Economist* Vol. 402 Issue 8766 p. 78.

Anon. (2013a) "British Film Is Booking but Not for Female Directors" *Telegraph. Co.UK* 24 July http://search.proquest.com.ezproxy.wlv.ac.uk/docview/1411981658?pq-origsite=summon (Accessed 28/05/2015).

Anon. (2013b) "Clubhouse News" *American Cinematographer* Vol. 94 Issue 12 pp. 114–115.

Anon. (2014) "Robust and Sobering Reflections of the Class War" *The Western Morning News* 19 September p. 25.

Anthony, Scott, and Russell, Patrick (2014) "Postwar Documentary: A New Way Forward (A Response to Brian Winston)" *Journal of British Cinema and Television* Vol. 11 Issue 2–3 pp. 252–261.

Anwar, Farrah (1994) "Review: Deadly Advice" *Sight and Sound* Vol. 4 Issue 5 pp. 40–41.

Armstrong, Franny (1998) "Why Won't British TV Show a Film About McLibel? Is It So Dangerous? Or Are Broadcasters Cowards, Asks Film-Maker Franny Armstrong" *The Guardian* 19 June T004.

Armstrong, Franny (2002) "The Truth Will Out" *The Guardian* 26 August p. 14.

Armstrong, Franny (2004) "Out and About: Culture Watch: Film Making: Money? Ha!" *The Guardian* 18 February p. 10.

Armstrong, Franny (2009) "The Challenge of Our Era Cannot Be Left to Governments: Stopping Climate Change Needs a Generation to Take Action, as Battles for Votes and Equality Once Did. Help Lead the Way" *The Guardian* 2 September p. 30.

Armstrong, Stephen (2013) "Film: Iron Ladies Have Golden Touch" *Sunday Times* 24 November p. 14.

Armytage, Marcus (2010) "Television Serves Up Two Winners to Whet the Appetite: Racing Diary …" *The Daily Telegraph* [London (UK)] 09 March p. 18.

Arnold, Andrea (2011) "Production Notes: Wuthering Heights" *Oscilloscope Laboratories Press Kit* pp. 1–15.

Ascher-Walsh, Rebecca (2009) "The Graduates" *Hollywood Reporter* Vol. 412 Issue 18 pp. 14–15.

Ashby, Justine, and Higson, Andrew (eds) (2000) *British Cinema Past and Present* London, New York: Routledge.

Auld, Tim (2014) "Public School Enemy Number One" *Stella* 14 September p. 36.

Austin, Thomas (2002) *Hollywood, Hype and Audiences: Selling and Watching Popular Film in the 1990s* Manchester: Manchester University Press.

Austin, Thomas, and de Jong, Wilma (eds) (2008) *Rethinking Documentary: New Perspectives, New Practices* Maidenhead, New York: MacGraw Hill, Open University Press.

Ayisi, Florence, and Brylla, Catalin (2013) "The Politics of Representation and Audience Reception: Alternative Visions of Africa" *Research in African Literatures* Vol. 44 Issue 2 pp. 125–141.

Badt, Karen (2005) "Festival Report: Cannes 2005" *Film Criticism* Vol. 29 Issue 3 p. 60.

Badt, Karin Luisa (2009) "Cannes 2009: Andrea Arnold's *Fish Tank* Makes the Most Waves" *Film Criticism* Vol. 33 Issue 3 pp. 67–71.

Bamigboye, Baz (2013) "Review: Gone Too Far" *Daily Mail* 21 June p. 52.

Barnard, Clio (2013) "Clio Barnard's Cannes Diary" *Sight and Sound* Vol. 23 Issue 7 p. 25.

Barnett, Vincent (2007) "Picturization Partners: Elinor Glyn and the Thalberg Contract Affair" *Film History* Vol. 19 pp. 319–329.

Barr, Charles (1986) *All Our Yesterdays* London: BFI.

Barr, Charles (2002) "Fries, Dam Lies and Videotape" *Vertigo* Vol. 2 Issue 4 p. 47.

Barsan, Tanya (2006) "Time Present and Time Past" in *Making History: Art and Documentary in Britain from 1929 to Now* Exhibition Catalogue, Tate Publishing, London: Tate Enterprises Ltd., pp. 9–26.

Basu, Paul (2008) "Reframing Ethnographic Film" in Thomas Austin and Wilma de Jong (eds) *Rethinking Documentary: New Perspectives, New Practices* Maidenhead, New York: MacGraw Hill, Open University Press, pp. 95–107.

Bell, James (2009) "Crop Row Revisited" *Sight and Sound* Vol. 19 Issue 6 p. 8.

Bell, Melanie, and Williams, Melanie (eds) (2009) *British Women's Cinema (British Popular Cinema)* London, New York: Routledge.

Belloni, Matthew, Fernandez, Jay, Kilday, Gregg, Kit, Borys, and Zeitchik, Steven (2009) "The A-List" *Hollywood Reporter* 14 January Vol. 408 Issue 8 pp. 20–21.

Benjamin, Alison (2010) "Society: Social Justice Films Get into the Fast Lane" *The Guardian* 24 March p. 2.

Benjamin, Julie (1993) "Direction: Margaret Thomson" *Spiral Productions: The Women's Gallery Inc.* http://personal.victoria.ac.nz/marian_evans/women-filmmaker/films/direction.html (Accessed 05/10/2015).

Benzine, Adam (2014) "Grace Under Pressure" *RealScreen* March/April p. 26.

Berger, Laura (2015) "Sundance Women Directors: Meet Louise Osmond – 'Dark Horse'" 21 January http://blogs.indiewire.com/womenandhollywood/sundance-women-directors-meet-louise-osmond-dark-horse-20150121 (Accessed 09/12/2015).

Bernbom, Maria (2001) "Copenhagen: Denmark's Hottest Director" *Europe* April Vol. 405 p. 38.

Berwick, Isabel (2013) "Gang of One" *Financial Times* 16 March p. 30.

Bevan, Tim (2003) "Success Through Diversity and Inclusion" *UKFC Diversity Action Group* pp. 1–28 in *UKFC Group and Lottery Annual Report and Financial Statements for the Year Ended 31 March 2003* TSO: The Stationery Office.

Black, Claire (2015) "Interview: Debbie Isitt" *The Scotsman on Sunday* 24 September http://www.scotsman.com/what-s-on/film/interview-debbie-isitt-i-m-proud-to-say-we-knocked-jim-carrey-and-disney-off-their-spot-1-2649320 (Accessed 24/09/2015).

Boon, Tim (2010) "Birthright" *Shadows of Progress: Documentary Film in Post-War Britain 1951–1977* DVD Booklet London: BFI, pp. 23–25.

Botting, Josephine (2015) "The Stranger Left No Card: Wendy Toye (UK, 1952)" *Sight and Sound* Vol. 25 Issue 10 p. 22–23.

Bradshaw, Jonathan (ed) (2011a) *The Well-Being of Children in the UK* (Third Edition) Bristol: Policy Press.

Bradshaw, Nick (2009a) "Phoning It In" *Sight and Sound* Vol. 19 Issue 10 pp. 38–39.

Bradshaw, Nick (2011b) "Angry Bastards" *Sight and Sound* Vol. 21 Issue 11 pp. 40–41.

Bradshaw, Nick (2012) "Forget Me Not" *Sight and Sound* Vol. 22 Issue 1 pp. 44–45.

Bradshaw, Peter (2009b) "Tilting at Windmills: A Passionate Documentary About Climate Change: The Age of Stupid" *The Guardian* 20 March p. 7.

Bradshaw, Peter (2010a) "Cannes Film Festival: Wordless Guide to a Breathtaking Project: Over Your Cities Grass Will Grow" *The Guardian* 17 May p. 7.

Bradshaw, Peter (2010b) "Cannes 2010: How Boris Beat the Bomb" *The Guardian* 18 May p. 22.

Bradshaw, Peter (2011c) "Scarier than a Horror Film" *The Guardian* 24 June p. 11.

Bradshaw, Peter (2013a) "Review: InRealLife" *The Guardian* 20 September p. 19.

Bradshaw, Peter (2013b) "Film: Magnetic North: Clio Barnard's Social Realist Tale of a Teen Scrap Scavenger Goes at It Like a Supercharged Ken Loach – And Packs in Bradford's Answer to Ben-Hur to Boot: The Selfish Giant" *The Guardian* 25 October p. 22.

Bradshaw, Peter (2014a) "Devils in Waistcoats" *The Guardian* 19 September p. 19.

Bradshaw, Peter (2014b) "Film: Gone Too Far" *The Guardian* 10 October p. 18.

Bradshaw, Peter (2015a) "Reviews: Film: Still Life 3/5" *The Guardian* 6 February p. 18.

Bradshaw, Peter (2015b) "Carol Morley and Tracey Thorn: Girls' School? They're a Hotpot of Urges" *The Guardian* 22 April p. 16.

Brady, Tara (2011) "Build Something Modern" *The Irish Times* 27 May p. 11.

Brady, Tara (2015) "Dizzy Rascals" *Irish Times* 17 April p. 8.

Brockes, Emma (2000) "Silent Witness" *The Guardian* 11 February p. 8.

Brooke, Michael (2013) "Review: McCullin" *Sight and Sound* Vol. 23 Issue 1 p. 101.

Brown, Kimberley (2006) "Franny Armstrong Takes Stock" *RealScreen* January p. 38.

Brown, Maggie (2007a) *A Licence to be Different: The Story of Channel 4* London: BFI.

Brown, Maggie (2012) "Parade's End Director Says Sexism Is Still Rife in the Drama World" *The Observer* 8 September 2012 http://www.theguardian.com/tv-and-radio/2012/sep/08/parades-end-sexism-drama-industry (Accessed 16/02/2016).

Brown, Mark (2007b) "Wanted: Crystal or Council Home" *The Guardian* 15 January p. 14.

Brunsdon, Charlotte (2000) "Not Having It All: Women and Film in the 1990s" in Robert Murphy (ed) *British Cinema of the 90s* London: BFI, pp. 167–177.

Brunsdon, Charlotte (2012) "It's a Film: Medium Specificity as Textual Gesture in Red Road and The Unloved" *Journal of British Cinema and Television* Vol. 9 Issue 3 pp. 457–479.

Bruzzi, Stella (2000) *New Documentary: A Critical Introduction* London, New York: Routledge.

Bulkley, Kate (2010) "Is Crowd-Funding the Future for Documentaries?" *The Guardian* http://www.theguardian.com/Sheffield-doc-fest/funding-models-for-film-making (Accessed 11/11/2013).

Burton-Hill, Clemency (2011) "Taking a Turn: The Lady Who Is Not for Turning" *The Independent* 30 December p. 8.

Butler, Alison (2002) *Women's Cinema: The Contested Screen* London, New York: Wallflower Press.

C.A.W. (1949) "Review: The Flemish Farm" *To-Day's Cinema* 26 January p. 13.

Cardullo, Bert (2002) "Women and Children First" *The Hudson Review* Vol. 54 Issue 4 pp. 635–644.

Carpenter, Louise (2015) "Carol Morley Interview" *Telegraph.co.uk* 13 April http://www.telegraph.co.uk/culture/culturenews/11528106/Carol-Morley-interview-I-like-to-give-some-light-to-the-dark-side-of-life.html (Accessed 13/05/2015).

Carrington, Damian, and Carus, Felicity (2009) "National: Commons Motion Urges Public Services to Cut Gas Emissions" *The Guardian* 19 October p. 10.

Carruthers, Susan L. (2012) "The Iron Lady" *Cineaste* Spring p. 51.

Carter, Meg (2011) "Social Media Influences Documentary-Makers" *The Guardian*, 6 June http://www.theguardian.com/film/2011/jun/06/social-media-documentary-makers (Accessed 18/03/2014).

Caughie, John (2007) "Morvern Callar, Art Cinema and the 'Monstrous Archive'" *Scottish Studies Review* Spring Vol. 8 Issue 1 pp. 101–115.

Cave, Dylan (2015) "BAFTA Shorts 2015" *Sight and Sound* Vol. 25 Issue 4 pp. 70–71.

Chadha, Gurinder (2004) "Austen Power" *Sight and Sound* Vol. 14 Issue 10 pp. 36–37.

Chang, Chris (2010a) "Use Your Illusion: The World-Changing Art of Vik Muniz" *Film Comment* Vol. 46 Issue 6 p. 17.

Chang, Chris (2010b) "Nowhere Boy" *Film Comment* Vol. 46 Issue 5 p. 73.

Chang, Chris (2011) "Hot Ice: Sophie Fiennes, Anselm Kiefer, and György Ligeti Together at Last" *Film Comment* Vol. 47 Issue 2 p. 16.

Chang, Chris (2012) "Short Takes: Midnight's Children" *Film Comment* Vol. 49 Issue 2 p. 70.

Chapman, James (2008) *The British at War* London, New York: I. B. Tauris.

Chapman, James (2015) *A New History of British Documentary* Basingstoke, New York: Palgrave Macmillan.

Charity, Tom (2008) "Blindsight" *The Times* 9 August p. 9.

Cheshire, Ellen (2015) *Bio-Pics: A Life in Pictures* London, New York: Wallflower Press.

Child, Ben (2012) "Cannes 2012: Palme d'Or Diversity Debate Rumbles on with New Petition" *The Guardian* 18 May http://www.theguardian.com/film/2012/may/18/cannes-2012-palme-diversity-debate-petition (Accessed 18/04/2014).

Child, Ben (2015) "Only 6.4% of Hollywood Films Directed by Women, Finds Report" *The Guardian* 10 December http://www.theguardian.com/film/2015/dec/10/directors-guild-america-report-6-per-cent-of-hollywood-films-directed-by-women (Accessed 22/02/2016).

Christie, Brendan (2007) "Producer Profile: Cactus Three" *RealScreen* March/April p. 66.

Clark, Duncan (2009) "Retail Giants Take 10:10 Vow to Fight Climate Change in Stores" *The Guardian* 9 October p. 21.

Clark, Ashley (2013) "Peckham Wry" *Sight and Sound* Vol. 23 Issue 2 p. 20.

Clark, Ashley (2014a) "Penny Woolcock Talks to Gangsters" *Sight and Sound* online http://www.bfi.org.uk/news-opinion/sight-sound-magazine/interviews/penny-woolcock-talks-gangsters (Accessed 22/05/2015).

Clark, Ashley (2014b) "Portrait of a Lady" *Sight and Sound* Vol. 24 Issue 7 pp. 31–33.

Clarke, Donald (2003) "Big Brother's Little Sister" *Irish Times (Dublin)* 28 June p. 56.

Clarke, Donald (2013) "The Realist Delusion" *Irish Times (Dublin)* 25 October p. 9.

Cliche, Danielle (2005) "A Reel or a Raw Deal for Women in the Film Biz" http://www.gender-research.net/web/files/29/en/CB_FP_Cliche.pdf (Accessed 09/09/2011).

Coates, David, and Oettinger, Sarah (2007) "Two Steps Forward, One Step Back: The Gender Dimensions of Treasury Policy under New Labour" in Claire Annesley, Francesca Gains, and Kirstein Rummery (eds) *Women and New Labour: Engendering Politics and Policy?* Bristol: Policy Press, pp. 117–131.

Cochrane, Kira (2010) "Making Films Saved My Life" *The Guardian* 12 February p. 18.

Cocker, Emma (2007) "Unstable Truths" *The Art Book* November Vol. 14 Issue 4 pp. 73–4.

Collin, Robbie (2013a) "Review: The Selfish Giant" *Telegraph* online 17 May http://search.proquest.com.ezproxy.wlv.ac.uk/docview/1352781067?pq-origsite=summon (Accessed 02/03/2015).

Collin, Robbie (2013b) "Shining Tale of a Dark England: The New British Drama is Hauntingly Perfect and Skin Pricklingly Alive" *The Daily Telegraph* 25 October p. 32.

Con, Ada (2004) "Baked Alaska" *Library Journal* 1 May p. 151.

Cooke, Rachel (2009) "Do Not Adjust Your Set" *New Statesman* 25 May Vol. 138 Issue 4950 pp. 42–44.

Cooper, John (2005) "Two Films Focus on Trauma of Being a Victim of Crime" *The Times* 1 November p. 7.

Corbett, Kevin (2013) "'Gleaners' and 'Waste': The Post-Issue/Advocacy Documentary" *Journal of Popular Film and Television* Vol. 41 Issue 3 pp. 128–135.

Cosandey, Roland (2004) "Le Blond, Elizabeth Alice Francis" in Richard Abel (ed) *Encyclopedia of Early Cinema* London, New York: Routledge.

Cousins, Mark (2007) "The Power of Documentary: Shaking the World" Vol. 17 Issue 9 pp. 22–38.

Crace, John (2009) "Red Letter Day as Royal Mail Joins 10:10 Campaign: Biggest Organisation So Far to Back Emissions Effort: Customers and Employees Encouraged to Join in" *The Guardian* 10 September p. 18.

Craigie, Jill (1986) *Fifties Features – The Women Behind the Pictures.* Transcript of Interview with Jill Craigie. S8938. London: BFI.

Cranston, Ros "Marion Grierson 1907–1998" *BFI Screenonline* http://www.screenonline.org.uk/people/id/581811/ (Accessed 07/01/2016).

Cranston, Ros, and McGahan, Katy (2010) "Science and Society: Peter de Normanville, Sarah Erulkar" in Patrick Russell and James Piers Taylor (eds) *Shadows of Progress: Documentary Film in Post-War Britain* Basingstoke, New York: Palgrave Macmillan, pp. 230–245.

Cranston, Ros (2015) "Homes for the People: Kay Mander (UK, 1945)" *Sight and Sound* Vol. 25 Issue 10 pp. 21–22.

Creely, Niamh (2009) "Think Tank" *Film Ireland* http://filmireland.net/2009/09/01/issue-130-%E2%80%93-think-tank/ (Accessed 12/12/2014).

Cullen, Catherine (2001) "Details Are Acoustical" *Afterimage* Vol. 29 Issue 1 p. 12.

Curran, James, and Porter, Vincent (1983) *British Cinema History* London: George Weidenfeld and Nicholson Ltd.

Curtis, Chris (2010) "Honesty Best Policy for Queen of Docs" *Broadcast* 2 July pp. 30–31, 33.

Cutting, Sam (2012) "Film in the Classroom: Wuthering Heights and Jane Eyre" *Use of English* Spring Vol. 63 Issue 2 pp. 160–164.

Dalton, Stephen (2008) "Film Choice: Mischief Night" *The Times* 15 March p. 49.

Dams, Tim (2004) "Moving Up the Budget Scale" *Screen International* 2 April Issue 1447 p. 15.

Dams, Tim (2011) "Q&A: Tanya Seghatchian, UKFC" *Televisual Blogs and Comments* http://www.televisual.com/blog-detail/QandA-Tanya-Seghatchian-UKFC_bid-225.html (Accessed 31/03/2014).

Darke, Chris (2010) "To the End of the Line" *Sight and Sound* Vol. 20 Issue 10 pp 46–47.

Davidson, Alex (2010) "Picture to Post" *Shadows of Progress: Documentary Film in Post-War Britain 1951–1977* DVD Booklet London: BFI, pp. 68–69.

Davie, Emma (2003) "Why I Make Documentary Films" *Documentary Film Magazine* Vol. 49 p. 4.

Davies, Sam (2015a) "Review: Gascoigne" *Sight and Sound* Vol. 25 Issue 7 p. 77.

Davies, Sam (2015b) "Review: Orion: The Man Who Would Be King" *Sight and Sound* Vol. 25 Issue 10 p. 92.

Dawtrey, Adam (2010) "Tanya Seghatchian to Head UK Film Council Film Fund" *The Guardian*, 10 February http://www.theguardian.com/film/2010/feb/10/tanya-seghatchian-uk-film-council (Accessed 20/03/2013).

de Lauretis, Teresa (1987) "Rethinking Women's Cinema: Aesthetics and Feminist Theory" in Teresa de Lauretis (ed) *Technologies of Gender: Essays on Theory, Film and Fiction* Bloomington, Indianapolis: Indiana University Press, pp. 127–148.

de Lauretis, Teresa (1990) "Guerrilla in the Midst: Women's Cinema in the 80s" *Screen* Vol. 31 Issue 1 pp. 6–25.

de Witt, Helen (2011) "Express Yourself" *Sight and Sound* Vol. 21 Issue 9 pp. 12–13.

Delgado, Maria (2008) "Review: Mamma Mia!" *Sight and Sound* Vol. 18 Issue 9 pp. 67–68.

Denny, Ned (2002) "World of Interiors" *New Statesman* Vol. 131 Issue 4588 pp. 40–41.

Dickinson, Margaret, and Street, Sarah (1985) *Cinema and State: Film Industry and the Government 1927–1984* London: BFI.

Doane, Mary Ann (1987) *The Desire to Desire: The Woman's Film of the 1940s* Bloomington: Indiana University Press.

Doyle, Gillian (2014) "Film Support and the Challenge of 'Sustainability': On Wing Design, Wax and Feathers, and Bolts from the Blue" *Journal of British Cinema and Television* Vol. 11 Issue 2–3 pp. 129–151.

Doyle, Gillian, Schlesinger, Philip, Boyle, Raymond, and Kelly, Lisa (2015) *The Rise and Fall of the UK Film Council* Edinburgh: Edinburgh University Press.

Dupin, Christophe (2012) "The BFI and Film Production: Half a Century of Innovative Independent Film-Making" in Geoffrey Nowell-Smith and Christophe Dupin (eds) *The British Film Institute, the Government and Film Culture, 1933–2000* Manchester, New York: Manchester University Press.

Dupin, Christophe (nd) "Free Cinema" http://www.screenonline.org.uk/film/id/444789/index.html (Accessed 30/10/2015).

Easen, Sarah (a) (nd) "Ruby Grierson 1904–1940" http://www.screenonline.org.uk/people/id/561579/ (Accessed 07/01/2016).

Easen, Sarah (b) (nd) "Margaret Thomson 1910–2005" http://www.screenonline.org.uk/people/id/581902/ (Accessed 20/11/2015).

Easen, Sarah (c) (nd) "Mary Field 1896–1968" http://www.screenonline.org.uk/people/id/581940/ (Accessed 04/09/2014).

Easen, Sarah (d) (nd) "Kay Mander 1915–2013" http://www.screenonline.org.uk/people/id/559726/ (Accessed 08/09/2014).

Edström, Maria, and Mølster, Ragnhild (eds) (2014) *Making Change* NORDICOM.

Elieas, Juanita, and Ferguson, Lucy (2007) "The Gender Dimension of New Labour's International Development Policy" in Claire Annesley, Francesca Gains, and Kirstein Rummery (eds) *Women and New Labour: Engendering Politics and Policy?* Bristol: Policy Press, pp. 211–228.

Elliott, Katy (2005) "The African Queen" *Screen International* 10 June Vol. 1504 p. 9.

Elmhirst, Sophie (2009) "We're Right at the End of the Time When We Can Still Do Something" *New Statesman* 26 October Vol. 138 Issue 4972 p. 26.

Elsey, Eileen (2003) "Her Stories" *Vertigo* Vol. 2 Issue 4 pp. 14–15.

Enright, Robert (2011) "Gillian Wearing: The Art of Everyday Illumination" *Border Crossings* Vol. 30 Issue 3 pp. 26–43.

Enticknap, Leo (2001) "Postwar Urban Redevelopment, the British Film Industry, and *The Way We Live*" in Mark Shiel and Tony Fitzmaurice (eds) *Cinema and the City: Film and Urban Societies in a Global Context* London: Blackwell, pp. 233–243.

E.O. (1943) "Review: The Flemish Farm" *Monthly Film Bulletin* Vol. 10 Issue 16 p. 88.

Evans, Barbara (nd) "Evelyn Spice 1904–1990" *BFI Screenonline* http://www.screenonline.org.uk/people/id/581923/index.html (Accessed 06/10/2015).

Fairbairn, Marty (2006) "Intrusion of the Real: An Interview with Sophie Fiennes, Director, *The Pervert's Guide to Cinema* (2006)" *Film-Philosophy* Vol. 10 Issue 3 pp. 38–49.

Fay, Liam (2010) "Clear of the Field" *Sunday Times* 21 March p. 32.

Feldman, Shelley, and Menon, Gayatri (2010) "Drowned Out" *Visual Anthropology* Vol. 23 pp. 55–58.

Felperin, Leslie (2003) "Review: Hoover Street Revival" *Sight and Sound* Vol. 13 Issue 8 p. 46.

Felperin, Leslie (2005) "Review: Yes" *Sight and Sound* Vol. 15 Issue 8 pp. 83–4.

Fiennes, Sophie (2011) "Over Your Cities Grass Will Grow" DVD Special Features: Audio Commentary with Sophie Fiennes and Ian Haydn Smith.

Fischer, Lucy (1989) *Shot/Counter Shot: Film Tradition and Women's Cinema* London: BFI.

Fisher, Mark (2011) "Review: Self Made" *Sight and Sound* Vol. 21 Issue 10 p. 76.

F.J. (1957) "Review: Windom's Way" *The Daily Cinema* 18 December Vol. 7928 p. 3.

Forde, Leon (2008) "Funny, Sad and Unusual" *Screen International* 25 April p. 12.

Forde, Leon (2009) "Awards Countdown: The Debutantes' Ball" *Screen International* 4 December pp. 14–21.

Forde, Leon (2010) "Amanda Posey, Finola Dwyer: Producers, Best Picture, An Education" in Michael Goodridge "Awards Countdown: And Then There Were 10" *Screen International* 12 February pp. 5–6, 8, 10, 12.

Fordy, Tom (2015) "London Film Festival: Why 2015 Is the Year for Strong Women" *Daily Telegraph* 9 October http://www.telegraph.co.uk/women/womens-life/11907336/London-Film-Festival-Why-2015-is-the-year-for-strong-women.html (Accessed 09/10/2015).

Forrest, David (2010) "Better Things (Duane Hopkins, 2008) and New British Realism" *New Cinemas* Vol. 8 Issue 1 pp. 31–43.

Forrest, David (2014) "The Films of Joanna Hogg: New British Realism and Class" *Studies in European Cinema* http://dx.doi.org/10.1080/17411548.2014.903102 (Accessed 22/07/2015).

Fowler, Claire (1998) "Under the Skin: Interview with Carine Adler" *Filmwaves* http://www.filmwaves.co.uk/index.php?option=com_content&view=article&id=56:under-the-skin-interview-with-carine-adler&catid=14:filmwaves-29&Itemid=2 (Accessed 06/10/2015).

Fowler, Catherine (2003) "Cinefeminism in Its Middle Ages, or 'Please, Please, Please Give Me Back My Pleasure': The 1990s Work of Sally Potter, Chantal Akerman, and Yvonne Rainer" in Jacqueline Levitin, Judith Plessis, and Valerie Raoul (eds) *Women Filmmakers: Refocusing* London, New York: Routledge, pp. 51–61.

Fowler, Catherine (2010) "The Day I Will Never Forget: An Interview with Kim Longinotto" *A Cultural Review* Vol. 15 Issue 1 pp. 101–107.

Fox, Charlie (2015) "Review: The Falling" *Sight and Sound* Vol. 25 Issue 5 pp. 76–77.

Fox, Jo (2013) "'To Be a Woman' Female Labour and Memory in Documentary Film Production, 1929–50" *Journal of British Cinema and Television* Vol. 10 Issue 1 pp. 584–602.

Fox, Killian (2015) "Rebecca Johnson on Honeytrap" *The Guardian* 17 May http://www.theguardian.com/film/2015/may/17/rebecca-johnson-honeytrap-interview-teenagers-brixton-london (Accessed 28/09/2015).

French, Philip (2010) "Over Your Cities Grass Will Grow" *The Observer* 17 October p. 27.

French, Philip (2011) "One Day" *The Observer* 28 August p. 26.

Friedman, Lester (1993) *British Cinema and Thatcherism* London: UCL Press Ltd.

Fuller, Graham (2007) "Red Road" *Film Comment* March/April Vol. 43 Issue 2 pp. 71–72.

Fuller, Graham (2011) "Misery Loves Company" *Film Comment* November/December Vol. 47 Issue 6 pp. 36–43.

Fuller, Graham (2012a) "The Iron Lady" *Film Comment* Vol. 48 Issue 1 pp. 67–68.

Fuller, Graham (2012b) "Possessed" *Film Comment* Vol. 48 Issue 5 pp. 76–79.

Gall, Michaela (2000) "Frieze-Wrapped" *New Statesman* Vol. 129 Issue 4489 pp. 45–46.

Galpin, Shelley Anne (2014) "Auteurs and Authenticity: Adapting the Brontës in the Twenty-First Century" *Journal of British Cinema and Television* Vol. 11 Issue 1 pp. 86–100.

Gant, Charles (2008) "Abba Hit Top Note" *Sight and Sound* Vol. 18 Issue 9 p. 9.

Gant, Charles (2010) "Birth of a Star" *Sight and Sound* Vol. 20 Issue 1 p. 11.

Garcia, Maria (2015) "Demanding to Be Heard" *Film Journal International* Vol. 118 Issue 10 p. 28.

Gardner, Lynn (2015) "Jennie Lee's Vision for the Arts Is as Relevant Today as It Was 50 Years Ago" *The Guardian* 23 February http://www.theguardian.com/stage/theatreblog/2015/feb/23/jennie-lee-policy-arts-white-paper-funding (Accessed 17/02/2016).

Gavron, Sarah (2015) "The Making of the Feature Film Suffragette" *Women's History Review* Vol. 24 Issue 6 pp. 985–995.

Gedalof, Irene (2011) "Finding Home in Bend It Like Beckham and Last Resort" *Camera Obscura* Vol. 26 Issue 1 pp. 131–157.

Geoff, Andrew (2010) "Cannes 2010: Ashes to Ashes, Dust to Dust" *Sight and Sound* Vol. 20 Issue 7 p. 21.

Gilbey, Ryan (2011a) "Known Unknown" *New Statesman* 19 December Vol. 140 Issue 5084/5 p. 85.

Gilbey, Ryan (2011b) "Stormy Heath" *New Statesman* 14 November Vol. 140 Issue 5079 p. 52.

Gilbey, Ryan (2006) "Fear and Loathing in Glasgow" *New Statesman* 30 October Vol. 135 Issue 4816 p. 45.

Gilbey, Ryan (2009) "The Land that Cinema Forgot" *New Statesman* 14 September Vol. 138 Issue 4966 p. 47.

Gilbey, Ryan (2010) "Estate of Shock" *New Statesman* newstatesman.com/blogs/cultural-capital 21 October p. 42. http://www.newstatesman.com/film/2010/10/lorraine-dunbar-arbor-life (Accessed 23/02/2016).

Gilbey, Ryan (2014) "Mad Dogs and Englishmen" *New Statesman* 19 September Vol. 143 Issue 5228 p. 83.

Giles, Jane (2015) "Review: Fifty Shades of Grey" *Sight and Sound* Vol. 25 Issue 4 pp. 64–65.

Gillett, Lizzie (2003) "Fries, Dam Lies and Videotape" *Vertigo* Vol. 2 Issue 4 p. 47.

Gledhill, Christine (1987) *Home Is Where the Heart Is: Studies on Melodrama and the Women's Film* London: BFI.

Gledhill, Christine (1994) "Image and Voice", in Diane Carson, Linda Dittmar, and Janice Welsch (eds) *Multiple Voices in Feminist Film Criticism* Minneapolis, London: University of Minnesota Press, pp. 109–123.

Gledhill, Christine (2003) *Reframing British Cinema* London: BFI.

Gledhill, Christine (2007) "Reframing Women in 1920s British Cinema: The Case of Violet Hopson and Dinah Shurey" *Journal of British Cinema and Television* Vol. 4 Issue 1 pp. 1–17.

Gold, John R., and Ward, Stephen V. (1997) "Of Plans and Planners: Documentary Film and the Challenge of then Urban Future 1935–52" in David B. Clarke (ed) *The Cinematic City* London: Routledge, pp. 59–82.

Goldrich, Robert (2014) "Lucy Walker: Chat Room" *Shoot* Vol. 55 Issue 1 p. 25.

Goodey, Jan (2008) "Film and Music: Brief Encounters: For Sale: A Warm Fuzzy Feeling" *The Guardian* 27 June p. 4.

Gordon, Christopher, and Stark, Peter (2010) "Funding of the Arts and Heritage – Culture, Media and Sport Committee Contents" September http://www.publications.parliament.uk/pa/cm201011/cmselect/cmcumeds/464/464vw31.htm (Accessed 16/09/2014).

Goodridge, Michael (2010) "Awards Countdown: And Then There Were 10" *Screen International* 12 February pp. 5–6, 8, 10, 12.

Goodwin, Christopher (2010) "The Blonde's Bombshell" *Sunday Times* 16 May p. 24.

Grant, Barry Keith (ed) (2008) *Auteurs and Authorship: A Film Reader* Malden, Oxford, Victoria: Blackwell Publishing.

Greene, Naomi (2007) *The French New Wave: A New Look* London, New York: Wallflower Press.

Grey, Tobias (2013) "We Have to tell Bigger Stories" http://search.proquest.com.ezproxy.wlv.ac.uk/printviewfile?accountid=14685 (Accessed 07/07/2015).

Gritten, David (2011a) "Throwaway Society" *The Daily Telegraph* 5 February p. 44.

Gritten, David (2011b) "Great Films Should Be Commercial Too" *The Daily Telegraph* 1 April p. 30.

Grove, Martin (2009) "Scherfig Was Seduced by an Education; Will Oscar Voters Fall under Its Spell Too?" *Hollywood Reporter* 15 October Vol. 411 Issue 45 p. 9.

Guano, Emanuela (2004) "She Looks at Him with the Eyes of a Camera: Female Visual Pleasures and the Polemic with Fetishism in Sally Potter's *Tango Lesson*" *Third Text* Vol. 18 Issue 5 pp. 461–474.

Haigh, Christine, and Vallely, Bernadette (2010) "Gender and the Climate Change Agenda" *Women's Environmental Network London* pp. 1–63. https://www.google.co.uk/search?client=qsb-win&rlz=1R3GUEA_en-GBGB352GB353&hl=en-GB&q=haigh+vallely+women+and+climate+change&gws_rd=cr&ei=lh7AV7rOOeWZgAbW5o3QBA (Accessed 12/11/2012).

Hallam, Julia, and Marshment, Margaret (2000) *Realism and Popular Cinema* Manchester, New York: Manchester University Press.

Hammond, Philip, and Ortega Breton, Hugh (2014) "Bridging the Political Deficit: Loss, Morality, and Agency in Films Addressing Climate Change" *Communication Culture and Critique* Vol. 7 Issue 3 pp. 303–319.

Hammond, Wally (2013) "Review: The Crash Reel" *Sight and Sound* Vol. 23 Issue 11 p. 73.

Harper, Sue (2000) *Women in British Cinema: Mad, Bad and Dangerous to Know (Rethinking British Cinema)* London, New York: Continuum.

Haskell, Molly (1974) *From Reverence to Rape: The Treatment of Women in the Movies* New York: Holt, Rinehart and Winston.

Haskell, Molly (1977) "Are Women Directors Different?" in Karyn Kay and Gerald Peary (eds) *Women and the Cinema: A Critical Anthology* New York: E.P. Dutton, pp. 393–406.

Haun, Harry (2009) "Educating Carey" *Film Journal International* Vol. 112 Issue 10 pp. 14–16.
Hawcock, Neville (2011) "Beeban Kidron Talks About Her Career" *Financial Times* 11 January http://search.proquest.com.ezproxy.wlv.ac.uk/docview/840360639?pq-origsite=summon (Accessed 27/05/2015).
Herbert, Stephen, and McKernan, Luke (1996) *Who's Who in Victorian Cinema: A Worldwide Survey* London: BFI.
Hickman, Leo (2009) "National: Missile Firm Pledges to Hit Target as It Joins 10:10 Climate Campaign" *The Guardian* 26 November p. 21.
Higgins, Charlotte (2010a) "Runaway Success" *The Guardian* 8 June p. 22.
Higgins, Charlotte (2010b) "British Filmmakers Lauded at Cannes Forced to Seek Overseas Backing" *The Guardian* 16 May http://www.guardian.co.uk/film/2010/may/16/british-film-industry-fund-women (Accessed 6/07/2011).
Higgins, Charlotte (2013a) "No Sexism Please, We're Swedish – Cinemas Classify Films by Representation of Women: Rating Movies by Gender Equality May Be a Blunt Tool but It Raises Serious Issues" *The Guardian* 7 November p. 3.
Higgins, Charlotte (2013b) "British in Cannes: The Selfish Giant" *The Guardian* 18 May p. 3.
Higson, Andrew (2011) *Film England: Culturally English Filmmaking Since the 1990s* London, New York: I.B. Tauris.
Hill, Amelia (2012) "Where Are the Women in Film?" *The Guardian* 19 May p. 42.
Hill, Clare (2006) "Ghetto Life and Women Bring Fresh Spirit of Adventure" *Western Mail* 6 March p. 26.
Hill, John (1996) 'British Film Policy" in Albert Moran (ed) *Film Policy: International, National and Regional Perspectives* London, New York: Routledge, pp. 101–113.
Hill, John (1999) *British Cinema in the 1980s: Issues and Themes* Oxford: Clarendon Press.
Hill, John (2000) "Failure and Utopianism: Representations of the Working Class in British Cinema of the 1990s" in Robert Murphy (ed) *British Cinema in the 90s* London: BFI, pp. 178–187.
Hill, John (2011) *Ken Loach: The Politics of Film and Television* London: BFI.
Hill, John (2012) "This Is for the *Batmans* as Well as the *Vera Drakes*: Economics, Culture and UK Government Film Production Policy in the 2000s" *Journal of British Cinema and Television* Vol. 9 Issue 3 pp. 333–356.
Hockenhull, Stella (2012) "Wednesday's Child: Adolescent Outsiders in Contemporary British cinema" in Debbie Olson and Andrew Scahill (eds) *Lost and Othered Children in Contemporary Cinema* Plymouth: Lexington, pp. 47–66.
Hockenhull, Stella (2013a) "An Age of Stupid?: Sublime Landscapes and Global Anxiety Post-Millennium" in Graeme Harper and Jonathan Rayner (eds) *Cinema and Landscape* (Vol. 2) Newcastle upon Tyne: Cambridge Scholars Publishing, pp. 106–120.

Hockenhull, Stella (2013b) *Aesthetics and Neo-Romanticism in Film: Landscapes in Contemporary British Cinema* London: I.B. Tauris.
Hockenhull, Stella (2015a) "Damsels in Distress?" *Film International* Vol. 13 Issue 1 pp. 6–19.
Hockenhull, Stella (2015b) "Jill Craigie (1911–1999)" in Jill Nelmes and Jule Selbo (eds) *Women Screenwriters: An International Guide* London, New York: Palgrave Macmillan, pp. 639–646.
Hockenhull, Stella (2016) "Picturesque, Pastoral and Dirty: Uncivilised Topographies in *Jane Eyre* and *Wuthering Heights*" in Paul Newland (ed) *British Rural Landscapes on Film* Manchester, New York: Manchester University Press, pp.148–161.
Hoggard, Liz (2011) "Treasures in the Trash" *The Evening Standard* 10 February pp. 31–32.
Honeycutt, Kirk (2011) "One Day" *Hollywood Reporter* Vol. 417 Issue 30 p. 48.
Hope-Jones, Mark (2008) "Fathers of the Bride" *American Cinematographer* August pp. 38–47.
Hopkins, David (2003) "'Out of It': Drunkenness and Ethics in Martha Rosler and Gillian Wearing" *Art History* Vol. 26 Issue 3 pp. 340–363.
Hornby, Nick (2009) "Life vs Education" *Sight and Sound* Vol. 19 Issue 11 p. 49.
Horsefield, Martin (2014) "Jeanie Finlay: It's the Small Moments that Make a Bigger Story" *The Guardian* 20 June http://www.theguardian.com/film/2014/jun/20/jeanie-finlay-its-the-small-moments-that-make-a-bigger-story (Accessed 23/09/2015).
Hunter, Allan, and Neiiendam, Jacob (2003) "Case Study: Wilbur Wants to Kill Himself" *Screen International* 6 January p. 27.
Hunter, Allan (2005) "The Brit Factor" *Screen International* 7 January pp. 14–24.
James, Christopher (2001) "Another Fine Fiennes" *Evening Standard* 13 July p. 29.
James, Nick (2000) "In Bed with the Film Council" *Sight and Sound* Vol. 11 Issue 1 pp. 14–17.
James, Nick (2009) "Prospect Recommends: An Education" *Prospect* Issue 164 p. 8.
James, Nick (2010a) "BFI London Film Festival: British Invention" *Sight and Sound* Vol. 20 Issue 11 pp. 18–40.
James, Nick (2010b) "Clio, Andrea and Lorraine Too" *Sight and Sound* Vol. 20 Issue 11 pp. 25–26.
James, Nick (2014) "The Look of Love: Naked Cinema" *Sight and Sound* Vol. 24 Issue 5 pp. 104–5.
J.G.W. (1953) "Review: The Million Pound Note" *To-Day's Cinema* Wednesday 30 December p.10.
Johnson, Liza. (2004) "Perverse Angle: Feminist Film, Queer Film, Shame" *Signs: Journal of Women in Culture and Society* Vol. 30 Issue 1 pp. 1361–1384.

Johnston, Claire (ed) (1975) *The Work of Dorothy Arzner: Towards a Feminist Film Critisicm* London: BFI.
Johnston, Claire ([1973]2008) "Women's Cinema as Counter Cinema" in Barry Keith Grant (ed) *Auteurs and Authorship: A Film Reader* Malden, Oxford, Victoria: Blackwell Publishing, pp. 119–126.
Johnston, Trevor (2009) "Review: Horses" *Sight and Sound* Vol. 20 Issue 3 pp. 66–67.
Johnston, Trevor (2010) "Almost Famous" *Sight and Sound* Vol. 20 Issue 1 pp. 48–49.
Johnston, Trevor (2012a) "Review: I Am Breathing" *Sight and Sound* Vol. 23 Issue 7 pp. 80–76.
Johnston, Trevor (2012b) "Review: Good Vibrations" *Sight and Sound* Vol. 23 Issue 4 pp. 91–92.
Johnston, Trevor (2013) "Review: InRealLife" *Sight and Sound* Vol. 23 Issue 10 pp. 80–81.
Johnston, Trevor (2014) "Review: 20,000 Days on Earth" *Sight and Sound* Vol. 24 Issue 10 pp. 87–88.
Johnston, Trevor (2015) "Review: Honeytrap" *Sight and Sound* Vol. 25 Issue 6 p. 76.
Jones, Emma (2015) "British Horseracing Tale Wows Sundance" *BBC News* 2 February http://www.bbc.co.uk/news/entertainment-arts-31006259 (Accessed 9/12/2015).
Jones, Kristin Marriott (2002) "Review: Morvern Callar" *Film Comment* Vol. 38 Issue 6 p. 74.
Jones, Kristin Marriott (2010) "Fish Tank" *Film Comment* Vol. 46 Issue 1 p. 77.
Kaplan, E. Ann (1977) "Interview with British Cine-Feminists" in Karyn Kay and Gerald Peary (eds) *Women and the Cinema: A Critical Anthology* New York: E.P. Dutton, pp. 393–406.
Kay, Jeremy (2008) "Here Come the Summer Hits" *Screen International* 4 April pp. 6, 8.
Kay, Karyn, and Peary, Gerald (eds) (1977) *Women and the Cinema: A Critical Anthology* New York: E.P. Dutton.
Kazimuddin, Ahmed, and Young, Zoe (2003) "Drowned Out: We Can't Wish Them Away" *Organization and Environment* Vol. 16 Issue 3 pp. 390–392.
Keirstead, Thomas (1997) "Review: Dream Girls and Ripples of Change" *American Historical Review* Vol. 102 Issue 1 pp. 251–2.
Kelly, Gabrielle, and Robson, Cheryl (2014) *Celluloid Ceiling: Women Film Directors Breaking Through* London: Supernova Books.
Kelly, Richard (2001) "Review: Italian for Beginners" *Sight and Sound* Vol. 12 Issue 4 p. 47.
Kemp, Philip (2004) "Review: Wants to Kill Himself" *Sight and Sound* Vol. 14 Issue 1 p. 64.

Kemp, Philip (2009) "Review: The Age of Stupid" *Sight and Sound* Vol. 19 Issue 4 p. 50.

Kemp, Philip (2012) "Review: The Iron Lady" *Sight and Sound* Vol. 22 Issue 2 pp. 67–68.

Kemp, Philip (2013) "Review: One Mile Away" *Sight and Sound* Vol. 23 Issue 4 p. 99.

Kemp, Stuart (2011) "Over-Emotional? Director Hits Back at Iron Lady Critics" *The Hollywood Reporter* Vol. 417 Issue 43 p. 16.

Kennedy, Steven (2014) "Child Poverty Act 2010: A Short Guide" in *House of Commons Library* Hansard Reports pp. 1–15.

Kermode, Mark (2004) "Big Girls' Pants: Bridget Jones: The Edge of Reason" *New Statesman* 15 November p. 45.

Kermode, Mark (2013) "Film of the Week: Boys from the Scrapheap: The Selfish Giant" *The Observer* 27 October p. 32.

Kermode, Mark (2015) "And the Rest ...: Dreamcatcher" *The Observer* 8 March p. 23.

Kerr, Paul (2013) "Making Film Programmes for the BBC and Channel 4: The Shift from In-House 'Producer Unit' to 'Independent Package-Unit' Production" *Historical Journal of Film, Radio and Television* Vol. 33 Issue 3 pp. 434–453.

Kerrigan, Finola (2010) *Film Marketing* Amsterdam, Boston, Heidelberg, London, New York, Oxford, Paris, San Diego, San Francisco, Singapore, Sydney, Tokyo: Elsevier Ltd.

Kidron, Beeban (2001) "What About Me?" in Penny Sumner (ed) *The Fruits of Labour: Creativity, Self-Expression and Motherhood* London: The Women's Press Ltd., pp. 96–104.

Kidron, Beeban (2011) "Education Shouldn't Be About Jumping Through Hoops" *The Times Educational Supplement* 4925 21 January p. 25.

Kidron, Beeban (2013) "Common People" *The Guardian* 3 September p. 12.

KM (2010) "The Princess and the Frog" *The Times* 29 January p. 36.

KM (2011) "Countdown to Zero" *The Times* 24 June p. 46.

Knight, Julia, and Thomas, Peter (2011) *Reaching Audiences: Distribution and Promotion of Alternative Moving Image* Bristol, Chicago: Intellect.

Kolozova, Katerina, and Milevska, Suzana (2007) "Casting Žižek: Manliness as a Masquerade" *The International Journal of the Humanities* Vol. 5 Issue 8 pp. 157–163.

Kothari, Priya, Whitham, Graham, and Quinn, Thomas (2014) "A Fair Start for Every Child: Why We Must Act Now to Tackle Child Poverty in the UK" *Save the Children* 1–40. https://www.google.co.uk/search?client=qsb-win&rlz=1R3GUEA_en-GBGB352GB353&hl=en-GB&q=Kothari,+Priya,+Whitham,+Graham,+and+Quinn,+Thomas+%282014%29+%E2%80%9CA+Fair+Start+for+Every+Child:+Why+We+Must+Act+Now+to+Tackle+Child+Poverty+in+the+UK&gws_rd=cr,ssl&ei=NArMVoe_BcLuUNz6ulg (Accessed 23/02/2016).

Kuhn, Annette (1982) *Women's Pictures: Feminism and Cinema* London: Routledge and Kegan Paul.

Kuhn, Annette (2008) *Ratcatcher* London: BFI.

Kuhn, Annette (2015) "Knowing Men: Elinor Glyn (UK, 1930)" *Sight and Sound* Vol. 25 Issue 10 p. 20.

Lamont, Tom (2013) "The New Review: Cover Story: Is British Film on the Crest of a New Wave?: 'I Have an International Audience in Mind': Clio Barnard" *The Observer* 15 October p. 8.

Lant, Antonia (1993) "Women's Independent Cinema: The Case of Leeds Animation Workshop" in Lester Friedman (ed) *British Cinema and Thatcherism* London: UCL Press Ltd., pp. 161–187.

Lawrenson, Edward (1999) "Review: Fanny and Elvis" *Sight and Sound* Vol. 9 Issue 12 p. 45.

Lay, Samantha (2002) *British Social Realism: From Documentary to Brit Grit* London, New York: Wallflower Press.

Lee, Benjamin (2015) "Former Film4 Head Tessa Ross to Launch Production Company" *The Guardian* 9 June http://www.theguardian.com/film/2015/jun/09/former-film4-head-tessa-ross-launch-production-company (Accessed 22/07/2015).

Leeds Animation Workshop http://www.leedsanimation.org.uk/index.html (Accessed 22/06/2015).

Leggott, James (2008) *Contemporary British Cinema* London, New York: Wallflower Press.

Leigh, Jacob (2002) *The Cinema of Ken Loach: Art in the Service of the People* New York: Columbia University Press.

Levitin, Jacqueline, Plessis, Judith, and Raoul, Valerie (eds) (2003) *Women Filmmakers: Refocusing* London, New York: Routledge.

Lewis, Helen (2015) "These Were Voiceless Women. We Gave Them a Voice" *New Statesman* 16–22 October Vol. 144 Issue 5284 pp. 40–43.

Lewis, Malcolm (2006) "Red Road" *New Internationalist* Issue 395 pp. 26–27.

Lewis, Paul, and Evans, Rob (2013) "McLibel Leaflet Was Co-Written by Undercover Police Officer Bob Lambert" *The Guardian* 21 June http://www.theguardian.com/uk/2013/jun/21/mclibel-leaflet-police-bob-lambert--mcdonalds (Accessed 22/02/2016).

L.H.C. (1949) "Review: Blue Scar" *To-Day's Cinema* 8 April p. 8.

Lisotta, Christopher (2010) "War of the Words" *Hollywood Reporter* 1 May Vol. 412 Issue 41 pp. 8–11.

Longinotto, Kim (2003) "Why I Make Documentary Films" *Documentary Film Magazine* Vol. 49 p. 4.

Longinotto, Kim (2004) "In Het Huis Van Mijn Vader (In My Father's House)" *Documentary Film Quarterly* Vol. 50 p. 32.

Loomis, George (2008) "Nuclear Switchover" *Financial Times* 11 October p. 15.

Lord, Catherine Mary (2012) "Precarious Planet: Ecological Violence in *The Age of Stupid*" *Excursions Journal* Vol. 3 Issue 1 http://wlv.summon.serialssolutions.com/#!/search?ho=t&q=franny%20armstrong&l=en (Accessed 13/03/2015).

Low, Rachael (1971) *The History of the British Film 1918–1929* London: George Allen and Unwin Ltd.

Low, Rachel (1973) *The History of the British Film 1914–1918* London: George Allen and Unwin Ltd.

Low, Rachel (1979) *Documentary and Educational Films of the 1930s* London: George Allen and Unwin Ltd.

Low, Rachel (1985) *Film Making in 1930s Britain* London: George Allen and Unwin Ltd.

Lucca, Violet (2015) "Review: Love Is All" *Sight and Sound* Vol. 25 Issue 3 p. 82.

Luckett, Moya (2000) "Image and Nation in 1990s British Cinema" in Robert Murphy (ed) *British Cinema in the 90s* London: BFI, pp. 88–99.

Lynas, Mark (2008) "Coming to a Screen Near You – Me!" *New Statesman* 4 August Vol. 137 Issue 4908 p. 18.

Macaulay, Scott (2002) "25 New Faces of Independent Film: Lucy Walker" *Filmmaker* Vol. 10 Issue 4 p. 61.

MacCabe, Colin (2009) *Critical Quarterly* October Vol. 51 Issue 3 pp. 111–115.

Macnab, Geoffrey (1993) *J. Arthur Rank and the British Film Industry* London, New York: Routledge.

Macnab, Geoffrey (2002) "Film: Spreading the Word" *The Independent* 16 August p. 10.

Macnab, Geoffrey (2003a) "Killing Me Softly" *Sight and Sound* Vol. 13 Issue 12 pp. 24–25.

Macnab, Geoffrey (2003b) "Lone Scherfig: Suicide for Beginners" *Sight and Sound* Vol. 13 Issue 12 p. 25.

Macnab, Geoffrey (2004) "Review: The Principles of Lust" Vol. 14 Issue 2 p. 56.

Macnab, Geoffrey (2005a) "Review: On a Clear Day" *Sight and Sound* Vol. 15 Issue 9 pp. 73–74.

Macnab, Geoffrey (2005b) "New Kids on the Block" *Screen International* 7 January p. 10.

Macnab, Geoffrey (2006a) "Making Mischief" *Screen International* 10 November p. 12.

Macnab, Geoffrey (2006b) "Nina's Heavenly Delights" *Sight and Sound* Vol. 16 Issue 10 pp. 74, 76.

Macnab, Geoffrey (2009a) "Blindsight" *Sight and Sound* Vol. 19 Issue 5 p. 85.

Macnab, Geoffrey (2009b) "Perfect Pitch" *Screen International* 31 July pp. 10–11.

Macnab, Geoffrey (2013a) "Grim but Gripping Up North" *The Independent* 25 October p. 44.

Macnab, Geoffrey (2013b) *J. Arthur Rank and the British Film Industry* London, New York: Routledge.

Maher, Kevin (2009) "Is It Climate Change or Eco Films that We Need Saving From?" *The Times* 14 March p. 6.
Maher, Kevin (2011) "Postcards from the Edge of the Edge" *The Times* 18 February p. 10.
Malcolm, Derek (2008) "Behind the Scenes in Bollywood" *The Evening Standard* 17 January p. 41.
Marciniak, Katarzyna (2007) "Palatable Foreigness" in Katarzyna Marciniak, Anikó Imre, and Áine O'Healy (eds) *Transnational Feminism in Film and Media* New York, Basingstoke: Palgrave Macmillan, pp. 187–206.
Marcus, Greil (2011) "The Night Has a Thousand Eyes: Red Road and Look" *Aperture* Issue 202 pp. 28–30.
Marking, Hannah (2010) "Kim Longinotto's Hold Me Tight, Let Me Go" *Documentary* Vol. 10 Issue 4 p. 44.
Martin, Angela (2014) "Becoming Sheffield Film Co-op" *Women's Film and Television History* https://womensfilmandtelevisionhistory.wordpress.com/2014/04/04/becoming-sheffield-film-co-op/ (Accessed 22/06/2015).
Mattar, Mira (2011) "Out of the Past: An Interview with Cinenova" *Mute*http://www.metamute.org/editorial/articles/out-past-interview-cinenova (Accessed 06/08/2015).
Mayer, Sophie (2006) "Review: Sisters in Law" *Sight and Sound* Vol. 16 Issue 9 p. 73.
Mayer, Sophie (2008) "Expanding the Frame: Sally Potter's Digital Histories and Archival Futures" *Screen* Vol. 49 Issue 2 pp. 194–202.
Mayer, Sophie (2009a) *The Cinema of Sally Potter: A Politics of Love* London, New York: Wallflower Press.
Mayer, Sophie (2009b) "Review: Rage" *Sight and Sound* Vol. 19 Issue 12 pp. 69–70.
Mayer, Sophie (2010a) "Across the Great Divide" *Sight and Sound* Vol. 20 Issue 10 pp. 42–45.
Mayer, Sophie (2010b) "Review: Rough Aunties" *Sight and Sound* Vol. 20 Issue 9 p. 74.
Mayer, Sophie (2010c) "Review: The Unloved" *Sight and Sound* Vol. 20 Issue 3 p. 81.
Mayer, Sophie (2012) "Bomb Culture" *Sight and Sound* Vol. 22 Issue 11 pp. 34–35.
Mayer, Sophie (2015a) "Review: Dreamcatcher" *Sight and Sound* Vol. 25 Issue 3 p. 64.
Mayer, Sophie (2015b) "Things Fall Apart" *Sight and Sound* Vol. 25 Issue 5 pp. 29–31.
Mayer, Sophie (2016) *Political Animals: The New Feminist Cinema* London, New York: I.B. Tauris.
Mayne, Judith (1990) *The Woman at the Keyhole: Feminism and Women's Cinema* Bloomingtom, Indianapolis: Indiana University Press.

Mayne, Judith (2008) "Female Authorship Reconsidered" in Barry Keith Grant (ed) *Auteurs and Authorship: A Film Reader* Malden, Oxford, Victoria: Blackwell Publishing, pp. 263–279.

McCarthy, John P. (2012) "Heathcliff 2.0." *America* Vol. 207 Issue 10 pp. 26–28.

McClintock, Pamela (2011) "A Glance at the Season's Other Female Directors" *Hollywood Reporter* 16 December Vol. 417 Issue 45 pp. 50–54.

McDonald, Paul (2010a) "The Cultural Impact of UK Film: Questions and Evidence Birkbeck College, University of London, 27 November 2009" *Journal of British Cinema and Television* Vol. 7 Issue 2 pp. 324–328.

McDonald, Paul (2010b) "What's On? Film Programming, Structured Choice and the Production of Cinema Culture in Contemporary Britain" *Journal British Cinema and Television* Vol. 7 Issue 2 pp. 264–298.

McFarlane, Brian (2003) *The Encyclopaedia of British Film* London: Methuen.

McGahan, Katy (nd) "Sarah Erulkar 1923–2015" http://www.screenonline.org.uk/people/id/1397348/ (Accessed 06/10/2015).

McGill, Hannah (2003) "White Girl in the Ghetto" *The Herald* 3 July p. 20.

McGill, Hannah (2006) "Mean Streets" *Sight and Sound* Vol. 16 Issue 11 pp. 26–28.

McGill, Hannah (2011) "We Need to Talk About Kevin" *Sight and Sound* Vol. 2 Issue 11 pp. 16–19.

McGown, Alistair (nd) "The Children's Film Foundation 1951–1987" http://www.screenonline.org.uk/film/id/1148379/index.html (Accessed 6/10/2015).

McGrath, Melanie (1998) "Review: Stella Does Tricks" *Sight and Sound* Vol. 8 Issue 2 p. 50.

McIntyre, Steve (1996) "Art and Industry: Regional Video Policy in the UK" in Albert Moran (ed) *Film Policy: International, National and Regional Perspectives* London, New York: Routledge, pp. 215–233.

McIver, Brian (2015) "Into the Lion's Mouth" *The Guardian* 11 January p. 20.

McKernan, Luke (1992) *Topical Budget* London: BFI.

McKernan, Luke (2010) "Jessica Borthwick" *Women and Silent British Cinema* https://womenandsilentbritishcinema.wordpress.com/the-women/jessica-borthwick/ (Accessed 02/02/2015).

McRobbie, Angela (2007) "Postfeminism and Popular Culture: Bridget Jones and the New Gender Regime" in Yvonne Tasker and Diane Negra (eds) *Interrogating Post-Feminism* Durham, London: Duke University Press, pp. 27–39.

Mermin, Liz (2010) "My Year of the Horse" *Daily Mail* 16 March p. 26.

M. H. (1954) "Review: Man with a Million" *Motion Picture Herald* Vol.195 Issue 9 p. 9.

Merz, Caroline (1991) "The Tension of Genre: Wendy Toye and Muriel Box" *Film Criticism* Vol. 16 Issue 1–2 pp. 84–94.

Millward, Rachel (2008) "Sisters Are Doing It for Themselves" *Vertigo* Issue 3 Issue 8 p. 15.

Millward, Rachel (2010) "Women Directors on the Right Track" *The Independent*, 5 March http://www.independent.co.uk/arts-entertainment/films/features/women-directors-on-the-right-track-1916154.html (Accessed 06/07/2011).

Millward, Rachel (2011) "BEV News" http://www.birds-eye-view.co.uk/news/2011/10/26/no-festival-in-2012 (Accessed 07/12/2011).

Millward, Rachel (nd) http://birds-eye-view.co.uk/about-us/history-people/ (Accessed 07/10/2015).

Minns, Adam (2000) "British Screen to Be Folded into Film Council" *ScreenDaily* http://www.screendaily.com/british-screen-to-be-folded-into-film-council/401087.article (Accessed 08/09/2015).

Minns, Adam (2004) "Reason to Be Cheerful" *Screen International* 3 September p. 8.

Mitchell, Wendy (2006a) "Death Trip" *Screen International* 25 August Vol. 1560 p. 13.

Mitchell, Wendy (2006b) "Black Magic" *Screen International* 13 October p. 10.

Mitchell, Wendy (2008) "Making a Mega-Hit: The Key Ingredients" *Screen International* 7 November pp. 6–7.

ML (2011) "Review: Wuthering Heights" *New Internationalist* November p. 41.

ML (2012) "Review: Ginger and Rosa" *New Internationalist* Issue 457 November p. 35.

ML (2013) "InRealLife" *New Internationalist* October p. 35.

ML (2015a) "Review: The Falling" *New Internationalist* Issue 482 p. 35.

ML (2015b) "Review: Dreamcatcher" *New Internationalist* March, p. 35.

Modleski, Tania (1999) *Old Wives' Tales: Feminist Re-Visions of Film and Other Fictions* London, New York: I.B. Tauris.

Monahan, Mark (2003) "Humour to Die For" *The Daily Telegraph* 29 November p. 7.

Monk, Claire (1997) "Review: The Tango Lesson" *Sight and Sound* Vol. 7 Issue 12 pp. 54–55.

Monk, Claire (2000a) "Underbelly UK: The 1990s Underclass Film, Masculinity and the Ideologies of 'New' Britain" in Justine Ashby and Andrew Higson (eds) *British Cinema Past and Present* London: BFI, pp. 274–287.

Monk, Claire (2000b) "Men in the 90s" in Robert Murphy (ed) *British Cinema of the 90s* London: BFI, pp. 156–166.

Monk, Claire (2001) "Sexuality and Heritage" in Ginette Vincendeau (ed) *Film/Literature/Heritage: A Sight and Sound Reader* London: BFI, pp. 6–11.

Monk, Claire (2002) "The British Heritage-Film Debate Revisited" in Claire Monk and Amy Sargeant (eds) *British Historical Cinema: The History, Heritage and Costume Film* London, New York: Routledge, pp. 176–198.

Monk, Claire, and Sargeant, Amy (eds) (2002) *British Historical Cinema: The History, Heritage and Costume Film* London, New York: Routledge.
Monk, Claire (2011a) "Eyre Conditioning" *Sight and Sound* Vol. 21 Issue 10 pp. 44–45.
Monk, Claire (2011b) *Heritage Film Audiences: Period Films and Contemporary Audiences in the UK* Edinburgh: Edinburgh University Press.
Monserrate, Carey (2004) "Trembling Playground: Two Young Directors Discuss Film, Faith, and the Challenges of Documenting Religion" *Crosscurrents* Vol. 54 Issue 1 pp. 84–95.
Moore, Lindsey (2005) "Women in a Widening Frame: (Cross) Cultural Projection, Spectatorship, and Iranian Cinema" *Camera Obscura* Issue 59 p. 24.
Moran, Albert (ed) *Film Policy* London, New York: Routledge.
Morey, Anne (2006) "Elinor Glyn as Hollywood Labourer" *Film History* Vol. 18 Issue 2 pp. 110–118.
Morley, Carol (2011) "Reportage: Joyce Vincent Was Beautiful, Intelligent and Popular" *The Observer* 9 October p. 16.
Morley, Carol (2012) "Two Deaths, One Story: The Case of Joyce Vincent and Michelle Conroy Speak of a Social Isolation Linked to Housing, or the Lack of It" *The Guardian* 3 December p. 32.
Morley, Carol (2015a) "Mass Hysteria Is a Powerful Group Activity" *The Observer* 29 March p. 8.
Morley, Carol (2015b) "They Should Have Been Contenders ...: Carol Morley: Director, Dreams of a Life, The Falling" *The Observer* 25 January p. 12.
Morley, Carol (2015c) "Carol Morley Interview: I Like to Give Some Light to the Dark Side of Life" *Telegraph.co.uk* http://www.telegraph.co.uk/culture/culturenews/11528106/Carol-Morley-interview-I-like-to-give-some-light-to-the-dark-side-of-life.htm (Accessed 13/05/2015).
Morrow, Fiona (2000) "Going Back to the Bottle" *The Guardian* 5 June pp. 2, 7.
Mortimer, Claire (2010) *Romantic Comedy* London, New York: Routledge.
Mundy, John (1999) *Popular Music on Screen: From Hollywood Musical to Music Video* Manchester: Manchester University Press.
Muir, Kate (2013a) "Teenagers Share, Therefore They Are" *The Times* 20 September p. 6.
Muir, Kate (2013b) "The Instability of Truth" *Sight and Sound* Vol. 23 Issue 11 pp. 32–33.
Mullen, Lisa (2009) "Estate of Mind" *Sight and Sound* Vol. 19 Issue 10 pp.16–19.
Mullen, Lisa (2010) "Over Your Cities Grass Will Grow" *Sight and Sound* Vol. 20 Issue 11 pp. 69–70.
Mullen, Lisa (2012) "Review: Ginger and Rosa" *Sight and Sound* Vol. 22 Issue 11 pp. 88–9.
Mullen, Lisa (2013) "Review: The Pervert's Guide to Ideology" *Sight and Sound* Vol. 23 Issue 10 p. 87.

Mullen, Lisa (2014) "Review: Gone Too Far" *Sight and Sound* Vol. 24 Issue 11 p. 75.
Mullen, Lisa (2015) "Review: Second Coming" *Sight and Sound* Vol. 25 Issue 6 pp. 64–65.
Mulvey, Laura (nd) http://www.underwirefestival.com/about-us/ (Accessed 08/09/2015).
Mulvey, Laura (1975) "Visual Pleasure and Narrative Cinema" *Screen* Vol. 16 Issue 3 pp. 6–18.
Murphy, Robert (ed) (2000) *British Cinema in the 90s* London: BFI.
Murphy, Robert (ed) (2006) *Directors in British and Irish Cinema* London: BFI.
Murphy, Robert (2001) "Citylife: Urban Fairy-Tales in Late 90s British Cinema" in Robert Murphy (ed) *The British Cinema Book* London: BFI, pp. 292–300.
Nagra, Dalijit (2014) "A Conversation with Gurinder Chadha" *Wasafiri* Vol. 29 Issue 3 pp. 24–30.
Nahra, Carol (2004) "Documenting Women's Rites: Interview with Filmmaker Kim Longinotto" *International Documentary* Vol. 23 Issue 1 pp. 8–9.
Nahra, Carol (2008) "Raising Half a Million by Crowd Funding" *Documentary Film Quarterly* Vol. 77 pp. 4–5.
Napper, Lawrence (2001) "A Despicable Tradition? Quota-Quickies in the 1930s" in Robert Murphy (ed) *The British Cinema Book* London: BFI, pp. 45–59.
Nelmes, Jill, and Selbo, Jule (2015) *Women Screenwriters: An International Guide* Basingstoke, New York: Palgrave Macmillan.
Newland, Paul (2013) "Phantom Rides: Journeys and Disappearances in Perestroika" in DVD Booklet, *Essays* London: LUX.
Newman, Kim (2015) "Review: Northern Soul" *Sight and Sound* Vol. 25 Issue 1 pp. 86–87.
Newsinger, Jack (2009) "The 'Cultural Burden': Regional Film Policy and Practice in England" *Journal of Media Practice* Vol. 10 Issue 1 pp. 39–55.
Newsinger, Jack (2012) "British Film Policy in an Age of Austerity" *Journal of British Cinema and Television* Vol. 9 Issue 1 pp. 133–144.
Nichols, Bill (1991) *Representing Reality: Issues and Concepts in Documentary* Bloomington, Indianapolis: Indiana University Press.
Nichols, Bill (1994) *Blurred Boundaries* Bloomington, Indianapolis: Indiana University Press.
Nichols, Bill (2010) *Introduction to Documentary* Bloomington, Indianapolis: Indiana University Press.
Nowell-Smith, Geoffrey, and Dupin, Christophe (eds) (2012) *The British Film Institute, the Government and Film Culture, 1933–2000* Manchester, New York: Manchester University Press.
Ogborn, Kate (2000) "Pathways into the Industry" in Robert Murphy (ed) *British Cinema of the 90s* London: BFI, pp. 60–67.
Ogborn, Kate (2016) Email Correspondence with Author Dated 29 February 2016.

O'Pray, Michael (2003) *Avant-Garde Film* London, New York: Wallflower.
Pantazis, Christina, Gordon, David, and Levitas, Ruth (eds) (2006) *Poverty and Social Exclusion in Britain* Bristol: Policy Press.
Parker, Alan (2004) *UKFC Group and Lottery Annual Report and Financial Statements for the Year Ended 31 March 2004* TSO: The Stationery Office.
Patterson, Hannah (2009) "Women on the Verge" *Sight and Sound* Vol. 19 Issue 2 p. 84.
Peretti, Jacques (2000) "Shame of a Nation" 26 May http://www.theguardian.com/film/2000/may/26/1 (Accessed 08/09/2015).
Perkins, Jasper (2009) "Arts Around the World" *FT.com*http://search.proquest.com.ezproxy.wlv.ac.uk/printviewfile?accountid=14685 (Accessed 07/07/2015).
Perkins, Sean (2012) "Film in the UK, 2001–10: A Statistical Overview" *Journal of British Cinema and Television* Vol. 9 Issue 3 pp. 310–332.
Petley, Julian (1989) "Background and Development of Film and Video Workshops" in *Landmarks* London: British Council, pp. 6–10.
Petley, Julian (2002) "From Brit-Flicks to Shit-Flicks" *Vertigo* http://www.close-upfilmcentre.com/vertigo_magazine/volume-2-issue-2-spring-2002/from-brit-flicks-to-shit-flicks/ (Accessed 31/05/2015).
Petrakis, John (2012) "On Film: We Need to Talk About Kevin" *Christian Century* 22 February p. 52.
Petrie, Duncan, (2004) "British Film Education and the Career of Colin Young" *Journal of British Cinema and Television* Vol. 1 Issue 1 pp. 78–92.
Petrie, Duncan (2012) "Creative Industries and Skills: Film Education and Training in the Era of New Labour" *Journal of British Cinema and Television* Vol. 9 Issue 3 pp. 357–376.
Phoca, Sophie (2010) "Filming the Alternative" *Art Monthly* 10–11 December–January Issue 342 pp. 7–10.
Pidd, Helen (2006) "Culture Briefing: The Invisible Woman" *The Guardian* 14 March p. 23.
Pierson, Michelle (2005) "Amateurism and Experiment: The BFI's Experimental Film Fund (1952–1966)" *The Moving Image* Vol. 5 Issue 1 pp. 68–94.
Pinet, Carolyn (2006) "Translating Tango: Sally Potter's Lessons" *Romance Notes* Vol. 46 Issue 3 pp. 377–85.
Porter, Vincent (2001) "Methodism Versus the Market Place" in Robert Murphy (ed) *The British Cinema Book* London: BFI.
Porton, Richard (2001) "Beyond Hollywood at the Toronto International Film Festival" *Cineaste* Vol. 27 Issue 1 pp. 47–48.
Porton, Richard (2005) "McLibel" *Cineaste* Vol. 30 Issue 4 p. 80.
Porton, Richard (2011) "Documentary Cinema and Reality Hunger" *Cineaste* Vol. 36 Issue 3 pp. 10–14.
Potter, Edward (2006) "Mischief Night" *Sunday Times* 5 November p. 12.
Price, Stuart (2003) "TV Opera Comes of Age" *The Independent* 22 May p. 15.

Price, Karen (2005) "Strong Women's Stories to be Screened at Cannes" *Western Mail* 30 April p. 21.

Pulver, Andrew (2010) "Film Reviews: Horses" *The Guardian* 29 January p. 9.

Quinn, Judy (1999) "Fiennes Times for Bloomsbury USA" *Publishers Weekly* Vol. 246 Issue 33 p. 31.

Quinn, Anthony (2004) "Bridget Hits Rock Bottom: Bridget Jones: The Edge of Reason" *The Independent* 12 November pp. 6–7.

Quinn, Anthony (2008) "Also Showing" *The Independent* 18 January p. 8.

Radner, Hilary (2011) *Neo-Feminist Cinema* London, New York: Routledge.

Radner, Hilary, and Stringer, Rebecca (2011) *Feminism at the Movies: Understanding Gender in Contemporary Popular Cinema* London, New York: Routledge.

Rahimieh, Nasrin (2009) "Divorce Seen Through Women's Cinematic Lens" *Iranian Studies* Vol. 42 Issue 1 pp. 97–112.

Ramachandran, Naman (2004) "Review: Bride and Prejudice" *Sight and Sound* Vol. 14 Issue 10 pp. 43–44.

Ramachandran, Naman (2008) "Review: Shot in Bombay" *Sight and Sound* Vol. 18 Issue 3 p. 80.

Ramanathan, Geetha (2006) *Feminist Auteurs* London, New York: Wallflower Press.

Rahman, Mai Abdul (2006) "The Beauty Academy of Kabul Documentary Screened in DC" *Washington Report on Middle East Affairs* Vol. 25 Issue 5 pp. 67–8.

Ramsay, Lynne (2002) Interview on DVD Release *Ratcatcher* Pathé Pictures and BBC Films in Association with Arts Council of England, Lazennec and Le Studio Canal+ a Holy Cow Films Production. BFI.

Raphael, Amy (2011) "Love Will Tear Us Apart" *Sight and Sound* Vol. 21 Issue 12 pp. 34–36.

Rapold, Nicolas (2008) "Mahindra Indo-American Arts Council Film Festival" *Village Voice* Vol. 53 Issue 45 p. 52.

Rapold, Nicolas (2011a) "Eyes Wide Open: The Up Close and Personal Films of Kim Longinotto Rethink the Documentary Ethos of Dispassionate Engagement" *Film Comment* Vol. 47 Issue 6 pp. 32–34.

Rapold, Nicolas (2011b) "Review: Waste Land" *Sight and Sound* Vol. 21 Issue 3 p. 77.

Rapold, Nicolas (2013) "Short Takes: Ginger and Rosa" *Film Comment* Vol. 49 Issue 2 p. 70.

Renée, V. (2013) "Why Are Female Directors Having (Relative) Success in Independent Film, but Not in Hollywood?" 6 May http://nofilmschool.com/2013/05/female-directors-indie-film-hollywood (Accessed 02/04/2014).

Reynolds, Lucy (2010) "Behind the Mask" *Sight and Sound* Vol. 20 Issue 11 pp. 26–27.

Richards, Beryl (2013) "British Film Is Booming but Not for Female Directors" *Telegraph.co.uk* 24 July http://search.proquest.com.ezproxy.wlv.ac.uk/docview/1411981658?accountid=14685 (Accessed 28/05/2015).

Risov, Vadim (2015) "Sundance: Park City Lights" *Sight and Sound* Vol. 25 Issue 3 p. 19.

Ritman, Francis (2006) "Review: Destricted" *Sight and Sound* Vol. 16 Issue 10 pp. 49–50.

Ritrosky-Winslow, Madelyn (2006) *Quarterly Review of Film and Video* Vol. 23 pp. 237–56.

Roberts, Ben (2013) "A Public Inquiry: BFI Film Fund Insights" *Sight and Sound* Vol. 23 Issue 8 p. 16.

Roberts, Ben (2014) "Panel Beaten: BFI Fund Insights" *Sight and Sound* Vol. 24 Issue 1 p. 16.

Roberts, Rex (2012) "Review: The Iron Lady" *Film Journal International* Vol. 115 Issue 1 p. 45.

Roddick, Nick (2009) "Do We Know Where We Are Going?" *Sight and Sound* Vol. 19 Issue 10 pp.19–20.

Roddick, Nick (2010) "The Pleasure Principle" *Sight and Sound* Vol. 20 Issue 1 p. 11

Roddick, Nick (2011) "Mystery of a Life" *Evening Standard* 22 September p. 28.

Roddick, Nick (2013) "Fairytale Film-Maker: Writer-Director Clio Barnard's Poetic and Hauntingly Beautiful The Selfish Giant Will Surely Go Down as a Milestone of British Film. Her Aim, She Tells Nick Roddick, Was to Put the Artifice Next to the Real" *Evening Standard* 17 September p. 28.

Roddick, Nick (2015) "Tait of Grace" *Sight and Sound* Vol. 25 Issue 6 p. 54.

Rodgers, Jude (2008) "The Late, Late Show" *New Statesman* Vol. 137 Issue 4887 p. 47.

Rogers, Susan (2007) "A Report Produced for the UK Film Council: British Films: Who Writes British Films and How Are They Recruited?" Royal Holloway, University of London 27 June pp. 1–58. https://www.google.co.uk/search?client=qsb-win&rlz=1R3GUEA_en-GBGB352GB353&hl=en-GB&q=Rogers,+Susan+%282007%29+%E2%80%9CReport+for+UKFC:+British+Films:+Who+writes+British+films+and+how+are+they+recruited%3F%E2%80%9D%3F%3F%3F%3F&gws_rd=cr,ssl&ei=JRHMVsKVGISxUbvLgrgI#hl=en-GB&q=Rogers%2C+Susan+Report+for+UKFC:+British+Films:+Who+writes+British+films+and+how+are+they+recruited%3F%E2%80%9D%3F%3F%3F%3F (Accessed 23/02/2016).

Rollyson, C. (2005) *To Be a Woman* London: Aurum.

Romney, Jonathan (2004) "It's a Hard Knock Life" *The Independent on Sunday* 29 February p. 7.

Romney, Jonathan (2010) "The Scilly Season" *Sight and Sound* Vol. 20 Issue 11 p. 27.

Romney, Jonathan (2011) "Review: *Archipelago*" *The Independent* 6 March http://www.independent.co.uk/arts-entertainment/films/reviews/archipelago-joanna-hogg-114-mins-15-2233413.html (Accessed 14/02/2012).

Romney, Jonathan (2013) "Review: The Selfish Giant" *Sight and Sound* Vol. 23 Issue 11 pp. 89–90.

Romney, Jonathan (2014) "Coming Apart" *Film Comment* Vol. 50 Issue 4 pp. 40–43.

Rooney, David (2011) "The Iron Lady" *Hollywood Reporter* Vol. 417 Issue 44 p. 76.

Roper, Danielle (2014) "Film Maker Returns to Her Roots for Festival" *Manchester Evening News* 23 October p. 43.

Rose, Steve (2012) "The Guide: Film: Made in Britain London" *The Guardian* 31 March p. 25.

Rosenblum, Robert (1994) *Modern Painting and the Northern Romantic Tradition: Friedrich to Rothko* London: Thames and Hudson.

Rosser, Michael (2014) "Clio Barnard: Wellcome Research Inspired New Film *Trespass*" *ScreenDaily* 24 November http://www.screendaily.com/news/clio-barnard-wellcome-research-inspired-new-film/5080330.article (Accessed 02/02/2016).

Rosser, Michael (2015) "Seetha Kumar Named Creative Skillset CEO" *ScreenDaily* 6 July http://www.screendaily.com/news/seetha-kumar-named-creative-skillset-ceo/5090122.article (Accessed 09/09/2015).

Rummery, Kirstein, Gains, Francesca, and Annesley, Claire (2007) "New Labour: Towards an Engendered Politics and Policy?" in Claire Annesley, Francesca Gains, and Kirstein Rummery (eds) *Women and New Labour: Engendering Politics and Policy?* Bristol: Policy Press, pp. 231–249.

Ruskin, John (1906) *Modern Painters Vol. III* London: George Allen.

Russell, Jamie (2004) "Revival Meeting" *Sight and Sound* Vol. 14 Issue 6 p. 79.

Russell, Patrick, and Taylor, James Piers (eds) (2010) *Shadows of Progress* London: BFI.

Said, S. F. (2003) "Gospel According to Sophie" *The Daily Telegraph* 30 June p. 17.

Sanderson, David, and Blakely, Rhys (2013) "Sexist Hollywood? It's a Magic Time to Be a Woman in Films, Says Watson" *The Times* 17 May p. 7.

Sandhu, Sukhdev, and Robey, Tim (2006) "Must See: Mischief Night" *The Daily Telegraph* 4 November p. 16.

Saner, Emine (2011) "G2: 100 Inspiring Women: Franny Armstrong Film-Maker" *The Guardian* 8 March p. 11.

Saner, Emine (2013) "Blood on the Snow" *The Guardian* 24 September p. 16.

Sandhu, Sukhdev (2012) "Best Exotic Movie Hell" *The Guardian* 17 February p. 10.

Sandon, Emma (2010) "Women, Empire, and British Cinema History" *Framework: Journal of Cinema and Media* Vol. 51 Issue 2 pp. 324–33.

Sandon, Emma (nd) "Stella Court-Treatt" *Women and Silent British Cinema* https://womenandsilentbritishcinema.wordpress.com/the-women/stella-court-treatt/ (Accessed 2/10/2015).

Sargeant, Amy (2012) "Crossing Borders: Artist Film-Makers in the New Decade" *Journal of British Cinema and Television* Vol. 9 Issue 3 pp. 502–520.

Sauma, Luiza (2008) "Storyville: Shot in Bombay" *The Independent on Sunday* 19 October p. 81.

Saunders, D. (1992) "The National Gallery at War", in Pamela B. Vandiver (ed) *Material Issues in Art and Archaeology III. Materials Research Society Symposium Proceedings, cclxvii* Pittsburgh, pp. 101–10.

Sayad, Cecilia (2013) *Performing Authorship: Self-Inscription and Corporality in the Cinema* London, New York: I.B. Tauris.

Schlotterbeck, Jesse (2008) "Trying to Find a Heartbeat" *Journal of Popular Film and Television* Vol. 36 Issue 2 pp. 82–90.

Schwarzbaum, Lisa (2006) "The Beauty Academy of Kabul" *Entertainment Weekly* Issue 870 p. 43.

Seymour, Tom (2013) "I Couldn't Tell My Stories" *The Guardian* 30 August p. 14.

Shackleton, Liz (2004) "Production: On Location with Bridget Jones and Alexander in Thailand" *Screen International* 5 March Vol. 14/15 pp. 19–20.

Shiel, Mark (2006) *Italian Neo-Realism: Rebuilding the Cinematic City* London, New York : Wallflower Press.

Sharp, Rob (2006) "Gormley Goes Up in Flames for Movie Art in Margate" *The Observer* 1 October p. 19.

Shoard, Catherine (2011) "The Laugh-Out-Loud Nightmares of Joanna Hogg" *The Guardian* 24 February http://www.theguardian.com/film/2011/feb/24/joanna-hogg-archipelago (Accessed 10/12/2013).

Sheridan, Dorothy (ed) (1990) *Wartime Women: A Mass Observation Anthology, The Experiences of Women at War* London: Mandarin.

Shilling, Jane (2010) "Storyville: Race Horses" *Evening Standard* 11 March p. 46.

Silverstein, Melissa (2008) "The Success of Women Documentary Filmmakers" http://www.alternet.org/story/88642/the_success_of_women_documentary_filmmakers (Accessed 02/04/2014).

Skidelsky, William (2006) "Food: The Mind May Forget Nauseous Trauma, But the Body Never Does" *New Statesman* 20 February Vol. 135 Issue 4780 p. 62.

Smaill, Belinda (2009) "The Documentaries of Kim Longinotto: Women, Change and Painful Modernity" *Camera Obscura* Vol. 24 Issue 2 pp. 42–75.

Smith, Anna (2009) "Review: 1 Day" *Sight and Sound* Vol. 19 Issue 9 p. 77.

Smith, Justin, and Mayne, Laura (2014) "The Four Heads of Film4" *Journal of British Cinema and Television* Vol. 11 Issue 4 pp. 517–551.

Smith, Murray (1994) "Character and Emotional Response in the Cinema" *Cinema Journal* Vol. 33 pp. 34–56.

Smyth, J. (2015) "The Past, Present and Future of Women's History on Screen" *Cineaste* Vol. 41 Issue 1 pp. 18–21.

Solomons, Jason (2010) "Terrorists and Ghosts Don't Fill Me with Adoration" *Mail on Sunday* 31 January, p. 16.

Spencer, Liese (1999) "What Are You Looking At?" *Sight and Sound* Vol. 9 Issue 10 pp.17–19.

Spicer, Andrew (nd) "Muriel Box 1905–1991" *BFI Screenonline* http://www.screenonline.org.uk/people/id/479374/ (Accessed 05/10/2015).

Stables, Kate (2009) "Lessons in Life" *Sight and Sound* Vol. 19 Issue 11 pp. 48–49.

Stables, Kate (2012) "Review: Dreams of a Life" *Sight and Sound* Vol. 22 Issue 1 pp. 64–65.

Stables, Kate (2013) "From the Sea to the Land Beyond" Vol. 23 Issue 3 p. 117.

Stables, Kate (2014) "Review: The Riot Club" *Sight and Sound* Vol. 24 Issue 11 pp. 87–88.

Stafford, Roy (2007) *Understanding Audiences and the Film Industry* London: BFI.

Staiger, Janet (1992) *Interpreting Film Studies in the Historical Reception of American Cinema* Princeton: Princeton University Press.

Steele, David (2013) "Succès de plume? Female Screenwriters and Directors of UK Films, 2010–2012" *BFI Statistical Yearbook* www.bfi.org.uk%2Fsites%2Fbfi.org.uk%2Ffiles%2Fdownloads%2Fbfi-report-on-female-writers-and-directors-of-uk-films-2013-11.pdf&usg=AFQjCNHTRRjUHYYUJOdk1SHqVt9c9HisjQ&cad=rja (Accessed 12/11/2014)

Steele, Francesca (2010) "The Special Relationship" *The Independent* 12 May p. 12.

Stevens, Isabel (2010) "Into the Labyrinth" *Sight and Sound* Vol. 20 Issue 11 p. 11.

Stevens, Isabel (2011) "In the Garden of Trash" *Sight and Sound* Vol. 21 Issue 3 p. 9.

Stevens, Isabel (2012) "The Female Gaze" *Sight and Sound* Vol. 25 Issue 10 p. 18.

Stevens, Isabel (2013) "At the End of the World" *Sight and Sound* Vol. 23 Issue 6 p. 109.

Stewart, Michael (2012) "Falling, Looking, Caring: Red Road as Melodrama" *Journal of British Cinema and Television* Vol. 9 Issue 4 pp. 548–568.

Street, Sarah (1997) *British National Cinema* London, New York: Routledge.

Stuart, Julia (2004) "Beauty and the Burqa" *The Independent* 1 September pp. 6–7.

Stubbs, David (2010) "On the Streets" *The Guardian* 8 November p. 26.

Study by the Institute for Media Research at University of Rostock, February 2015. https://www.google.co.uk/search?client=qsb-win&rlz=1R3GUEA_en-GBGB352GB353&hl=en-GB&q=German+feature+film+directors+finds+that+women+are+underrepresented+with+only+22%25+of+films+made+between+2009+and+2013+directed+by+women&gws_rd=cr,ssl&ei=BGXNVdTnHMuSavncipgL (Accessed 06/11/2015).

Sturges, Fiona (2001) "The Reality Effect" *The Independent* 19 May p. 47.

Sumpter, Helen (2014) "Q&A Joanna Hogg: Exhibition" *Art Review* http://artreview.com/features/feature_qa_joanna_hogg_exhibition_2014/ (Accessed 20/01/2016).

Sylvester, Rachel (2013) "The Internet Is an Addictive Place that Is Grooming Our Children" *The Times* 14 September p. 30.

Tasker, Yvonne, and Negra, Diane (eds) (2007) *Interrogating Post-Feminism* Durham, London: Duke University Press.

Taubin, Amy (2010) "Coming Up on the Outside" *Final Cut* Vol. 46 Issue 1 pp. 54–55.

Tay, Sharon Lin (2009) *Women on the Edge: Twelve Political Film Practices* Basingstoke, New York: Palgrave Macmillan.

Taylor, Lib (2013) "Voice, Body and the Transmission of the Real in Documentary Theatre" *Contemporary Theatre Review* Vol. 23 Issue 3 pp. 368–379.

Taylor, Richard (2001) "Obituary: Alison de Vere" *The Guardian* 15 January http://www.theguardian.com/news/2001/jan/15/guardianobituaries (Accessed 15/09/2015).

Teasley, Sarah (2000) "Interview with Kim Longinotto" *Documentary Box* Vol. 16 pp. 17–27.

Thomson, Patricia (2012) "Wild Passion" *American Cinematographer* Vol. 93 Issue 5 pp. 42–51.

Thornham, Sue (2012) *What If I Had Been the Hero?* Basingstoke, New York: Palgrave Macmillan.

Thornham, Sue (2015) "'A Hatred so Intense…' *We Need to Talk About Kevin*. Postfeminism and Women's Cinema" *Revista Lusófona de Estudos Culturais* Vol. 3 Issue 1 pp. 43–63.

Thorpe, Vanessa (2013) "National: Dispatch: Cannes; Festival Taps into the Power of Nostalgia to Fight Back Against Global Competition: For Decades Its Conspicuous Excess Dazzled the World, but Film-Makers Are Increasingly Turning to Television to Show Off Their Wares" *The Observer* 19 May p. 2.

Till, Stewart (2003) "A Bigger Future Report" UKFC/Skillset Report www.bfi.org.uk/sites/bfi.org.uk/files/…/uk-film-council-bigger-future-report.pdf (Accessed 06/12/2014).

Till, Stewart (2006) *UKFC Group and Lottery Annual Report and Financial Statements for the Year Ended 31 March 2006* TSO: The Stationery Office.

Tourmarkine, Doris (2015) "The Riot Club" *Film Journal International* Vol. 118 Issue 5 p. 176.

Townsend, Ian (2008) "The 2004/05 Child Poverty Target: What Happened?" in *House of Commons Library* Hansard Reports pp. 1–8.

Tracy, Andrew "Review: Exhibition" *Sight and Sound* Vol. 24 Issue 5 pp. 62–63.

Travers, Peter (1993) "Review: Used People" *Rolling Stone* 21 Jan Issue 648 p. 56.

Trotter, David (2010) "Lynne Ramsay's *Ratcatcher*" *Critical Quarterly* Vol. 52 p. 156–170.
Turner, Sarah (2010) "Ghost in the Machine" *Sight and Sound* Vol. 20 Issue 10 p. 47.
Turvey, Gerry (2009) "Constrained Emancipation: The Career of Ethyle Batley, Britain's Pioneering Woman Film Director" *Film History* Vol. 21 Issue 4 pp. 359–372.
UK Film Policy Review (2012) *A Future for Britain: It Begins with the Audience* PDF Document. https://www.gov.uk/government/consultations/film-policy-review-*consultation* (Accessed 12/12/2014).
UKFC Report (2000) *Towards a Sustainable UK Film Industry* http://www.bfi.org.uk/sites/bfi.org.uk/files/downloads/bfi-towards-a-sustainable-film-industry-2014-10-31.pdf (Accessed 14/04/15).
Urry, John (1990) *The Tourist Gaze: Leisure and Travel in Contemporary Society* London: Sage.
Vallance, T. (1999) Obituaries: Jill Craigie http://www.independent.co.uk/arts-entertainment/obituaries-jill-craigie-1132511.html (Accessed 20/09/2011).
Vanmeenan, Karen (2005) "Out of the West" *Afterimage* Vol. 33 Issue 2 pp. 16–17.
Vary, Adam (2009) "Making Noise" *Entertainment Weekly* 24 July Issue 1057 pp. 13–14.
Verve Pictures: *Red Road* www.vervepics.com/docs/rrnotes.doc (Accessed 02/12/2014).
Vidal, John (1997) *McLibel: Burger Culture on Trial* London: Macmillan.
Vidal, John (2009) "Society: Environment: Eco Soundings: You'd Be Stupid Not To" *The Guardian* 13 May p. 7.
Vineberg, Steve (2009) "On Film: An Education" *Christian Century* 17 November Vol. 126 Issue 23 p. 43.
Vollmer, Ulrike (2005) "Towards an Ethics of Seeing: Sally Potter's *The Tango Lesson*" *Literature and Theology* Vol. 19 Issue 1 pp. 74–85.
Wakefield, Thirza (2014) "Life in a Day" *Sight and Sound* Vol. 23 Issue 10 pp. 26–30.
Waldman, Diane, and Walker, Janet (eds) (1999) *Feminism and Documentary* Minneapolis, London: University of Minnesota Press.
Walker, Janet, and Waldman, Diane (1999) "Introduction" in Diane Waldman and Janet Walker (eds) *Feminism and Documentary* Minneapolis, London: University of Minnesota Press, pp. 1–35.
Walker, Lucy (2011) "All They Talk About Is What I'm Wearing" *The Observer* 6 March p. 17.
Walsh, John (2011) "Prime Mover" *The Independent* 31 December p. 34.
Watson, Wallace (2001) "Misogyny and Homoerotic Hints Feminized and Romanticized: Conrad's 'Amy Foster' and Kidron's 'Swept from the Sea'" *Literature Film Quarterly* Vol. 29 Issue 3 pp. 179–195.

Ward, Paul (2005) *Documentary: The Margins of Reality* London, New York: Wallflower Press.
Wearing, Sadie (2013) "Dementia and the Biopolitics of the Biopic: From Iris to the Iron Lady" *Dementia* Vol. 12 Issue 3 pp. 315–325.
Wheatley, Catherine (2008) "Review: Blindsight" *Sight and Sound* Vol. 18 Issue 9 pp. 52–53.
Wheatley, Catherine (2011a) "Review: Countdown to Zero" *Sight and Sound* Vol. 21 Issue 7 pp. 60–61.
Wheatley, Catherine (2011b) "Review: One Day" *Sight and Sound* Vol. 21 Issue 9 pp. 71–72.
White, Patricia (2006) "Cinema Solidarity: The Documentary Practice of Kim Longinotto" *Cinema Journal* Vol. 46 Issue 1 pp. 120–128.
White, Patricia (2009) "Watching Women's Films" *Camera Obscura* Vol. 24 Issue 3 pp.153–161.
White, Patricia (2015) *Women's Cinema, World Cinema: Projecting Contemporary Feminisms* Durham, London: Duke University Press.
Williams, Sally (2014) "A Toff Act to Follow" *Telegraph Magazine* 30 August p. 40.
Williams, Sally (2015) "Force-Feeding, Police Surveillance and Assault: On the Set of Suffragette" *Telegraph* 3 October p. 66.
Williamson, C. H. B. (1953) "About British Films" *ToDay's Cinema* Vol. 80 Issue 6740 p. 18.
Wilson, Angelia R. (2007) "New Labour and 'Lesbian-and-Gay-Friendly' Policy" in Claire Annesley, Francesca Gains, and Kirstein Rummery (eds) *Women and New Labour: Engendering Politics and Policy?* Bristol: Policy Press, pp. 193–209.
Wilson, Cheryl A. (2006) "Bride and Prejudice: A Bollywood Comedy of Manners" *Literature Film Quarterly* Vol. 34 Issue 4 pp. 323–331.
Winston, Brian (2008) *Claiming the Real: Grierson and Beyond* London: BFI.
Winter, Jessica (2004) "Review: Bridget Jones: The Edge of Reason" *Sight and Sound* Vol. 14 Issue 12 pp. 40–41.
Wiseman, Andreas (2013) "Screen and Broadcast Launch Diversity Programme" *Screendaily* 14 October http://www.screendaily.com/news/screen-and-broadcast-launch-diversity-forum/5062455.article (Accessed 10/02/2015).
Wiseman, Andreas (2015) "BFI Opens £1m Diversity Fund, More UK Funders Adopt Diversity Rules" *Screendaily* 15 October http://www.screendaily.com/news/bfi-opens-1m-diversity-fund-more-uk-funders-adopt-diversity-rules/5095551.article (Accessed 10/02/2016).
Wiseman, Andreas (2016) "Can the UK Film Industry Meet the Diversity Challenge?" *Screendaily* 31 January http://www.screendaily.com/features/can-the-uk-film-industry-meet-the-diversity-challenge/5099500.article (Accessed 10/02/2016).
Wollaston, Sam (2009) "Qatar's Junior Debating Team Are Geeky, Naïve and Incredibly Clever – Watching Them Is a Joy" *The Guardian* 12 May p. 27.

Women's Film & Television History Network-UK/Ireland https://womensfilmandtelevisionhistory.wordpress.com/tag/wftvn/ (Accessed 26/8/2016).

Women and Silent British Cinema "Peggy Hyland Home Page" https://womenandsilentbritishcinema.wordpress.com/the-women/peggy-hyland/ (Accessed 2/10/2015).

Women Make Movies http://www.wmm.com/ (Accessed 14/10/2015).

Women Make Movies Press Kit *Hold Me Tight* http://www.wmm.com/filmcatalog/pages/c713.shtml (Accessed 14/10/2015).

Women Make Movies Press Kit *Pink Saris* http://www.wmm.com/filmcatalog/pages/c789.shtml (Accessed 14/10/2015).

Wood, Jason (2008) *Talking Movies: Contemporary World Filmmakers in Interview* London, New York: Wallflower Press.

Woodward, Adam (2015) Rebecca Johnson: "Financiers Don't Want To Make Films With Black People In" *Little White Lies* 7 May http://www.littlewhitelies.co.uk/features/articles/rebecca-johnson-honeytrap-30108 (Accessed 29/09/2015).

Woodward, John (2004) *UKFC Group and Lottery Annual Report and Financial Statements for the Year Ended 31 March 2004* TSO: The Stationery Office.

Woodward, John (2006) *UKFC Group and Lottery Annual Report and Financial Statements for the Year Ended 31 March 2006* TSO: The Stationery Office.

Woodward, John (2007) *UKFC Group and Lottery Annual Report and Financial Statements for the Year Ended 31 March 2007* TSO: The Stationery Office.

Woodward, John (2008) *UKFC Group and Lottery Annual Report and Financial Statements for the Year Ended 31 March 2008* TSO: The Stationery Office.

Woodward, John (2009) *UKFC Group and Lottery Annual Report and Financial Statements for the Year Ended 31 March 2009* TSO: The Stationery Office.

Woodward, John (2010) *UKFC Group and Lottery Annual Report and Financial Statements for the Year Ended 31 March 2010* TSO: The Stationery Office.

Woolcock, Penny (2007a) "Sermon at the Seaside" *Broadcast* 7 November p. 29.

Woolcock, Penny (2007b) "Penny Woolcock on Exodus" *Vertigo* Vol. 3 Issue 4 pp. 48–49.

Woolcock, Penny (2009) "A Life of Grime" *Evening Standard* 16 October p. 36.

Woolcock, Penny (2010) "How to Make Bizet's Gem Shine Anew" *The Independent* 31 May p. 14.

Woolcock, Penny (2013) "The Woman Who Took on the Gangs" *The Times* 20 March p. 4.

Wright, Jonathan (2008) "Pick of the Day: Shot in Bombay – Storyville" *The Guardian* 18 October p. 71.

"Wuthering Heights Preliminary Press Notes" https://www.google.co.uk/search?client=qsb-win&rlz=1R3GUEA_en-GBGB352GB353&hl=en-GB&q=wuthering+heights+press+notes&gws_rd=cr,ssl&ei=C0PsVMONNsWC7QbxhoBA (Accessed 24/02/2015).

Wyver, John (2010) "A Boom of One's Own" *Sight and Sound* Vol. 20 Issue 12 pp. 38–39.

York, Ashley Elaine (2010) "From Chick Flicks to Millennial Blockbusters: Spinning Female-Driven Narratives into Franchises" *The Journal of Popular Culture* Vol. 43 Issue 1 pp. 3–25.
Young, Neil (2001) "Forever Amber: An Interview with Ellin Hare and Murray Martin of the Amber Film Collective" *Critical Quarterly* Vol. 43 Issue 4 pp. 61–80.
Zeitchnik, Steven (2009a) "Matching the Mood Will Matter" *Hollywood Reporter* 26 October Vol. 412 Issue 2 pp. 1–18.
Zeitchnik, Steven (2009b) "Times Are Lean for the Ladies" *Hollywood Reporter* 17 November Vol. 412 Issue 17 pp. 21–22.

BFI Special Collection: Unpublished Scripts

S13924 – BLUE SCAR – Release script
S8938 – FIFTIES FEATURES – THE WOMEN BEHIND THE PICTURES (1986)
Transcript of interview with Jill Craigie
Collection: Michael Balcon
H/83
Correspondence w/ Jill CRAIGIE 1954
I/45
Correspondence w/Jill CRAIGIE 1956–1958

Index

Note: Page numbers followed by "n" refer to notes.

S. Hockenhull, *British Women Film Directors in the New Millennium*, DOI 10.1057/978-1-137-48992-0

B

Printed by Printforce, the Netherlands

✓ Nature of Feminism in Andrea Arnold's the cinema of

-(A study of selected Films)

Locus of Control in this dissertation

centre of gravity

2:50